Derivatives and the Wealth
of Societies

Derivatives and the Wealth of Societies

EDITED BY BENJAMIN LEE
AND RANDY MARTIN

THE UNIVERSITY OF CHICAGO PRESS   CHICAGO AND LONDON

The University of Chicago Press, Chicago 60637
The University of Chicago Press, Ltd., London
© 2016 by The University of Chicago
All rights reserved. Published 2016.
Printed in the United States of America
25 24 23 22 21 20 19 . 18 17 16   1 2 3 4 5

ISBN-13: 978-0-226-39266-0 (cloth)
ISBN-13: 978-0-226-39283-7 (paper)
ISBN-13: 978-0-226-39297-4 (e-book)
DOI: 10.7208/chicago/9780226392974.001.0001

Library of Congress Cataloging-in-Publication Data

Names: Lee, Benjamin, 1948– editor. | Martin, Randy, 1957–2015, editor.
Title: Derivatives and the wealth of societies / edited by Benjamin Lee and Randy Martin.
Description: Chicago ; London : The University of Chicago Press, 2016. | Includes
    bibliographical references and index.
Identifiers: LCCN 2016008499 | ISBN 9780226392660 (cloth : alk. paper) | ISBN
    9780226392837 (pbk. : alk. paper) | ISBN 9780226392974 (e-book)
Subjects: LCSH: Derivative securities. | Derivative securities—Social aspects. | Markets—
    Mathematical models. | Markets—Philosophy. | Marxian economics.
Classification: LCC HG6024.A3 .D45 2016 | DDC 332.64/57—dc23 LC record available at
    http://lccn.loc.gov/2016008499

♾ This paper meets the requirements of ANSI/NISO Z39.48–1992 (Permanence of Paper).

THIS BOOK IS DEDICATED TO OUR COLLEAGUE,
FRIEND, AND COAUTHOR

RANDY MARTIN
1957–2015

Contents

Contributors

ARJUN APPADURAI, Goddard Professor of Media, Culture, and Communication, New York University. Former provost of The New School. Author of *Banking on Words*: *The Failure of Language in the Age of Derivative Finance.*

ELIE AYACHE, founding director, ITO 33, a company that makes financial software. Author of *The Blank Swan*: *The End of Probability* and *The Medium of Contingency: An Inverse View of the Market.*

EMANUEL DERMAN, director, Financial Engineering Program, Columbia University. Former director, Quantitative Strategies, Goldman Sachs. Author of *My Life as a Quant: Reflections on Physics and Finance* and *Models Behaving Badly: Why Confusing Illusion with Reality Can Lead to Disaster, on Wall Street and in Life.*

BENJAMIN LEE, University Professor of Anthropology and Philosophy and former provost, The New School. Author of *Talking Heads: Language, Metalanguage, and the Semiotics of Subjectivity*; coauthor of *Financial Derivatives and Globalization of Risk.*

EDWARD LIPUMA, professor of anthropology, University of Miami. Author of *Encompassing Others: The Magic of Modernity in Melanesia*; coauthor of *Financial Derivatives and the Globalization of Risk.*

RANDY MARTIN, professor of art and public policy and director of the Graduate Program in Arts Politics at New York University. Author of *Knowledge LTD: Toward a Social Logic of the Derivative.*

ROBERT MEISTER, professor of social and political thought, Department of History of Consciousness, University of California at Santa Cruz. Author of *After Evil: A Politics of Human Rights.*

ROBERT WOSNITZER, clinical assistant professor, New York University Stern School of Business. Vice president at Lehman Brothers, Banc One, and First Union. Director, Scotia Capital.

Preface

One of the most revealing moments of the global financial crisis occurred during Alan Greenspan's exchange with Henry Waxman at the hearings of the Government Oversight Committee of the House of Representatives held in the fall of 2008:

REP. HENRY WAXMAN: The question I have for you is, you had an ideology, you had a belief that free, competitive—and this is your statement—"I do have an ideology. My judgment is that free, competitive markets are by far the unrivaled way to organize economies. We've tried regulation. None meaningfully worked." That was your quote. You had the authority to prevent irresponsible lending practices that led to the subprime mortgage crisis. You were advised to do so by many others. And now our whole economy is paying its price. Do you feel that your ideology pushed you to make decisions that you wish you had not made?

ALAN GREENSPAN: Well, remember that what an ideology is, is a conceptual framework with the way people deal with reality. Everyone has one. You have to—to exist, you need an ideology. The question is whether it is accurate or not. And what I'm saying to you is, yes, I found a flaw. I don't know how significant or permanent it is, but I've been very distressed by that fact.

REP. HENRY WAXMAN: You found a flaw in the reality . . .

ALAN GREENSPAN: Flaw in the model that I perceived is the critical functioning structure that defines how the world works, so to speak.

REP. HENRY WAXMAN: In other words, you found that your view of the world, your ideology, was not right, it was not working?

ALAN GREENSPAN: That is—precisely. No, that's precisely the reason I was shocked, because I had been going for 40 years or more with very considerable evidence that it was working exceptionally well.

In his prepared testimony Greenspan had linked his worldview to the intersection between shareholder value, deregulation, and financial risk management, specifically Black-Scholes, the mathematical model for financial markets containing the derivative investment instruments that had collapsed in the 2008 crisis. Greenspan explained the flaw the crisis had exposed this way:

> [T]hose of us who have looked to the self-interest of lending institutions to protect shareholder's equity (myself especially) are in a state of shocked disbelief. . . . It was the failure to properly price such risky assets that precipitated the crisis. In recent decades, a vast risk management and pricing system has evolved, combining the best insights of mathematicians and finance experts supported by major advances in computer and communications technology. A Nobel Prize was awarded for the discovery of the pricing model that underpins much of the advance in derivatives markets. This modern risk management paradigm held sway for decades. The whole intellectual edifice, however, collapsed in the summer of last year because the data inputted into the risk management models generally covered only the past two decades, a period of euphoria.

By invoking worldview and ideology, Greenspan, if only for a moment, moved discussion beyond the two available explanations of the financial crisis. These focus either on technical failures (leaky Gaussian copulas and faulty value-at-risk measures) or narratives of greed and speculation. Technical explanations feed into the current hope of discovering some regulatory fix for derivative ills while tales of excess lead to calls for the abolition of derivatives as a form of wealth creation. For one side the goal is to return to some state of business as usual. For the other it is to construct a political economy free from the danger intrinsic to financial speculation with derivative instruments and thereby produce a more just and sustainable sociopolitical world order.

The collaboration this book represents proposes an integration of a social and a technical understanding of derivative finance within a single analytic and interpretive frame to allow discussion to escape the dead end produced by the irreconcilable solutions to the recent crisis offered by its alternative explanations. Our book proposes to use what was disclosed by the financial crisis to show that technical knowledge of derivative finance can be drawn upon to revalue and further people's capacity to act together constructively in innovative ways. Indeed it argues that new social, aesthetic, and political possibilities are already in play in the abundance of social wealth that derivative finance capitalism has placed within reach during the past forty years. How fundamental technical knowledge of both "the social" and of wealth production using derivative instruments can be woven into a single coherent interpretive and analytic language of human possibility and well-being in our time is the challenge this first volume to be published from our collaboration takes up.

To create a technically competent integrative framing of contemporary derivative global finance and "the social" dimension of everyday life in late modernity is ambition enough for any one book to undertake. Nevertheless many readers will want our answer to the question "What 'solution' to the crisis of global capitalism—whether conceived of as the socially catastrophic injustice of permanent and unrelenting inequality or the 'ecocide' from which its current productive logic seems to offer no escape—does your book and its new integrative language of social wealth creation and its revaluation provide?"

Our fundamental insight is that derivative financial instruments— in their existing forms—already attest to an abundance of social wealth whose real potential use for general well-being is just now, perhaps, coming into view. Capitalism has always justified its destructiveness by its claims to be transitional—a set of social arrangements and power relations necessary for the production of a universal abundance. That abundance is now here, the two volumes of our larger project will argue. A new form of wealth supplies the means, we believe, to accomplish a historical justice long thought to be impossible because of incalculability— a justice that revalues the violence, dispossession, and losses of the past through action and freedom of creation of value on behalf of all in the present and future.

This book is the work of many hands, yet it attempts to offer, in as coherent and unified a voice as possible, a general proposal for a new way to understand the social dimensions of derivative finance. This is the first volume of what we project will be a two-volume work. It represents the initial collaboration of a small group of eight scholars and finance practitioners, as well as an editor, assembled from a larger collaboration between two working groups of academics and finance professionals interested in the question of the social dimension of finance.

The Cultures of Finance Working Group at New York University was convened in the fall of 2009 and is directed by Arjun Appadurai and

Benjamin Lee. The Bruce Initiative on the Future of Capitalism was founded at the University of California at Santa Cruz in the spring of 2010 and is led by Stephen Bruce and Robert Meister. We who have written this book together call ourselves The Wealth of Societies Project. The names of some of the many colleagues, friends, and fellow working group members who have contributed so much to our efforts are listed in the acknowledgments. It is our deepest hope that this book will inspire others to respond to our effort by themselves finding new ways to put the value of the abundance of social wealth that derivative finance represents to better use.

The Wealth of Societies Project

Arjun Appadurai

Elie Ayache

Emanuel Derman

Peter Dimock, editorial and publishing consultant

Benjamin Lee

Edward LiPuma

Randy Martin

Robert Meister

Robert Wosnitzer

Introduction

Benjamin Lee

This book is part of an ongoing project to understand the implications of the derivative. Despite the unparalleled historical expansion of derivative finance—from an annual notional value of under a trillion dollars in the eighties to over a quadrillion at the present—it is still unclear whether this growth signals a qualitative or merely quantitative change in the nature of capitalism. For liberal critics, derivatives amplified tendencies latent in capitalism by providing increased leverage for speculative greed and excess. Their remedy is a combination of better regulation and redistribution. For Marxist critics, derivatives are examples of fictitious capital that produce enormous quantities of monetary wealth in a global capitalism whose core is still the production of labor-based value. One radical proposal made by David Graeber (2011) for mitigating the social volatilities of contemporary global capitalism is to transform finance capitalism via radical measures such as debt refusal.

Our derivative reading of the social employs a small set of financial concepts to understand certain defining dimensions of contemporary derivative capitalism. The central idea will be that of volatility and its relations to risk, uncertainty, hedging, optionality, and arbitrage. These technical and theoretical insights will be applied to classic anthropological discussions of the gift, ritual, and exchange and Marxist notions of capital and value. Our social reading of the derivative will involve anthropological discussions of the gift, ritual, play, dividuality, and performativity. These provide frames of embodiment for analyzing, through action and event, the ways derivatives do their work. Along the way we will show how our analysis of the social logic of the financial derivative naturally marries with the thought of the nineteenth- and early twentieth-century giants of social theory Marcel Mauss, Max Weber, and Karl Marx as well as Frank Knight and Fischer Black. By connecting the gift to the derivative, we create a framework that provides historical and comparative perspectives on a major question that has arisen over the debates about neoliberalism. That question is: How far should market thinking extend into our lives and social institutions? This book proposes another: Does derivative finance offer anything new to the old debates over what money can and can't buy?

The gift and the derivative share the property that both take the volatilities and uncertainties of social life and transform them into manageable risks by equating things that are different. The basis for innovation in derivative finance, the Black-Scholes formula, takes the cash flows of different assets (e.g., a stock and an option) and commensurates them by analogically equating their present and future volatilities. It is the play of the interval (unlike stocks, options have expiration dates) that produces the wealth that derivatives are capable of producing (what's known technically as "convexity"). Gift exchanges take different inherently risky "social flows" and commensurate them via ritualized performances. The interval of time between gift and countergift produces the "social convexity" that creates wealth in the form of new social claims and obligations. In both cases, a variety of social and cultural practices grow out of the volatilities that gift and derivative exchanges both presuppose and create, ranging from the collective effervescence of Durkheim's Arunta corroboree to the "flow" of traders in the derivatives markets (Zaloom 2006; Wosnitzer, this volume).

This volume brings together experts and expertise from very different intellectual backgrounds with what are usually considered different—even incomparable—trajectories of application. These include knowledge domains of financial engineering (designed for the use of traders, salespeople, and quants), sociology, anthropology, arts activism, media and cultural studies, design, and philosophy. The technical mathematical arcana of contemporary finance often prevent dialogue and interpretively accessible cross-fertilization among these disparate domains. But to avoid the technical leaves us in the dark about how derivative finance insinuates itself into the social. By bringing together such a diverse group of authors, we hope to initiate a discussion that will help readers understand the social dimensions of the derivative as well as the derivative dimensions of contemporary capitalism.

In reevaluating the theoretical vocabulary for understanding derivative capitalism we hope to pave the way for a reexamination of both financial capitalism's history and its future. The first step in crafting a social reading of the derivative that incorporates its technical dimensions was the pathbreaking work by Donald MacKenzie and Michel Callon on the "performativity of finance." They showed how the Black-Scholes options pricing model initially helped to create the financial reality that it purported to model. Their work called into question the independence of model and reality presupposed by the natural sciences. Drawing upon the anthropological research on the performativity of ritual, the chapters by Arjun Appadurai, Edward LiPuma, and Benjamin Lee construct a social reading of the derivative by using the work on ritual, gift, and exchange to show the contingent claims of gift exchange, the role of ritual performativity in objectifying economic imaginaries, and the centrality of the *dividual* person to the making of collectivities such as "the market." The wealth of societies lies in social relationships and social interconnections and new forms of social wealth are created by performatively connecting previously independent flows and exchanges. What emerges from using this approach is a derivative reading of the social. The gift contains an immanent foreshadowing of the derivative form itself. There is a swap-like relation between gift and countergift and an "optionality" involved in the timing of the return.

To advance this discussion, Robert Meister and Randy Martin directly confront the theorization of the role of finance in capital's making of capitalism. They investigate and reassess Marx's delineation of capital, locating an arbitrage logic at the heart of Marx's account of relative surplus value. Meister employs the language of puts and calls used by Robert Merton (1974) to analyze the capital structure of companies to refigure Marx's account of relative surplus value. The combination of this protoderivative structure of relative surplus value and arbitrage allows the reader to see how Marx's approach might encompass the new derivative design of capital markets. Randy Martin builds upon Meister's insights by looking at Marx's account of the falling rate of profit in volume 3 of *Capital*. He outlines how hedging the countertendencies to the falling rate of profit creates the immanent possibility for the development of a nonlinear and nondirectional dynamic within Marx's account of capital that can be understood as the precursor to the derivative logic of finance capitalism.

In the last section of the book Emanuel Derman investigates the technical dimensions of the logic of the derivative. He shows how the Black-Scholes formula gives access to volatility by hedging away directional risk. Elie Ayache approaches the question of value from the standpoint of a market already in motion. He begins by understanding the event of wealth creation as an encounter between the market maker and the act of pricing the derivative. Robert Wosnitzer then analyzes how a complex sociality—coded as relations linking agents, machines, and models—underwrites the Black-Scholes pricing model and the execution of trades. Emanuel Derman writes as a quant representing the theoretical side of finance, while Elie Ayache and Robert Wosnitzer draw upon their experience as traders and market makers to illuminate the social act of trading and its implications for embodied subjectivity. The subject of derivative finance, it turns out, may be most strongly felt in the way it recombines the social and the subjective in novel ways.

It is this book's contention that the breakthrough in derivative finance is the discovery and pricing of volatility. This moment is enshrined in the Black-Scholes formula, commonly agreed to be the starting point for derivative finance and still used to price trillions of dollars of derivatives every day. Volatility is the randomness in things that is felt as the intensity of change. In finance this instantaneous or "actual" volatility is transformed into a historically based statistical measure, the standard deviation of price movements over some fixed time frame such as a year.

The concept of volatility exists in a no man's land between finance and the social sciences. Despite the explosion of interest in risk and uncertainty created by works such as Anthony Giddens's "Risk and Responsibility" and Ulrich Beck's *Risk Society*, most social science research does not clearly distinguish risk and uncertainty from volatility. The distinction is the fundamental insight of Black-Scholes and is foundational for contemporary financial capitalism. At the same time, financial work on volatility tends to focus on its mathematical aspects, eschewing the social and cultural dimensions of volatility that trading and market activity presuppose. Indeed most of the standard introductory finance textbooks present a continuous historical march from portfolio theory to CAPM to Black-Scholes. This obscures the magnitude of the intellectual break from directional risk to volatility, which in Black-Scholes is captured by the key insight that in order to have access to volatility you have to hedge away, or neutralize, all directional risk (this is highlighted in Derman's derivation of Black-Scholes in this volume). The magnitude of the breakthrough is nicely captured in the following quote from Salih Neftci's *Principles of Financial Engineering*:

> In the traditional textbook approach, options are introduced as *directional* instruments. . . . For an end investor or retail client, such *directional motivation* for options may be natural. . . . In fact motivating options as directional tools will disguise the fundamental aspect of these instruments, namely that options are tools for trading *volatility*. (2004, 193)

Like many key concepts in finance, volatility has both formal and everyday usages. The seeming clarity created by the precision of its mathematics rests upon a grasp of pragmatic phenomenology. Much of contemporary financial engineering is the formalization of a small set of concepts whose phenomenological roots are captured in aphorisms and maxims that are linked to embodied practices and sensibilities. For example, arbitrage is the idea of a riskless profit, and the nonarbitrage principle, presupposed by most pricing models, is captured by the idea of "there are no free gifts." The maxim "no pain, no gain" characterizes the relation between risk and return that is the starting point for portfolio theory. This quickly leads to the idea of diversification or "don't put all your eggs in one basket" that is the guiding insight for the invention of index funds. In each case financial practices developed around sophisticated mathematical models presuppose common-sense understandings that ground them in everyday practice. It is this interaction between the formal side of finance and its phenomenological embodiment that we explore in our dual readings of the derivative and the social.

The Gift of Black-Scholes

Knowing the long story of the development of Black-Scholes within derivative finance allows a coherent picture of the integration of these diverse aspects of contemporary financialization to emerge. Black-Scholes starts out as a mathematical model of option prices that has remained in continuous use to the present despite the fact that financial analysts know that it doesn't work. There are, in fact, more sophisticated and accurate pricing models. Nevertheless Black-Scholes remains the gold standard. Its relative failure is part of the reason for its current success as the way to calculate what is known as "implied volatility." This has become the standard measure of volatility in derivative pricing. Yet the calculation of implied volatility continually violates one of the basic assumptions of the model. This would seem to confirm MacKenzie and Callon's contention that there is no "physics of finance" and that derivative finance has an important constructivist moment. But another interpretation, raised by LiPuma in his chapter of this book, is that the belief in Black-Scholes is more akin to religion or ideology. This conclusion reinsinuates the dimension of performativity into finance and reasserts wealth creation's connections to ritual and collective faith. This book argues that understanding the social dimensions of derivative finance gives us a way to take seriously Alan Greenspan's comments at the 2008 House hearings that the financial crisis brought about the collapse of his "view of the world" and his "ideology." Both, he openly admitted, were based upon faith in Black-Scholes and "the modern risk management paradigm" it helped create.

In the Black-Scholes equation, the price of an option is calculated by a differential equation with five variables: the strike price and expiration date of the option, the risk-free interest rate, and the price and volatility of the underlying stock. The basic idea is brilliantly simple. Hedging out directional risk (the stock price going up or down) results in a riskless financial instrument whose expected return is the risk-free interest rate. The price of the option is the cost of the hedge. The only "unknown" in the formula is the volatility of the stock. This can be estimated via historical data or the calculation of what is known as "implied volatility."

Black-Scholes relies upon equating the risk profiles of the stock and its option, a process known as "dynamic replication." By matching the risk profiles of an unknown instrument with that of a known one, one can price and thus create new financial instruments, in a potentially unending chain of dynamic replication in which new instruments are created by matching volatilities. Emanuel Derman characterizes the breakthrough:

> Before Black and Scholes and Merton no one had even guessed that you could manufacture an option out of simpler ingredients. Anyone's guess for its value is as good as anyone else's; it was strictly personal. The Black-Scholes Model . . . revolutionized modern finance. Using Black and Scholes's insight, trading houses and dealers could value and sell options on all sorts of

securities, from stock to bonds to currencies, by synthesizing the option out
of the underlying security. (2011, 176)

All of these are implications of Black-Scholes as a theoretical model for
options pricing. However, in practice it is used in a way that deconstructs
its own claims to accuracy and seems to undermine any pretense that a
"physics of finance" is possible. Since there are options markets, the various options for a given stock already have market prices at which they
are bought and sold. If one inverts Black-Scholes and then runs it backwards by inserting the market price of the option, one can then calculate
the "implied volatility" of the underlier. This is the market's estimate of
the forthcoming volatility of the stock. In the theoretical model, a stock
can only have constant volatility. But it turns out that calculating the implied volatilities of options on the same stock with different strike prices
will yield different volatilities, producing what is known as the volatility
smile (see Derman in this volume). In options markets, when people talk
about volatility they are usually referring to implied volatilities—option
prices are expressed in implied volatilities not dollar amounts. But the
result is that the actual practice of derivatives trading constantly violates
one of the basic assumptions of the model used to price derivatives. This
leads to Ayache's remarkable conclusion that "if implied volatility is followed through all its implications, we find that it perpetually leads to the
devastation of its concept" (Ayache 2005, 32–33).

The practice of trading the derivative brings a theoretical model of
pricing and turns it into a model for trading by inverting the model and
suspending disbelief in its failure. These moves suggest that the faith
in the market is more religious or ideological than scientific. The shift
from theory to practice also moves from abstract decision making to embodied sensibilities. The latter are more the domain of a true believer
and trained athlete than the "animal spirits" of behavioral finance. Elie
Ayache's first day as a market maker was on Black Monday, October 19,
1987, when global markets fell more than twenty percent. Therefore perhaps it's not surprising that his descriptions of trading reveal the existential dimensions of its embodiment:

> Through the dynamic delta-hedging and the anxiety that it generates (Will
> I execute it right? When to rebalance it, etc.), the market-maker penetrated
> the market. He penetrated its volatility and he could now feel it in his guts. In

a word, he became a *dynamic trader*. He now understood—not conceptually, but through his senses, through his body—the inexorability of time decay, the pains and joys of convexity. (Ayache 2008, 36–37)

As Wosnitzer relates in his chapter on trading the derivative, the trader sits in his "turret" as part of a huge global information processing machine. He trades as much by instinct as by calculation. The technical aspects of finance lie both "inside" and "outside" of him. Bloomberg machines flash the implied volatilities of options while his "delta hedging" is a mixture of training, experience, and a suspension of disbelief. Finding the social in the derivative isn't restricted to the performativity of pricing. It also lies in the performativity of religious belief and ideological conviction.

Finding the Derivative in the Gift

From the performativity of pricing it is a short step to the performativity of ritual and the gift. The gift touches upon issues at the heart of contemporary economics and finance. What can and can't money buy? How far should markets encroach upon social life?

Although the rise of capitalism is usually analyzed in terms of the expansion of commodity production and markets, the gift points to an existential moment in which what money can't buy plays a crucial role in its development. In his *The Protestant Ethic and the Spirit of Capitalism*, Max Weber argues that the spirit of capitalism is born out of an existential uncertainty over salvation. The existential anxiety over the uncertainty of God's gift of grace compels the Calvinist to a lifetime of ascetic productivity in the name of God. But the connection between capitalism and the existential continues into the age of derivative finance. This becomes particularly evident in times of crisis.

But how do we find the derivative in the social, particularly in the gift? One definition of derivatives is that they are contingent claims. This is to say that they are contracts among counterparties with a payout that depends upon some uncertain future event. Shifting the emphasis from "contingent" to "claim" highlights a feature of the derivative that locates its tie to the gift. Derivatives and gifts create social claims and obligations between people. An option is a financial instrument that gives the buyer the right but not the obligation to buy (a call) or sell (a put) an underlying asset at a specified (strike) price at or by a specified time. Derivatives embed "direct" social claims and obligations within networks of "stranger-mediated" social relationships that are connected to the uncertainty of future cash flows.

Options also have a special property that distinguishes them from the underlying stock from which they are created. The combination of a strike price and expiration date produce what is known mathematically as "convexity." This term designates the asymmetric bias towards the upside. It results from the fact that the strike price caps the loss at the price of the option while its upside is theoretically unlimited. Its price behavior will therefore differ from that of its underlying stock whose return is linear. Options create a relation between the future and the present that allows future cash flows to have a calculable value in the present by commensurating risk profiles.

Anthropological accounts of ritual performativity inevitably go back to the gift. As elaborated in the works of Marcel Mauss, Claude Lévi-Strauss, and Pierre Bourdieu, ritual constitutes a foundational alternative to Hobbes's contract theory (performative in its own "rite" as the exchange of promises) as a way to conceptualize the origins of society. Ritual exchanges foreground the connections among volatility, uncertainty, and circulation. What, for instance, were the implications of exchanging women with other social groups with whom you were in competition? Ritual exchanges were seen as moments of danger but also opportunities to increase wealth, especially in the form of new social relations. Cross-culturally and transhistorically, social wealth always consists of a portfolio of claims and obligations that require constant care and upkeep.

Ritualized exchange creates new forms of social wealth by creating new social relations among idealized social groups. Rituals create a template or inscription of an idealized social form. If the ritual is properly enacted, the benign, transcendent force of the idealized macrocosm is brought to bear upon the social group. Successful participation transforms the ritual event into an instance of the manifestation of the idealized macrocosm. Rituals achieve this goal partly by enabling exchanges that transform social uncertainty (what does it mean if cross-cousins marry?) into manageable risks.

At the core of these exchanges is the interplay of gift and counter-gift. A gift is like a derivative swap in which two cash flows (in ritual, two sets of social claims and obligations) are exchanged. Gift and countergift must not be identical and have to be separated by an interval of time. This allows the possibility of strategic manipulation as does the optionality embedded in all derivatives. Like an option, the key to ritual is the existence of a temporal interval for the play of strategy and timing to capture the upside of the volatility and uncertainty that the ritualized exchange helps to mitigate. Both gift and derivative produce wealth (new social relations in the former and monetary wealth in the latter) by commensurating different social/cash flows and embedding them in a structure of optionality created by the possibility of expiration. The gift contains, in immanent protoform, the two major types of derivatives, the swap and the option.

Both the gift and the derivative are ways of creating new claims and obligations by performatively creating equivalences between "value flows" that are in principle different. The gift and the derivative both create social wealth in the form of claims and obligations. In the case of the gift, these are based upon direct social relationships in which monetary exchanges can be embedded. In the case of an option, the option is an exercisable claim to a cash flow, not another social relationship. The option embeds the sociality of the gift as a "contingent claim" within a monetary exchange that takes place between "counterparties" who are in principle strangers to one another.

The gift and countergift cannot be simultaneous. Especially among high status competing groups the immediate return of a countergift is a refusal of a social relationship and thus potentially an insult. The interval between gift and countergift creates the possibility of new forms of social claims and obligations allowing ritual exchanges to contain a "social convexity" in which the successful performance of the ritual creates social wealth in the form of new social relationships that wouldn't have existed without the ritual. The "play" of the interval between gift and countergift also creates an optionality that intersects with its social convexity to produce the new social wealth that successful ritual exchanges can produce; the productive potential of the stranger-mediated derivative is immanent in the sociality of the gift.

Marx and the Derivative

The chapters by Lee, Meister, and Martin fill out the trajectory between the gift and the derivative through their readings of Marx. Marx suggests the first part of this trajectory in volume 1 of *Capital* when he traces the development from inalienable exchange to simple forms of value and then the ensuing stages of the money and value dialectic. Marx even uses the example of the "Indian commune" to discuss societies in which things are not yet alienated from the people who exchange them. This is a point that Appadurai emphasizes in his account of *dividualized* exchange in traditional and contemporary India. Marx emphasizes that alienable exchange in the form of barter first starts at the boundaries of society and then moves toward the center. Money gradually becomes a form of generalized social mediation that only becomes value after labor power has become a commodity. The "convexity" of capital lies in its ability to create more of itself through its consumption. This becomes manifest in two forms, absolute and relative surplus value. The former increases in a linear fashion, by increasing the labor time involved in production. The latter, however, is nonlinear and convex and is driven by technological competition and innovation.

Marx's account of the development of value borrows heavily from Hegel's Absolute Concept represented by the first person pronoun "I." "I" is a one-word performative. Its utterance creates and refers to the person uttering it. Its utterance creates the role of speaker and makes her the topic of discourse. The self-referential creativity of "I" provides the model for Marx's idea of a self-moving substance that creates itself out of its own movement. The value that capital substantiates is the creation of a performative social mediation that takes time itself as its object. Meister and Martin point out that Marx's account of relative surplus value, already the performative subject of capitalism, is also a value arbitrage. This understanding combines social and derivative readings of Marx and paves the way for the development of derivative finance not as fictitious capital but as the immanent potential of production-centered capitalism.

Arbitrage is a fundamental concept in finance. It takes the idea of making a profit by buying low and selling high and turns it into a riskless profit or a "free gift" by taking advantage of an asset or commodity having two prices at the same time. (The price of the dollar in different markets would be an example of this.) Buying at the lower price and simultaneously selling at the higher is the realization of the speculator's dream, an instantaneous, riskless profit. Arbitrage also has a kind of negative performativity. As soon as an arbitrage opportunity appears, it cancels itself out by closing the discrepancy as people take advantage of it.

In Marx's account of relative surplus value the technological innovation sells at the same price as its competitor but takes less labor time to produce it. The innovator takes advantage of this value arbitrage but at the same time sets in motion the process of its destruction as the new price/value standard replaces the old. The destruction of competitive advantage through innovation inserts a process of creative destruction at the heart of capitalism. The nonarbitrage principle is one of the fundamental presuppositions of modern finance. (It's sometimes referred to as the "fundamental theorem of finance.") It is part of the formal methodology supporting Martin's insight that the immanent potential for derivative finance already exists in Marx's account of capital once it is understood as the key to the technical ability to hedge the countertendencies in the falling rate of profit described in part 3 of volume 3.

Conclusion

This book outlines a new way of understanding the long history of value and wealth creation stretching from the gift to the derivative. Our hope is that it contributes to an understanding of contemporary derivatives that will help us better navigate the volatilities of contemporary capitalism. Value, we think, is best seen as starting with the inalienable circulation of things among *dividuals*, their gradual transformation into alienable exchanges, and then money-mediated transactions among individualized agents. From the very start, we believe it is possible to see the immanent potential and trajectory of the derivative in the gift. That potential becomes realized in the performative arbitrage structure of relative surplus value. Relative surplus value makes technological innovation a structuring principle of capitalism. In it lie the seeds of financial innovation that will eventually take volatility as its object. With the ascendance of Black-Scholes, volatility becomes a new source of wealth creation in a derivative capitalism driven by commensurating the risk and volatility profiles of future circulations and bringing them into the present as sources of wealth.

The Great Moderation (the long period of reduction in the volatility of business cycle fluctuations beginning in the early 1960s and continuing until 2007) showed us that derivatives are capable of not only producing great wealth but also of changing our values and status hierarchies. The financial crisis of 2007–8 reminded us that neoliberal policies of deregulation and privatization do not bring the benefits they promise. Policies that turn their back on the wealth that derivatives are capable of producing are counterproductive in an age of diminishing resources. The derivative moves in a direction opposite to debt by giving everyone a common stake in a future that all must acknowledge is volatile and uncertain. Revaluing the social implications of derivatives may give us a way not to fear the future we confront. What are the policies that would allow us to harness the potential of financial capital for larger social benefit?

Appadurai's opening chapter sets the tone by suggesting that the "slicing and dicing" of derivatives might be the basis for new forms of *dividualized* sociality that could support progressive alternatives to neoliberal agendas. In *The Gift*, Mauss discussed the Maori term *hau*, the Maori principle of vitality and productivity. Viewing the subsequent anthropological research on *hau*, the anthropologist Marshall Sahlins concludes that it refers to the yield or excess that was produced by exchange and that "benefits taken by man ought to be returned to their source" (in Schrift 1997, 83). If A gives something to B and B gives it to C who uses it to produce some surplus, some of that "profit" should be returned to A. In this seemingly *dividualized* "primitive" exchange there is the outline of a lesson for our age of the derivative. Neoliberal policies deregulated and privatized the wealth produced by derivatives that tapped future cash flows and turned them into present assets. The message behind *hau* is that some of the wealth produced by exchange should go back to its source to ensure future fecundity for all.

Randy Martin, to whom this volume is dedicated, saw a similar potential in the derivative. He wouldn't have been surprised to find insight and inspiration in Maori rituals, as he saw the wealth produced by volatility in everything from dance and skateboarding to the arts and social media. The derivative taps into and makes more explicit the fundamental role of volatility, risk, and uncertainty in our lives; its financial form is merely the monetary realization of social processes in which future volatilities and uncertainties are transformed into present assets of all sorts. The gift reminds us that, even in stranger-mediated contemporary capitalism, the workings of the derivative rest upon a social foundation of shared claims and obligations that is its ultimate source of wealth. The potential of the derivative is not simply as a new source of wealth for a particular set of (directional) tasks and purposes but instead as a model for how to fashion ways in which the "benefits taken by man" could be "returned to their source" for the future benefit of society. Could we fashion a social system of derivatives that not only taps the wealth of the future for present use but invests much of that new abundance according to a revalued understanding of social wealth's capacity to create the futures we need to flourish?

PART I

CHAPTER ONE

The Wealth of Dividuals

Arjun Appadurai, New York University

Finance and Dividualization

One of the pernicious effects of the era of financialization has been the erosion of the status of the individual.[1] By this I do not mean simply that the individual has been alienated, dispossessed, exploited, mystified, or marginalized, though there is some truth to each of these claims. But there is nothing new about this order of social cost paid for the benefits of industrial capitalism.

I am referring to a more radical and less visible process whereby the broad social canvas in which the Western individual (both as category and as social fact) dominated society has been eroded and thinned out in favor of a more elementary level of social agency, which some have called the "dividual." The dividual is not an elementary particle (or homunculus) of the individual but something more like the material substrate from which the individual emerges, the precursor and precondition of the individual, more protean and less easy to discern and to name than the individual, which is one of its structural products.

I hope to show that the erosion of the individual and the rise of the dividual is largely an effect of the workings of financial capitalism since the early 1970s and in particular a collateral effect of the spread of the derivative form as the quintessential tool of making money out of uncertainty in this era of financialization. The form of dividualism produced by financial capital is ideal for the masking of inequality, for the multiplication of opaque quantitative forms that are illegible to the average citizen, and for the multiplication of profit-making tools and techniques, which can escape audit, regulation, and social control. In short, the dividualism that financialization both presumes and enhances is counter to the interests of the large majority of society. But it is also irreversible. Thus, rather than argue for a return to the era of the composite (or canonic, or classical) individual, I propose a new form of politics, which can create radically new forms of collective agency and connectivity that can replace the current predatory forms of dividualism with truly socialized dividualism. To make this journey, one needs a fuller understanding of the idea of the dividual.

To think the dividual, we must unthink the individual. This is no easy task, but one way to understand the post-Enlightenment conception of the individual, on which much ink has been spilled, is to see it as the crystallized product of many centuries of gradual convergence, in the West, between the idea of the actor, the agent, the person, the self, the human soul, and the human being. Each of these categories can be provided with a distinct Western genealogy, composed of elements that can be traced back variously to the Greeks, the Romans, the Christians, the Jews, and a multitude of subtraditions, countertraditions, and hybrid traditions that have grown up around these major traditions. With Descartes and his idea of the *cogito* and its resident "I," the basis was laid for these ideas to be amalgamated to the point of mutual fungibility. Starting in the eighteenth century, it became hard to set apart ideas of humanity, agency, personality, and selfhood, which only recently have begun to reveal their contingent and composite architecture. This was all the more forcefully naturalized as the dominant Western ideas of property, political voice, wealth, and market interests all began to reinforce the idea that some sort of individual was the isomorphic site of agency, natural rights, biological coherence, and moral value. The individual became the invisible condition of possibility for all Western political, economic, and moral thought.

Anthropology as a discipline was well situated to unravel this composite idea of the individual at the beginning of the twentieth century, as its practitioners encountered ideas of soul, technique, religion, and politics that appeared not to revolve around the idea of the individual that Western ethnographers and scholars had come to view as natural and universal. Still, it was fairly late in the twentieth century when two very different anthropological giants, Marcel Mauss (1985) and Meyer Fortes (1973), dealt separate blows to the common sense about the universality of the individual. Mauss was the most important pupil (and nephew) of Durkheim and is arguably the single most important thinker of the founding period of anthropology for all anthropologists today. Fortes was a giant in the midcentury context of British social anthropology, whose primary concern was with the ways in which individuals and collectivities were formed through other entities that he, for the first time in the history of anthropology, used the term "dividual" to describe, in 1973. Mauss deserves the credit for distinguishing the category of the person from that of the self, the latter in his view being not a social artifact but a moral one. But Fortes identified the "dividual" as a more elementary and foundational element of agency (both human and animal) than the individual. For this he deserves credit.

But the most important figure, and the least remembered, at least in this regard, is McKim Marriott, who in the early 1970s at the University of Chicago formulated a theory of the "dividual" that was the most explicit, radical, and generative statement of the relativity and parochialism of our own naturalized idea of the individual in the West. Marriott, in collaboration with a younger historian at Chicago, Ronald Inden, wrote an important essay (1974) that built upon the earlier work of David Schneider on "code" and "substance" in American kinship, to offer a radical new theory of South Asian caste systems, which had hitherto been seen as extreme versions of Western social forms such as class and race. Synthesizing a vast array of empirical ethnographic studies of rural South Asia, as well as a variety of historical, philosophical, and religio-legal sources from the archive of Indic civilization, Marriott and Inden argued that South Asian social systems were built on a wholly different architecture from those of the West, whose foundation was the "dividual," an agent of action and transaction that was continually transferred by contact with other dividuals to create new arrays of rank, purity, and potential liberation from the material world. This idea emerged as part of a debate between Marriott and Louis Dumont, whose pathbreaking study of caste, *Homo Hierarchicus* (1970), had made the case for a radical contrast between Western individualism and Indic holism, without any reference to the idea of the "dividual." Much later, Marilyn Strathern (1988) made an ostensibly independent discovery of the idea of the "dividual" and generated a substantial Melanesian dialogue about this category, which was oddly indifferent to its earlier anthropological lineages.

Entirely outside of the anthropological tradition, we have another emergent line of thought, best articulated by Gilles Deleuze, who developed a radical cosmology of rhizomic networks, man-machine assemblages, and nomadic social forms with its roots in Bergson and Spinoza (Deleuze and Guattari 1987). Deleuze's thought, partly developed in collaboration with the psychoanalyst Felix Guattari, ranged from studies of ecology and biopolitics to studies of cinema and the unconscious, which were regarded with the greatest of respect by his major contemporaries, such as Foucault and Derrida. The implications of Deleuze's ideas about energy, machinic forms, and human agency are only now beginning to be fully explored, notably in what are now referred to as the "new materialisms."[2] Deleuze's ontology may be described as dynamic, vitalist, and processual, and constitutes a radical metaphysical critique of the Cartesian world-picture. Especially in its linkage of the vitalist tradition of Spinoza and Bergson to current interests in machinic agency and ecopolitics, Deleuze is the crucial link. It is noteworthy that the only explicit reference to the "dividual" in Deleuze's oeuvre occurs in a short and prescient article published in English in 1992, where Deleuze distinguished what he calls the emerging societies of control from what were earlier disciplinary societies (with explicit reference to Foucault). Deleuze draws the distinction in many dimensions but especially when he says:

> We no longer find ourselves dealing with the mass/individual pair. Individuals have become "*dividuals*," and masses, samples, data, markets, or "banks." Perhaps it is money that expresses the distinction between the two societies best, since discipline always referred back to minted money that locks gold as numerical standard, while control relates to floating rates of exchange, modulated according to a rate established by a set of standard currencies. The old monetary mole is the animal of the space of enclosure, but the serpent is that of the societies of control. We have passed from one animal to the other, from the mole to the serpent, in the system under which we live, but also in our manner of living and in our relations with others. The disciplinary man was a discontinuous producer of energy, but the man of control is undulatory, in orbit, in a continuous network. Everywhere surfing has already replaced the older sports. (1992)

Though this statement by Deleuze is even more compressed and aphoristic than is usual for him, it allows us to recognize the momentous way in which contemporary finance has produced (or at least catalyzed) a dramatically contemporary form of the dividual, which is directly linked to quantification in all its pervasive forms, one of which is monetization.

What contemporary finance does is to monetize all the other forms of quantification that surround us today, by taking advantage of the dividual forms that such quantification continuously produces. To move from the idea of the dividual to an argument about contemporary finance requires three steps: (a) examining the way in which finance has created a predatory mode of dividuation; (b) showing how the idea of the dividual illuminates the workings of ritual in precapitalist societies; and (c) demonstrating that this dividualized ritual logic underpins the social form of the derivative and can be used to move from predatory dividuation to progressive dividuation. These steps are the subjects of the next three sections.

The Subprime Mortgage and Predatory Dividuation

Let us now look at housing mortgages in the United States. The bizarreness of this form of mediated financial materiality has only risen to public attention because of the meltdown of 2008, in which new forms of bundled mortgage derivatives played a massive role in the market collapse, the effects of which are still very much with us.[3]

Housing loans (mortgages) are an essential part of the material life of financial objects in the United States because they take a mythic element of the contemporary cosmology of capitalism, in which your "own" house is treated as the mark of financial adulthood and security, all housing values are always supposed to rise, and though what you own is a piece of paper, you are led to believe that you actually own a house. The bizarre materiality of the mortgage-backed American house is that while its visible material form is relatively fixed, bounded, and indivisible, its financial form, the mortgage, has now been structured to be endlessly divisible, recombinable, saleable, and leverage-able for financial speculators, in a manner that is both mysterious and toxic.

The fact is that this financial rematerialization of the American home is made possible not merely through the mechanism of the mortgage (which is, after all, simply a particularly complex long-term loan) but through the most complex form of financial mediation the world has known, the derivative. The global financial crisis of 2008 was in no small part created by the crash of housing prices (of the underlying commodity, in other words), which had been leveraged into a complex and massive set of traded derivatives whose values were out of all proportion to the actual value of homes. This yawning gap between home values and derivative prices was in large part due to the creation of certain derivatives, which allowed a large number of subprime mortgages to be made to first-time homeowners. The big question about the mortgage crisis of 2007–8, which was a primary driver of the financial meltdown of that year in the United States, is: Why did so many banks make so many weak or risky loans?

The answer is that in the decades that preceded the global financial crisis, and especially after 1990, the housing market was identified by the financial industries as being capable of yielding far more potential wealth than it had historically done through the mediation of new derivative instruments. The principal two new instruments that allowed banks to do this were mortgage-backed securities (MBS), which are a specific form of something called asset-backed securities (ABS). These securities allowed "bundling" of large numbers of mortgages into a single tradable instrument whose value depended on different ideas about the future value of such bundles between buyers and sellers. This bundling also had another feature: subprime mortgages could be bundled together with mortgages with superior credit ratings and, with the connivance of the credit rating agencies, toxic loans were in effect laundered by bundling them together with better loans, disguising them under an overall superior rating. This meant that many lenders could make money by originating subprime loans so that they could be bundled and resold by being mixed in with higher quality loans. A second derivative instrument that enabled this dangerous alchemy was called a collateralized default obligation (CDO), which allowed these bundles of mortgages to be divided into tranches, or levels, that had different credit ratings. What is important, though technically a shade more obscure, is how the higher value tranches were used to bury, obscure, or disguise the more toxic tranches.

Imagine selling a house with a beautiful view from the upper floor and a leaky basement, which is hidden from view by some mysterious financial instrument that groups all the houses and uses the grading of the top stories to disguise all the leaky basements. This is what allowed the trading of mortgage-based securities and collateralized debt obligations to be a roaring business through the first few years of this millennium, riding the wave of belief that the rising value of all housing would indefinitely postpone the flooding of many millions of basements. Well, housing prices did eventually fall precipitously and the metaphorical basements did flood, leaving hundreds of lenders holding toxic assets and hundreds of homeowners holding mortgages (rightly called underwater mortgages) on which they owed more to the bank than the house was worth at that time. And because these and other derivative instruments connected the massive collapse of the mortgage market to all other credit markets, the entire financial system of the United States was on the brink of disaster until the government pumped in a vast amount of public funds to secure this avalanche of bad loans and debts, in the first weeks of the new Obama administration.

So what is the moral of this story for our purposes today? The moral is that the derivative is above all a new form of mediation. What it mediates by the endless exploitation of the spreads between emergent prices and the unknown future values of commodities is the always-evolving distance between the commodity and the asset, the latter being the commodity as its unrealized potential for future profit. In this process, derivatives are not mere financial instruments (however exotic). They are practices of mediation that yield new materialities, in this case the materialities of the asset, which are potentially available in all commodities. Notice how far this chain of mediations has brought us from the house as a simple materiality. Mediated in the capitalist market, the house becomes the mortgage; further mediated, the mortgage becomes an asset, itself subject to trading as an uncertainly priced future commodity. Mediated yet again, this asset becomes part of an asset-backed security, a new derivative form, which can be further exchanged in its incarnation as a debt obligation. At every step, the financial form serves as mediating practice, which produces a new order of materiality. Notice that in our current financial world this iterative chain of financial derivations also affects other materialities, apart from housing, such as food, health, education, energy, the environment, and virtually everything else that can be mediated into new forms of materiality. So the home—as a material fact—does not exist in our highly financialized world apart from its availability to the mediation of the derivative form. Conversely, it is only by materializing new wealth out of assets such as housing, food, health, and education, among many other assets, that the mediating powers of the derivative become realized, and real.

The relationship between the mortgage crisis and the derivative form cannot fully be understood without understanding the much more radical and widespread way in which financialization relies on a variety of forms of quantification of the person that correspond precisely to

Deleuze's (1992) idea of the dividual in societies of control. There are, of course, other scoring tools in wide use in American society for a variety of purposes, ranging from security alerts to SAT examinations to various insurance protocols for defining risk properties to pools of customers. This feature of contemporary finance would be unviable except in the context of a sweeping process through which contemporary Western individuals have been rendered subjects of a vast array of data search, collation, pattern seeking, and exploitation, some of which has been captured in the recent category of "Big Data."[4] Big Data pervades the activities of the state, private corporate enterprises, and many varieties of security apparatus. Point-of-sale information has been mined for several decades to refine consumer demographics; point-of-use data is critical for the NSA's telephonic surveillance activities both within and outside the United States; social media companies generate troves of interactional information of value to both the state and to the corporate world.

It has been widely observed that these multiple and massive inventories of data are the object of complex new forms of pattern seeking, mining, and strategic application. What has been less noticed is the tectonic shift that these data industries imply in the conception of the individual as the foundation of modern Western ethics, ontology, and epistemology. The most critical implication of these new forms of data gathering and analysis, for the present argument, is the ways in which they atomize, partition, qualify, and quantify the individual so as to make highly particular features of the individual subject or actor more important than the person as a whole. Numbers are attached to consumer purchases, discrete interactions, credit, life chances, health profiles, educational test results, and a whole battery of related life events, so as to make these parts of the individual combinable and customizable in such ways as to render moot or irrelevant the idea of the "whole," the classical individual. This logic of dividuation has natural and historical roots in the machineries of insurance, risk management, and behavioral analysis that pool these quantified parts into larger quantified categories, which can then be further searched, combined, and reaggregated so as to maximize knowledge, profits, and risk minimization for various large-scale institutional actors who have no interest in the idiosyncrasies of the classical individual. I call this logic predatory because its interests are narrow and control oriented, with no regard for individuals except as holding addresses for a large variety of dividual features and possibilities. Contemporary finance lies at the heart of these dividualizing techniques, because it relies on the management and exploitation of risks that are not the primary risks of ordinary individuals in an uncertain world but the derivative or secondary risks that can be designed in the aggregation and recombination of large masses of dividualized behaviors and attributes from credit scores to SAT results.

The multiple derivative instruments that were developed by slicing and dicing individual mortgages so as to generate profit for financial institutions exemplify this predatory logic and have the effect of making dividualized actors incapable of any concerted critique, resistance, or reform with regard to these predatory logics. Thus the many varieties of antidebt movement (exemplified by the Occupy movement) are doomed to fail because they seek to oppose dividualizing logics with strategies of mobilization, persuasion, and critique that rely on the politics of the individual. To create a strong politics to oppose the predatory dividualism that drives the current logic of the derivative requires an alternative approach to politics, a topic addressed in the concluding section of this essay. But now we must consider the dividual logic that underpins classic precapitalist societies, largely unmonetized worlds whose approach to risk and uncertainty can be seen in their ritual machineries.

The Dividual in Ritual Societies

I have elsewhere shown that Durkheim's ideas about religion were radically secularizing (Appadurai 2016) and allow us to see the market as a sacralizing force in contemporary society, and also referred to the well-established "hedging" view of ritual, which lives on today in the most colloquial uses of the word. I further proposed there that the Austinian view of performatives was the most important innovation on this hedging view. Subsequently, Judith Butler's work introduced the idea of what I now refer to as retroperformativity, which allows us to see that ritual can be regarded as a framework for the costaging of uncertainty and certainty in social life. I concluded that argument by referring to the classic work of Arnold van Gennep on *The Rites of Passage* (1960) and some of his modern followers about rituals with a sacrificial element, in which a person, or a part of the person, is sacrificed in the interest of reproducing a social and cosmological whole.

The logic of sacrifice can, in one important respect, illuminate all rituals, and that is in the way sacrifice relies on the critical role of dividuals in order to accomplish its goals. *Sacrifice can only work when what is offered, or given up, usually to a God or ancestor, is a dynamic part of some apparent whole.* In other words, the parts that are given up by one actor to another, in the world of precapitalist sacrifice, are dynamic parts, which also carry their own energies, vitalities, and strivings (in the sense that Spinoza used the term *conatus*). They are not inert shreds or samples of a prior whole. Consider the logic of sorcery, which frequently relies on human bodily leavings (such as nails, hair, skin, or other elements of an actor), to be operated on at a distance by the sorcerer, so as to provide malign or deadly effects on the original source of these leavings. Or consider offerings of human hair to enshrined deities in many parts of India, as gifts that are part of vows to these deities, ventured in the hope of receiving boons, such as a child for a barren woman. Many distinguished anthropologists, such as Lévi-Strauss (1976), Tambiah (1968), and Leach (1976), have pointed out that the efficacy of rituals relies on a special combination of the logics of metaphor (the partial likeness of unlike things) and the logic of metonym (contiguity, connectivity, participation) that connects parts to wholes: head to body, hair to head, organs to other organs, bodies to their effluvia. Metonym is no simple logic of part and whole. It is a logic of dividuation, in which personhood rests not in the stable crystallization of body, soul, intention, and affect in a single bodily envelope but in the highly volatile relationship between those substances (flesh, blood, vitality, energy, essence, and effluvia) that are always in the process of interacting and recombining to produce temporary assemblages of sociality, identity, and affect. This is the dividual logic of noncapitalist societies described by McKim Marriott (1976), Marilyn Strathern (1988), and others who have followed them in the ethnography of South Asia, Melanesia, and other places outside the capitalist orbit. This is dividuation without exploitation because it lacks the monetized and predatory logic by which the derivative form exploits the *dividuation of the many for the individuation (by profit making) of the few.*

Indeed, if we look more closely at retroperformativity, now widely regarded as the underlying logic of many ritual worlds, it can be shown that dividuation is the underlying condition of possibility of retroperformativity in ritual. Because this argument is not a familiar or generally accepted view among anthropologists, it requires an explicit argument. Let us look at the classic instance of the gift (*le don*), first made a canonic concern of anthropology by Marcel Mauss, and then elaborated and debated by a distinguished sequence of French thinkers, including Claude Lévi-Strauss, Émile Benveniste, Pierre Bourdieu, Hélène Cixous, Luce Irigaray, and Jacques Derrida, as well as a host of ethnographers and ethnologists working in other academic traditions on a large range of noncapitalist societies.[5]

The idea of retroperformativity (also discussed in a much fuller way by Edward LiPuma in this volume) amounts in its essence to the following: ritual has its most powerful effect by bringing into effect a change of state in its prime actors as well as in the cosmology that is its frame by realizing (making real) a world presumed as its precondition through a sequence of actions in which effects create causes or conditions of possibility that take shape only in retrospect. This retrocreativity (or performativity) has hitherto been seen primarily as a linguistic effect, which is a temporal reversal of the logic of the performative first identified by Austin with regard to utterances, which change the world by their mere utterance under certain conditions of felicity. This is a deep insight so far as it goes. But its implications for personhood have yet to be identified.

To examine these implications, let us return to the logic of the gift, in particular the force (or *hau*), which Mauss saw, generalizing the Maori concept, as a quality that links the gift, the giver, and the recipient in such a manner as to compel the receiver to make a countergift or a further gift, thus revealing a logic of reciprocity that precedes even the initial gift. Mauss saw *hau* as a quality that somehow linked the gift and the giver in a manner that compelled the countergift. We know that for Mauss this logic accounted for why gifts produced the obligation to return, after an interval of time that could not be reduced to a rule, a formula, or a legal contract. This interval of time is what allowed Pierre Bourdieu (1976) to posit the noneconomistic character of gift exchange and allowed Derrida (1992) to shift the entire focus of the gift away from exchange to the gift of time itself.

This mysterious force that binds gift to both giver and receiver was not further explored by anthropologists because it was not recognized that the gift here is an instance of the attachment of the dividual character of the giver to be attached to the gift and to spark a further tie to some dividual element of the receiver. Put another way, gifts and other objectified instruments in the ritual process do not create ties between "whole" individuals but rather between dividuals, who are in effect partial, volatile, and particular sorts of agents, capable of joining other dividuals in their capacity as kinsmen, traders, enemies, affines, ancestors, or descendants, all more like what we would today call roles rather than individuals. But the idea of role is itself so deeply anchored in the idea of a prior substrate or ground that we think of as the individual that it does not capture the ontology of a dividualized society, since dividuals are, in such societies, the elementary constituents of individuals (and of other larger social aggregations) rather than mere aspects, dimensions, or "personae" of a foundational individual. This ontological reversal is the very definition of the dividual.

Just as the power of the gift may be seen to lie in the capacity of dividuals to create assemblages between themselves and others by combining with things (the gifts as such), so all ritual processes as described by anthropologists from van Gennep to Clifford Geertz may be reinterpreted as the metaphoric and metonymic techniques through which dividuals enter into dynamic and volatile assemblages. It is because the key actors (or actants) in ritually organized societies are dividuals, rather than individuals, that these rituals are capable of acquiring retroperformative force. If named and stable individuals were the subjects of such ritual processes, their assemblage into desirable configurations would have no more than the force of ratification or recognition of established logics of role, status, and norm. In ritually organized societies, since ritual is about the costaging of uncertainty and certainty to handle volatility (in society, nature, and cosmos), retroperformativity benefits from the dynamic assemblage of dividuals, does not rely on the routinized confirmation of relations among individuals, as in our own societies of contract. The volatility of interactions among dividuals requires some form of retroperformativity because totalities (wholes) can only be retroengineered in a world composed of dividuals (parts).[6]

The Derivative and the Dividual

It remains now to link up the world of the financial derivative (embodying, as I have earlier suggested, a predatory logic of dividuation) to a more expansive view of the precapitalist ritual milieu, so as to open the door to a more radical, progressive, and socially generative view of finance, wealth, and risk. The best route to this argument is the recent work of Elie Ayache (2010), who is also a fellow contributor to this volume.

Ayache is at pains to argue that the market, so far as financial tools are concerned, is not a reflective or post hoc process for aggregating, mediating, or commensurating buyers and sellers (or demand and supply). Rather, it is a creative force, an ontological absolute that precedes and is the condition of all pricing. Ayache does not refer to Durkheim, but his argument may be seen as a radical version of Durkheim's view on the prior ontological reality of society, in his famous argument in *The Elementary Forms of Religious Life* (1995), about the social basis of the category of the sacred.

When we combine Ayache's view of the trading event, with his account of the body of the trader and of the importance of writing as the key tool for the making of contingent claims (Appadurai 2016), we can see the possibilities for a deep convergence between Durkheim's ideas about collective effervescence and Ayache's idea of the trading event as the real site of market making through agreements about price. The deep link here is between the trading floor or space (even when it is virtual or machine mediated) and those of the moment of collective effervescence in the ritual life of Australian aboriginal societies. The shared element is the electricity, the metasocial sensation of belonging, and the deep identifications (body-to-body), that attend the creation of society in ritual (for Durkheim).

Still, a major puzzle remains about both logic of the derivative and the logic of precapitalist ritual, and this is where the idea of the dividual can come to our assistance. Recall that Durkheim, and his numerous followers (including Mauss, Lévi-Strauss, and Bourdieu, as well as numerous other anthropologists of the twentieth century), did not really unsettle the category of the individual as the foundational element of all social interaction and social institutions. In this sense, Durkheim did not move away from Kant, with whose ideas about the origins of our primary categories (such as space and time) he took radical issue. It was not until the path-breaking work of Louis Dumont, in *Homo Hierarchicus* (1970) and a series of other books and essays, that the post-Renaissance idea of the individual was put into sharp comparative relief. But even Dumont contrasted Western individualism with Indic "holism" and did not really consider the idea of dividuality. This was the accomplishment of Marriott (1976) and, later, Marilyn Strathern (1988), as I have already argued. And these latter thinkers had, alas, little interest in the problem of performativity (even less in the issue of retroperformativity).[7]

If we now insert the idea of the dividual back into our reading of Durkheim, bearing in mind the link to Ayache's argument about derivative trading and its own logic of "backwardation" or retroperformativity, we can supply an answer to the peculiar way in which precapital-ist societies invented a major modality for dealing with uncertainty as the core predicament of human societies. *Rituals take their effect by the retroperformative creation of wholes out of parts, but the parts in question are dividuals, not individuals.* The reason that all rituals, however routinized, always carry an element of anxiety is that every ritual performance undertakes, as if for the first and last time, the effort to produce "wholes," such as individuals, clans, and tribes as well as affines, agnates, allies, and friends, out of inherently unstable, volatile, and contingent elements, namely dividuals. The momentary creation of "totalities," at any and all of these levels, is subject both to situational uncertainty (Will a counterparty be found to any ritual invitation? Will the gift be returned? Will the adolescent survive the wounds of the rite of passage? Will the new child be appropriately healthy? Will the crops actually grow?) as well as to a more primary uncertainty, which is whether the constituent dividual actors in any ritual scene, in any moment of collective effervescence, will stay stable enough to lend retrospective stability to an inherently volatile and contingent assemblage of dividuals.

In the case of market making in derivatives, as described by Ayache, this volatility, contingency, and unpredictability are wrapped into the derivative instrument itself and is a product of the slicing, dicing, and recombination that lies at the heart of the derivative form itself. *In both cases, the great accomplishment of backwardation[8] (in the case of derivative trading) or retroperformativity (in the case of ritual performance) is to create options and hedges in and through the same sequence of actions.* The option aspect of the event is its taking of the risk that some sort of whole can be created, even if temporarily, by the strategic assemblage of parts. The hedge aspect of the event is the reliance on some sort of routinized assumption that the larger model (of cosmological or market fundamentals) will guard against the inherent instability of the dividuals involved in the assemblage.

But there is also a critical difference between the ritual order and the market order. In the case of the ritual order, the dividuals entering into a performance are the *permanent* elements of the order who take the temporary risk of assembling themselves into wholes (whether individual or corporate). In the case of the financialized order, the dividuals are *temporary* products of predatory dividuation (ranking, scoring, enumeration, quantification, monetization) who are put at risk by actors (brokers, traders, managers, analysts) who reserve the right to behave as individuals *in their own interest.* In short, in the ritual order, all actors take the risk of entering into a risky assemblage, whereas in the financial order, the risk is asymmetrically distributed between professional risk takers (traders) at the expense of already dividuated actors who largely bear the downside risks of the market. This is the difference that is captured in the idea of predatory dividuation.

The Political Future

We are now in a position to raise the main political question that follows from this argument about dividuals, ritual, and derivative trading, which is: Is there a way to transform the derivatives markets (and by extension the contemporary financial markets) into sites of progressive or democratic dividuation rather than sites of the current exploitative, asymmetric, and antidemocratic financial order? In other words, can we leverage our argument about the dividual into a basis for a democratic politics of finance?

The answer to this question is not entirely within the scope of this essay, but an approach can be indicated. The only way to convert the dividual into a genuinely empowered subject in today's predatory financial context is not by any form of return to a nonmonetized, nonfinancialized order, or any "refusal" of our current forms of debt and wealth creation, both of which imply a reversal of history that is both unrealistic and undesirable. What is called for is a radical change in the architecture of our social thought.

What we need to do is to rethink our primary vocabulary for social consociation so as to reflect the irreversible effects of financialized dividuation. For us, as social scientists, this will mean a radical reconstruction of such categories as group, class, mass, crowd, and multitude, as well as qualitative terms such as "public," "collective," "free," and "social." These two sets of concepts, which provide the armature of much of our current social theory, will need rebuilding with the assumption being that the elementary building blocks of the social are not individuals but dividuals, the latter being a much more unstable, volatile, contingent, and open element than the canonic individual that has so far anchored our social thought.

If we are able to undertake this thoroughgoing reform of our basic social vocabulary, we might be able to take such phenomena as spreads,

volatility, liquidity, and risk, currently used to disenfranchise most dividuals, and imagine new forms of collective risk taking through which the
derivative will more closely approximate what Guy Debord called the
"dérive" (2007), that is, the practice of playful travel through urban land-
scapes that opens up the terrain of chance and serves as an antidote to
the deadening routinization of everyday experience in late capitalism.[9]

In simpler terms, a radical social theory built on a contemporary definition of the dividual has the potential for reintroducing the play of
chance into our social lives in a manner that allows *all of us* to engage
in the risk-taking possibilities for creating wealth, rather than reserving
this privilege to the 1 percent who reap the rewards of risk taking, with
the rest of us consigned to the status of risk bearers and collective losers.
This radical potential takes the derivative form to be a genuine instrument for the production of wealth in the present by taking risks on the
future. But it also requires us to see ourselves as partial, contingent, and
volatile beings who can leverage and resocialize our dividuality by ex-
ploiting the deep logic of the derivative form.

Concluding by Example

To imagine the political implications of the argument about the contras-
tive relationship between dividual and individual in capitalist and ritual-
based societies, I turn to a brief analysis of the housing market in Mumbai, where an activist movement of slum dwellers has been struggling to
establish rights to housing for the homeless of underhoused slum communities for more than three decades.

I have written extensively about the ritual, social, and political life of
this movement in a recent book (Appadurai 2013). In the present context,
what is striking is how dividuality expresses itself in a context where a
population of about six million persons lack legitimate access to housing
and where, as a consequence, financial markets, mortgages, and derivatives are essentially absent. At the same time Mumbai, with a growing
population of more than sixteen million persons, is a financial and corporate hub for India, which has a highly active stock market, many insurance companies, and a number of national and global financial firms
(banks, hedge funds, and nonformal lending institutions). The products
and services offered by these financial players directly affect the housing
development market in Mumbai, as well as the lives of numerous mem-

bers of Mumbai's middle classes who participate in banking, borrowing, stock investments, mortgages, and insurance. This financial market is in the process of developing and is only gradually becoming rationalized in the manner of its Western counterparts, in regards to regulation, risk, law, and data gathering.

In this respect, cities like Mumbai and societies like India occupy an intermediate and transitional space between the ritualized societies that I have been discussing in this essay and the advanced financial economies of the West. As a result, Mumbai (and India) also exhibit some dynamic contrasts and connections between the ritualized dividuation of small-scale, low-technology societies and the financialized dividuation of the contemporary West.

The slum activists with whom I worked in Mumbai are keenly aware of the dangers of the fully financialized environment in which they increasingly function, in a city whose square foot real estate prices rival those of New York, London, and Tokyo. They are surrounded by developers who transform slum areas into high-rise towers and middle-class housing, bankers who would like to draw them into the microsavings markets, and politicians who would like to use them as vote banks.

These slum communities, led by an alliance of activists, can be regarded as pursuing a progressive brand of dividualism, albeit in a powerful capitalist environment. This characterization is based on several observations. First, the slum dwellers I spoke to always expressed a strong ideology of anti-individualism, based on their sense that individualism was closely linked to selfishness, greed, and antisocial tendencies, which could be expressed in the behavior of members regarding money, personal possessions, or temporary housing. At the same time, they expressed strong aversion to descriptions of their collective identity in terms of class, interest group, party, or faction, all of which they regarded as misleading ways of talking about their sense of community. This resistance always puzzled me until recently, when I began to look at my decade-long experience with them in terms of the broader and deeper Indic idea of dividual actors and actions, as shown by McKim Marriott and many of his students. I have already discussed the key features of the idea of the dividual, but the relevance of this idea to Mumbai's slum dwellers needs further elaboration.

The slum dwellers of Mumbai are not a classical anthropological community. But they are all Indian and do come from a variety of linguistic, ethnic, and caste groups that have deep Indian roots. In this regard, they do share certain Indic ideas about health, wealth, and sociality. In Mumbai, they may be regarded as a quasicaste, because they share a situation into which they were mostly born, their destinies look fairly predetermined, and they are regarded as a biophysical category by other urban citizens, in often thinly biologized ideas about slum morality, hygiene, and disease. They react to this biologization by regarding themselves, to some extent, as a natural group, with common interests, obligations, and moralities. Poverty and slum dwelling have thus become partly accommodated to the lens of caste morality and ideology.

Part of this morality is the idea that moral agency is unstable, relational, and situational. At the same time such identities are regarded as rooted in some sort of natural, biophysical, and organic order. The primary insight of Marriott's ideas about the radical difference between Indian and Western moral cosmologies was that the Indian ones do not recognize a sharp line between mind and body, self and other, nature and culture, law and predisposition. Marriott called this point of view monistic (or nondualistic). While it might seem a long journey from Indic cosmological ideas to the political practices of the Mumbai slum dwellers, the connection is real. Its most clear expression is the refusal of these slum dwellers to allow themselves to be defined as individuals, in the common modern sense, and to insist on their collective identity. This in itself might be viewed as a conventional modern form of social solidarity, as expressed in the language of class, party, income group, or interest group. But the sense of collective identity among these slum dwellers is more radically attuned to the dynamic linkages between bodies, infrastructure, technical assemblages, and situational instability and is in fact expressive of a dividual cosmology.

This can most clearly be seen in their understanding of the importance of toilets and defecation in the struggle for rights for slum communities. I have written elsewhere (Appadurai 2001) of the ways in which toilet festivals (*sandas mela*) have been a key strategy of this urban movement to redefine defecation, sanitation, and sociality in the Mumbai context, as well as in many other locations in urban India where they work. The problem of toilets is a vital part of the politics of urban poverty throughout the world, and in India it bears the additional burden of highly valued notions of purity, pollution, stigma, and degradation, as evidenced in the powerful social bias against those Untouchables who historically served as scavengers, toilet cleaners, and night soil carriers in both rural and urban India. The toilet politics of the Mumbai slum dwellers have made community toilets, designed, built, and operated by the slum communities themselves, a site of empowerment and dignity rather than of exclusion and pollution. They have done this by making toilets more like community centers (in which the person charged with maintaining a new toilet block lives in a small unit above the community toilet) and have invited government officials and other political figures to launch these community toilets in a manner in which the inauguration of temples and deities in much of India is done, with flowers, coconuts, and public celebrations accompanying these events. This is part of a complex strategy to make defecation a publically recognized and valid platform for social dignity, in an environment where defecation in public is always a sign of radical dispossession, especially in urban India.

Behind this reclamation of toilets from being a site of deficit, disease, and degradation, there lies a complex view of how best bodies, bodily wastes, sociality, and community can be reassembled in situations where space, access to infrastructure, and privacy are always scarce. It requires a view of slum communities as formed of dividuals whose shared bodily practices are grounded in the capacity of such groups to recombine traditional Indian social categories. Here it is important to note that these slum communities come from diverse castes, ethnic groups, and religious communities throughout India, each of which would traditionally have placed great emphasis on their differences from one another, however minute. By redesigning and revalorizing community toilets, these communities create a radical bodily space in which a derivative and dividual logic is turned to the project of finding positive value (solidarity) where only negative value (shit) previously existed. This transformative and derivative operation can only occur in an environment where dividuals are always in an unstable, volatile, and relational environment of social and moral reproduction. To place toilets and sanitation at the center of a politics of "deep democracy" (Appadurai 2001) literally turns classic Indic dividualism on its head, and turns shit into social value and exclusion into empowerment.

This is thus a fascinating glimpse of a progressive politics of dividualism, equally distinct from modern Western possessive individualism and from classical Hindu dividualism, which has a powerful conservative thrust, insofar as it locks castes and other social categories into a persistent form of inequality. The Mumbai slum dwellers have assembled a different, and derivative, form of dividuality that may properly be called political and progressive in that it embodies an immanent critique both of classical Hindu thought as well as of the financialized individualism that surrounds them in modern Mumbai.

This instance is not likely to stand alone, either in India or in the rest of the world. I point to a possible third way for the politics of the dividual and the derivative to be reassembled in the interests of social justice. For if shit can be turned to positive value by a group on the margins of predatory capitalism in a city like Mumbai, surely other forms of labor, energy, and value can be similarly reclaimed for progressive and dividualized forms of social wealth, which are derivative in form but socially inclusive and expansive in spirit.

CHAPTER TWO

Ritual in Financial Life

Edward LiPuma, University of Miami

The ascension of financial derivatives and their markets has forcibly foregrounded circulation. Not just in its logistical mission as the filament that connects production to consumption, that represents how one pregiven form carries on a material and symbolic conversation with another, but as the means by which these forms, such as the ascendant financial markets, constitute themselves as such and do so in a sociohistorically specific manner. Following the contours of this transformation, this chapter originates in a shift of perspective: a 180-degree revolution from crystallized forms to circulatory structures. What appears to be a slight shift in the optic of understanding, an adjustment suggested by the globalizing processes now in train, reverberates theoretically, frequently in unexpected ways. Once we accord circulation equal ontological weight, categories such as rituality and performativity come suddenly into new perspective, and the canonized opposition between two presumably well-formed forms—primitive society and capitalist society—begins to dissolve. But also to reestablish itself on altogether different ground. From this different ground, the critical difference that separates capitalism from, even as it superimposes itself upon and encompasses, the diversity of noncapitalist forms of social life stems from the historically revised way in which capitalism uses production and circulation to create sociality. There is disciplinary resistance—that has always been the story—but the ascension of circulation, exemplified by the rise of the derivative and the growing power of financial markets globally, compels a reinterpretation of the concepts that we have used to apprehend the social.

There's no point in wasting time: in the land of power, time is seldom on the side of science. In a spirit of reinterpretation, what follows begins with an effort to undo a principle dualism upon which the social sciences' sociohistorically specific account of the social has resided. Thus the quasifoundational dualism between "primitive" and "modern" where the former rested upon socially robust but economically rationally compromised practices of ritualized exchange, while the modern market awaited only advances in science to be mathematized into an apparently objective and sovereign space, termed *the* economy, that brackets off and misrecognizes the very sociality that is the condition of its existence. This duality ultimately rests on a contrast and comparison between *the surface forms of capitalism and what primitive exchange would look like from the perspective of those forms.* The italics are important because the surface forms of capitalism, exemplified by production-centered commodity production, impart an objective, lawlike, and thus apparently economically rational character to commodity circulation. In contrast primitive exchange, with its overt reliance on kinship and community, appears to be guided by subjects that have no allegiance to assessments of risk, calculations of value and return, or strategies of how to use the interval between the giving of a gift and its future requital. A deeper reading of the ethnography would show that "primitive" subjects act in interested ways, a point Pierre Bourdieu stressed right from the beginning (e.g., 1972). It is also a misreading of the ethnography to think that primitive societies do not have markets, commodities, and wealth accumulation and that these surface categories constitute adequate grounds for differentiating them from capitalism. The real comparison must be between the deep sociostructures of capitalism and the real ethnographic character of social economies that feature ritualized gift exchange: even the apparently descriptive idea that there is the singularity called *the gift* is misleading. Such an interpretation attributes a totalization to the gift that is actually read off of the appearance of the commodity, whose underlying form is a striving toward a totality that can never be completed due to the dissembling effects of circulatory forces, such as the rise of derivatives (see LiPuma and Postone, unpublished manuscript, for a more comprehensive version of this argument). Primitive societies have markets, commodities, and wealth accumulation; they just constitute them differently in respect to the social.

In a synthesis of what once served as figure and ground, the present work will transit from an analysis of rituality in the context of primitive exchange to the rituality constitutive of the financial markets now roaming the earth. The critical links are the presumably noneconomic categories of performativity and rituality. The aim is to show how performativity operates throughout to socially instantiate a form(s)—such as a market—in such a way that its objectification can serve as the ground of practice (the trading of intertemporal derivative contracts). Developing the notion of performativity in respect to circulation will lead to a reconceptualization of totalities and the means by which they can serve as platforms for the production of wealth. The chapter then concludes with what, from this perspective, is the quintessential expression of rituality in the financial markets, the operation of the canonized Black-Scholes formula for pricing options. The force of the argument is to open an understanding of the circulatory object as a wealth-generating sociality.

Anthropology and Economic Disciplines

We begin with a conclusion put in service as an introduction to an alternative theorization of the structure of financial circulation: that we owe the bulletproof division between the anthropology of primitive societies and the formal economics of bourgeois capitalism more to the history of the self-positioning by the disciplines than to the actual economies found in the world. About this, there had long been an informal division of intellectual labor. Anthropologists worried about the typically nonwestern, marginally and partially capitalist, frequently still struggling postcolonial economies: community-based, primary production–centered, economies or economic enclaves lying on the margins of capitalism, places like the former Bantustans of South Africa, the remote, tribally ruled, mountain regions of Nepal and Ethiopia, or marginalized islands such as Haiti and New Caledonia. By contrast, economists focused on market-driven, capital-intensive, globally integrated economic sectors where they appeared. So, for example, anthropologists and rural sociologists studied the Amazonian Indian populations working on the rubber and coffee plantations in the interior of Brazil while economists were charged with studying Brazil's burgeoning finance and petroleum sectors. There are, of course, no disciplinary rules about economic subjects, but as a rule the division held with only a handful of scholars camping consistently on the other's terrain. More importantly, this division of intellectual labor corresponds to a theoretical vision of the social.

The idea is that sociality inundates the economies that anthropologists are wont to study; especially gift-based economies are so intrinsically social it is pointless to use concepts and tools developed for scalable, large-scale capitalist market-driven societies. The countervailing idea is that where capitalism reigns supreme the economic is an entirely independent domain that renders it possible to craft methods and models that isolate and fixate on the economic, as though the economic is a separate and thus separable dimension of social life. Embedded in this formulation was an agreement that the epicenter of formal economic analysis would be production whereas anthropologists would foreground the sociology of exchange (Sahlins 1972). An accepted disciplinary distinction between formal and substantive economics[1] enshrined this vision and division of the social world, which not coincidentally corresponded to two distinct and nonconversant literatures.

However, it turns out that an analysis of the semiotics and structures of financial circulation is only possible if we reject this theoretical division in favor of the view that all economies are necessarily substantive because they are inherently social. What is especially significant is that the original disciplinary division, occurring in the context of the rise of structuralism in anthropology and neoliberal economics, assisted in the entrenchment of two critical theoretical flaws. The first was the supposition of an irredeemable historical break between primitive noncapitalist societies and modern capitalist societies: Lévi-Strauss's distinction between hot and cold societies and the neoliberal supposition that a feature of modernity was the inevitable expression of the economically rational agent (that had been suppressed by tradition). Mainstream Marxists also implicitly endorsed this distinction by assuming that capitalism—founded on a commodity-driven, class-organized, market-based distribution of wealth—was so powerful and totalizing that it subsumed and vanquished primitive forms of social life. This distinction so conceived, the ritualized exchange of reproductive goods/gifts had nothing to do with the market exchange of labor-extracting commodities. This irredeemable break meant that there was no way to conceptualize the passages—that is, a historical interval that unfolds as a spread of possibilities—from noncapitalist primitive societies to capitalist social forms in respect to a genuine theory of the progressions from the former to the latter. What is missing is an archeology of transformed forms—that is, historically primitive forms of practice (such as and especially ritual)—that capitalism transforms in ways that recontextualize and reconfigure that phenomena while retaining its instrumentality in, for example, the reproduction of social totalities. What is apparent once we reconnect the forms of economic life is that analysis no longer has to treat Durkheim's constructivist account of ritual and Marx's immanent critique of capital as though they represent incommensurable analytical tracks. Weber is also brought back into the conversation through both his writings on ritual and his conceptions of social status and institutional position. The Weberian contribution reminds us that reproduction is mediated by persons whose economic positions and position-taking strategies (e.g., the allocation of capital) occur within and are oriented in respect to a collectively constituted space.

The second flaw is that the division between formal and substantive economics was conducive to slipping into a shadow account of the reproduction of a totality. What both substantivist and neoclassical economics had in common is that they bought into a capitalist ideology that suggests the integrity of social totalities—markets, clans, a culture, an economy— is ontological and thus preanalytical. While Lévi-Strauss (1969) and a whole generation of anthropologists focused on the exchanges of women and gifts, the analyses invariably presupposed the prior integrity and identity of the social groups conducting the exchange. As Bourdieu would later suggest (1976), once this ontology is rolled into place both the transgressions of the social groups and the interval between gift and countergift become irrelevant. By the same token, finance economics fixates on what the market does, in the process presupposing the market's integrity as the ungrounded ground of practice.

Through these moves, circulation is made to disappear. Specifically, all forms of circulation unfold in time, imbuing them with a temporality that is nothing less than a collectively anticipated forthcoming in which events of paying off punctuate, even as they generate, agents' sense of periodization (from an extended exchange cycle to a derivative's expiration date). This ontology brackets the reality that circulatory processes continually undermine and dissemble groups and other formations of totality, even as these circulatory processes are the source of the group's (the totality's) reproduction. We can see that reproduction depends on the volatility or change immanent in circulation but only on the condition that there are processes in place that mitigate volatility to the point where it does not threaten the functioning of liquidity and hence the totality's continuity. Inserted into this language, the bottom of Ayache's (2010) claims about the recalibration of derivatives is that the temporal interval permits, and is the reflection of, all manner of transgressions. Ayache's exchange-traded derivatives represent the point where the rituality of the market is so institutionalized and routinized that the social reproduction of the market appears to be each event's nonevent. All well and good, and so perfectly invisible, until normal "expected" volatility breaks down due to transgression and a market's liquidity disappears, thereby endangering its existence (exemplified by the crashes of 1987 and 2000).

In counterpoint to Ayache, Derman (2011) observes that the pricing models that drive the circulation of derivatives are prone to "behave badly" because they lack a real theory of the interval as a space-time of uncertainty in which the transgressive power of the exogenous factors the participants believe matter (e.g., change in the Fed's monetary policy), as well as the internal mechanics of the market, can and do make themselves felt. Derman's exotic "over the counter" derivatives name the point where the rituality of the market is so exteriorized that the market's social reproduction appears to be systemically natural.[2]

So our position is that while capitalism, exemplified by the market for financial derivatives, is qualitatively different from any other economic regime, it is nonetheless fundamentally social. Critically, the economic aspects of the social are also fundamentally different, but no less social for being so. Put another way, capitalism founds itself on a distinctive specific form of sociality, but this form of sociality is no less social for its distinctiveness (exemplified by its asocial appearance) nor is it less inclined to use the performative power of ritual to reproduce itself. The path from primitives to derivatives goes through the rituality constitutive of the social. Nothing illustrates this more than the social processes required to sanction agents to, provisionally, isolate the economic by placing themselves in contexts that valorize those dispositions that sublimate or eclipse their investments in the social.

Let it be said that if cultural anthropology has produced one incontrovertible conclusion, it is that for most of the history of humankind, societies did everything in their repertoire to produce persons who valued and valorized kinship and community above all else. The goal was to produce persons who radiate dividuality (above individuality) in that their "self"-interests are indistinguishable from the interests of the collectivity inasmuch as the crystallization of those interests arise in and through a person's relationality with others. Dividuality is a term derived from the Indian and Melanesian anthropological traditions to help explicate societies where persons' relationships to others are the primary constituent of their identity across most socially meaningful situations. Dividuality is not a kind of personhood; it is the functionality of being in the world that represents the collectivity's creation of a person's singularity. As such, dividuality and individuality are the twin inseparable dimensions of personhood. The critical question becomes, given the society in question, what are the socially constructed situations/conditions in which the partible aspects of persons become attached to others to create a collectively created singular person? What characterizes capitalism is that even those social situations that are redolent with dividuality are, on the model of the world read off of the commodity, cast as instances of individuality.

However natural it may now seem to those who tune in to CNBC and Bloomberg, entertain *Barron's* and the *Wall Street Journal*, or are schooled to an MBA, it requires a tremendous amount of social labor to produce persons (like those we encountered) who, enframed within the market, voluntarily sacrifice their relationship with their wives and their children to earn money speculatively on bets that, on account of their enormous piles of sequestered wealth, have little marginal value to them as a medium of exchange for other commodities. For the first time in social history, we have—through an intense process of socialization that begins with children's mass media and ends with MBA training and the initiation rites of investment firms—created persons defined by a deeply instilled monetized subjectivity: individuals whose core of self-esteem, identity, and self-worth is not centered around the creation of a family and a space of domesticity, the perpetuation of the family and lineage, the purchase of desirable commodities, the status rewards of social position, the attainment of public recognition, the satisfaction of intellectual achievement, discovering spiritual peace and fulfillment, or the reward of heavenly merit, but around the unending acquisition of money itself. What the common notion of greed distills, albeit in a deeply ideological form, is that the goals of self-actualization that have stood at the center of most cultures for most of the history of humankind, the goals that shine forth in ethnography after ethnography about cultures from all corners of the planet, are reduced to occasionally and conditionally important footnotes, as complements to one's life rather than the very core of personhood and self-identity. The quest is for money in the abstract, which is money in its electronic form as a cipher and surrogate for the self.

What defines those at the pinnacle of derivatives trading is that they are so preoccupied with and so deeply valorize their *acts of acquiring* money that money, once acquired, diminishes in value inasmuch as it can only be exchanged for the things that money can buy (e.g., houses, cars, boats). As Michael Lewis's investor portraits in *The Big Short* (2010) indicate, their return for being on the right (i.e., profitable) side of a trade that cut against the wisdom of the prevailing market (i.e., shorting collateralized mortgage obligations) was that it illustrated to their peers and above all to themselves that they were the embodiment of an uncommon level of diligence, courage, intelligence, and competitive fire. The noticeable trait that high-stakes poker players and derivative traders have in common—which helps to explain why many of finance's most prominent deal makers are such avid poker players—is that money counts and that there is accordingly never a limit or end to their desire to acquire it because money is the means of keeping score. Those in finance appear to be inordinately greedy, their desire for money seemingly insatiable, precisely because the sociospecific form of greed that defines the contemporary financial field is founded on the acquisition of money. It is founded on the performative creation of the subject through repeated acts of acquisition: a deep-seated nonconscious compulsion whose appearance in everyday practice takes the form of agents' competitive drive and their love for the financial game. Gobs of money are, of course, exquisitely useful because agents can deploy them to fabricate a new material world and index success, but only acts of acquisition repeated again and again can make the subject so deeply valorized by the financial field. Which begins to explain why derivative traders feel a compulsion to trade, making speculative bets and constructing new deals, working long-hour days and then into the weekend, often refusing to take a vacation or vacationing with the computer screen and cell phone ablaze, long after they have accumulated tens of millions of dollars. This observation becomes a kind of theory in the hands of behavioral economists, culminating in the notion that financial crises occur when our deeply Puritan animal spirits of avarice, envy, and lust emerge from hibernation, casting us into a diabolical world in which what we think is rational, following the crowd on its pilgrimage toward financial success, is actually the epitome of irrationality and folly. Note that in behavioral economics the notions of *following* and *the crowd* are surrogates for an account of the social, for these irredeemably ambiguous notions lie almightily at the intersection where the objective outcomes of a market (houses that have soared in value and been flipped for huge gains) inflect agents' collective forthcoming actions. The language of behavioral economics constitutes an admission of the power of the social, which it is powerless to understand so long as it lives in the netherland between the rational and irrational.

In essence, as analysis probes beneath the surface, it becomes evident that there is a deeper, more social story of the financial field, markets, and agents, a place where the distinction between the social and economic makes little sense. While these markets are powerfully economic in the most robust sense of the term, they equally and unmistakably implicate questions concerning the (re)production of the market, the creation of agents' subjectivities, senses of belonging and fairness, an ethos of speculation, nationalism, an imaginary of the market, notions of anonymous sociality, the agents' sense of immersion in a competitive game, and more that is intrinsic to financial markets but goes far beyond the economic realm. Our objective is not to convince anyone that the economic is less than it appears, rather, that creation and practices of the finance markets presume the presence, and depend on the power, of a sociality that the financial field conceals as a condition of its own sociospecific production.

To his lasting credit—although he hasn't been given credit for it—Robert Pisani, CNBC's eye on the floor of the New York Stock Exchange, got to the hidden heart of the conundrum when he ascertained that "liquidity is a religion" in which the market had "lost its faith" (27 September 2008). The participants once possessed a confidence of belief in the markets, a confidence not based on empirical proof but on their trust in its agents and institutions, and this was gone. What Pisani grasped was that liquidity is something that the participants in a market provide one another, but that they only do this under certain circumstances that have much more to do with their collective state of mind than with the clockwork of the market. Behind his remark is the idea that liquidity is a pseudonym and reification for the *social relations* that allow *individuated* agents to construct the *collective enterprise* that is a market, just as, in their own ways, are notions of counterparty and a homogenous (arbitrage-free) market. Perhaps ironically, this is nowhere more true than in respect to the derivative markets. However much they appear deliberately not so, derivative markets are an ultimate expression of a social imaginary brought into being by the play of concrete social relations. The exposition must ground itself in these relations because they interpolate and mediate—through, for example, the recalibration of prices—

the dialectical relationship between the always contingent and often un-
predictable flows of events and the construction of a market as a totality.

Now it also turns out that religion is an unexpectedly apt metaphor:
for the modern American, circulation of faith is an unregulated market
where all commitments are over-the-counter bets on salvation. Critically,
it declares what anthropologists steeped in gift-based exchange have
known since the pioneering work of their ancestors, especially Marcel
Mauss and Claude Lévi-Strauss: that totalities, including the market, are
social fictions made real by collective belief and sustained through the
name that we have canonized for the power and persistence of belief—
namely, faith. A financial market is a social imaginary, a deeply institutionalized imaginary to be sure, endowed with a name, ratified participants, bodies of received knowledge, registered firms, a codified history,
and so on, but it is an imaginary nonetheless. A market objectifies itself institutionally much in the manner that a nation institutionalizes itself through the creation of a state (such as the institutionalization of US
nationness in the Treasury Department or the Federal Reserve Bank).
From our standpoint, it is neither an accident nor some opportune metaphor that a crisis-torn market began to speak in prayers, its commentators drawn to formulations that suture the health of the market to in-
scriptions of faith and belief normally attributed to religion. Even more,
in calling for the restoration of faith and belief, these commentators are,
without intending to, invoking a performativity that attends religion's
celebrated accompanist: ritual. Indeed, we take the financial community's self-assessment seriously. We see its references to religion not as a
mistake but as a crisis-induced moment of self-reflexivity and thus a sign
of where to look analytically. We will not suggest the argument that re-
ligions in a capitalist society tend to fetishize ritual in order to hide its
economic dimension (though this is so, there being a real economy to
ritual)[3]; rather, we will suggest that the structuring of the financial field
and its markets turns on their rituality. Our reading and theorization of
the evidence leads to the argument that rituality underwrites the collective vision that founds the creation of socially imagined totalities. This
is anything but straightforward, for a market when viewed (and concep-
tualized) from the standpoint of the agents appears as an aggregation
of individuals (maximizing self-interested competitors), whereas agents,
when viewed from the standpoint of the totality that allows the market
to exist as such, appear as a network of dividuals whose connectivity
grounds their self-interested competition.

The notion of the transformed form calls forth two big questions, whose answers repair or at least clarify the flaws originating in the received view of the arc from primitives to derivatives, from noncapitalist into capitalist society. The first is, *What is the essential character of the rituality in its pre-capitalist incarnations?* and the second, *How is this rituality transformed and instrumentalized to the sociospecific context of modern financial capitalism?* Let us begin with the anthropological maxim that a careful consideration of particular instances can reveal more general considerations. Due to its almost universal importance in precapitalist societies, we will take *ritualized marriage exchange* as our ritual object and the highland societies of Papua New Guinea as our ethnographic subject (in large measure because there is extensive data on these societies prior to their encompassment by nation-state capitalism). Our objective is to illustrate how rituality is the engine of the performative objectification of totality.

Performativity and Ritual

So where to begin with performativity, especially as performativity has been much discussed across a range of disciplines, although certainly not with the sociostructural implications that we attribute to it. Let us start with the supposition that performativity is intrinsically social and social-life performative, making performativity a critical part of the foundational character of the social. The single reason for its centrality is that the objective structures of the social (including markets) can reproduce themselves only in and through the *performance* of agents who, acting on their own behalf (interestedness), do things whose collective result is to reinstantiate these structures in the face of the dissembling effects of circulatory forces. This point needs to be italicized because virtually all analyses' point of departure is the stabilized moment *after* the structure's reinstantiation. This objectivism substitutes what agents have objectified, a system of products (e.g., markets, financial instruments, etc.), for the principles and performative practices of their innovation and reproduction. Which takes place at the crossroads where production and circulation not only intersect but are mutually constitutive (e.g., the innovation of a derivative always carries the intent of its circulation just as insuring its future liquidity informs the production of that derivative). Accordingly, analysis cannot apprehend the structuring effect of agents' performances if its standpoint removes the implications of circulation, either by considering reproduction as a pregiven and preordained process that exists somehow prior to and thus external from the participants' practices (e.g., ritual) or, alternatively, as a vacant a priori framework that individuals fill in individually in whatever manner their preferences and circumstances dictate (e.g., the economistic account of the market as the crystallization of individual transactions).

So agents' performances are performative precisely because these performances reconstitute the sociostructure and functionality that circulatory forces are constantly compromising (to a greater or lesser degree). Performativity reobjectifies the form or sociostructure and conserves its functionality (the ability of a market to organize the flow of derivatives) in the face of the volatility and dissembling effects that the unknowns and uncertainties inherent in circulation invariably variably throw up. As to the structure, the objectification of the form is the recertification of the platform (e.g., a market) that the participants must mutually presuppose in order to create and execute the strategies (e.g., one agent selling a put, the other buying that same put) that constitute the event. The magic of performativity is that *the social* structures the event without being there as such, not least because traders trade so deeply in the moment that the social disappears: the social is existentially consequential only if it fails and liquidity stops. On the side of agency, the participants' existential interest in the event/performance is what imbues their lives with significance and purpose; it is what motivates them to willingly take on the uncertain risks animated by the event itself, which, due to the uncertainties (transgressions) that attend wagers on the future or the forthcoming, can never rule out the possibilities of failures or misfirings (everyone knows cautionary tales of the best laid plans, the locked-in-can't-miss wagers that ended in loss, disgrace, conflict); ultimately it is this existential interest that motivates the agents to invest in the event's outcome and, in so doing, to take actions that reproduce the objective structure.

Although many accounts of things social have invoked what amounts to an implicit theory of performativity, it is with the work of the twentieth-century philosopher John Austin that the subject gains the foreground. In *How to Do Things with Words* (1962), Austin observes that English has utterances (such as "I promise," "bet," and "baptize") that create the situation they instantiate. These performatives are distinct from ordinary descriptions in that they are not statements about

the world that may be judged as to their existential truth or falsity. Performatives work when agents correctly attach a specific utterance to a socially specific context (as when, at the signature of a marriage ceremony,
a justice of the peace says "I now pronounce you man and wife"). Analysts also observed that language performatives often noticeably appear
in social situations that are fully constructed rituals, such as baptism and
marriage, or are imbued with elements of rituality, such as court proceedings and oaths of office. Austin identified an often ritually infused
means by which the social performatively engenders itself, so not sur-
prisingly, specialists in ritual soon began an extended if uneven flirtation
with the concept.

Stanley Tambiah used the concept of performativity to link content
and context. He showed ethnographically that Thai coronation ceremonies posit and presuppose the cosmology that the ritual exemplifies
(1985). The coronation locates this king, here, now, as genealogically
linked to a heavenly cosmology that the ritual's performance presents
and represents as simply another chapter in the temporal continuity of a
hierarchical religious-political order. Another celebrated pioneer in ritual studies, Victor Turner, invokes performativity as the answer to the
problem of how rituals create "a time out of time," and a space of limin-
ality, in which they suspend, annul, or overturn the quotidian structures
of the social order (such as the status difference between king and com-
moners or between the clergy and the laity) in order to construct a meta-
commentary about that social order (Turner 1969). But perhaps the most
explicit appropriation of the notion of performativity lies in the work of
Roy Rappaport (1979; 1999). He argues that ritual's performativeness is
essential in creating social clarity (by turning symbolic statements into
indexical events), in canonizing the liturgical order (by performing a liturgical order, the participants demonstrate to themselves and to others
that they accept unconditionally that liturgical order), and in establish-
ing the social conventions that define what is right and righteous. Thus,
"rituals do more than achieve conventional effects through conventional
procedures; they establish the conventions in terms of which those effects are achieved" (1999, 126). The "logos" of performativity thus stands
at the epicenter of the social, leading Rappaport to view "ritual as the
basic social act" (ibid., 137), which, brought to its logical conclusion, ne-
cessitates that although there are as many "ritual contents" as there are
social systems, "the ritual form is universal" and necessarily so (ibid.,
31). What all these theorists appreciate is that the objectification of the

social and the structure of practice is tied to the performativity inherent in ritual. Nonetheless, the notion of performative has presented something of a conundrum: on the one hand, it excites because it appears to hold an extraordinary amount of theoretical potential; on the other, attempts to use the notion of performativity never seem to live up to their promise. What is missing is a theory of performativity of the social.

It turns out that it is rather unfortunate that the study of performativity began with analyses of the explicit linguistic performativity common to Indo-European languages. Most of the world's languages do not subscribe to this form of performativity, and even those that do rarely do so in the transparent and explicit manner of English. The Bantu languages of the southern cone of Africa have, to give one example, an extensive array of conditionals that can, under the right conditions, function as quasi-performatives. Indeed, there is a good argument to be made that the importance socially of linguistic performativity is directly related and proportional to the emergence of the social contract as a highly critical surface form of juridical, state-based capitalism (the promise codified in the contract, the baptism of a name/trademark, the awarding of a patent with its declaration of originality, or the pronouncement of a contract). In it all, the analysis of performativity has centered on language and the presumably enclosed space-time of ritual, only occasionally venturing out in ways that are ultimately socially mute—mute in the sense that they're not generative of further analytical advances.

The alternative history of performativity—which grants equal ontological status to production and circulation and thus refuses to privilege one over the other—begins with the understanding that performativity is ubiquitous and social, it being a precondition for the reproduction of sameness and a form's totality. Totality and the act of totalization have an extensive biography, though too often its conceptualization succumbs to the contours of capitalism's social epistemology and the notion is essentialized (on the template of the commodity). The alternative reading is a theoretical starting point that does not ontologically privilege either totality or circulation and, with this, a starting point that refuses to elevate objectification over performativity. On this approach, a totality is the product of agents' collective and therefore social imagination of an abstract space of events that the agents hypostatize to be closed, complete, and self-referential in order to ground and frame the eventfulness of practice. The totality is nothing less than an *ontologically real social fiction, fictive* in that they are historically contingent and socially created (e.g., it's conceivable that nation-states and derivative markets were never invented) and *ontologically real* in that they ground and enframe real world events (e.g., an official from the US Treasury endorses the domestic derivative markets). There is nothing about a social totality that guarantees its reproduction absent the collective labor of its participants (thus the European Union is a first imagination of an alternative platform in which the nation-state form is a less consequential totality as the ground and frame of practice). On the approach developed here, totality and circulation are paired, inseparable, and frequently syncopated temporal refractions on the production of actionable social spaces.

Performativity is a thus necessary dimension of the social due to the necessity of reproducing a form's integrity, to objectify the form as a totality graced with an identity (embodied in the transparency, segmentability, and giveness of a form's name such as the collateralized mortgage market, the Eagle clan, the city of Miami, or for that matter the Hells Angels) in the face of recurring volatility and potentially dissembling effects created by the circulatory processes necessary to carry out that reproduction. What this means is that performativity is not confined to ritual or certain linguistic events but is implicated and instrumental in the reproduction of all those social forms and sociostructures involved in circulation, which encompasses all the socially meaningful ones, from nations and financial markets to universities and street gangs. But so long as analytics understand the concepts underlying objectification, sameness, and totality, nonperformatively they (meaning all the analytical traditions founded on an objectivist account of objectification) are condemned to presupposing the objectification of the forms that they analyze. Presupposing a form's objectification is tantamount to naturalizing and neutralizing all the social labor—agents' strategies, risk taking, and maneuvering—required to sufficiently counteract (not always successfully) the volatility created by circulatory forces so as to preserve or restore a form's liquidity. This liquidity is nothing less than the capacity to reengage those processes of circulation necessary to its reproduction. The rise of a "derivative logic" (Martin 2012) as a principle of the production of the derivative (based on the dissembling and reassembling of capital) references the generative scheme (creation of an exotic derivative based on this principle) that agents (such as quants) employ that serve to performatively reproduce that derivative market. The nonperformative perspective is the dominant one defining the many theoretical traditions that privilege production over circulation, the form over its social reproduction in sociohistorical time, the logic of theory over the logic of practice, and the pointillist position over the actions that agents take across an interval of position taking in respect to a spread of possibilities. The only way to put this is that an adequate account of financial practice demands a theory of performativity and that apprehending performativity requires an immanent account of objectification.

To foreground circulation, the temporality of reproduction, the logic of practice, and agents' strategizing across the interval is to rediscover the force of risk, uncertainty, and volatility. Indeed, what makes performativity so socially indispensable is that it works to counteract and ameliorate the threat to a form's integrity wrought by volatility and risk/uncertainty. The rituality of an event is performatively successful precisely when it reproduces a form's integrity and thus the maintenance of its liquidity in the face of whatever volatility is instigated by the unfolding of circulation. This may range from the threat to a patriclan's identity brought on by the influx of nonagnates, to the threat of a security having multiple simultaneous prices, to the threat of a derivative's market terminating due to the withdrawal of buyers and sellers, all of which result in a loss of liquidity. So the critical concern is the reproduction of the form's form in the face of the extant volatility and the risk/uncertainty of future volatility due to the strategies that are being implemented today. Performativity reobjectifies the form's form, albeit as a transformed form that appears ideologically as a conservation of identity, so as to conserve a form's liquidity. Inasmuch as circulatory forces dissemble all social forms, these forms must continually reobjectify themselves, from major practices such as full-tilt rituals to the iteration of a proper name designator (e.g., the x market, the y clan).

Reunification of performativity and objectification leads to a reconceptualization of totality that turns it from a permanently installed crystalline form to one that needs to be continually reobjectified. This continual process of reobjectification has its own social consequences: it means that the forms thus formed will be provisional, positional, and perspectival. Some examples are helpful. A clan's integrity and identity as a social form is provisional insofar as its internal composition changes over time as a condition of its reproduction (people come and go); its identity is positional in that the clan's formness is in respect to other clans' recognition of its form as a genuine example of clanness (it has a legitimate genealogical structure); and it is perspectival in that a clan's formness depends on one's standpoint in social space (a clan's boundaries appear as a spread ranging from unconditionally permeable to impermeable under all conditions). Capitalist markets follow a comparative logic. A derivative market is provisional in that its financing, liquidity, and participants are changing constantly (sometimes to the point of disappearing altogether); it is positional in that its definition and position as a market is in respect to other markets (so that derivative markets were once recognized as little more than venues for gambling); and it is perspectival in that its integrity depends on one's position in financial space. The forms objectified serve as ontologically real fictional spaces for launching both the flows that destabilize them and the performatives that reobjectify them. All, and this is a big all, that's required is that the agents implicated maintain their collective belief in the form's integrity amidst the destabilizing effects of circulatory forces. This maintenance is dependent on the small rituality of everyday acts—such as advertisements for a market, anthropomorphic reports of a market's behavior, the serial execution and posting of derivative trades—and, on special occasions, the grand rituality of full-tilt ceremonies and (only apparently paradoxically) the rituality inscribed in counterceremonial—i.e., crisis—events such as the Federal Reserve's celebrated infusion of liquidity to help stave off systemic failure of the *commercial paper market.*

Performativity is simultaneously positive and negative performativity. One might say that the simultaneity of the plus and the minus is what makes performativity perform. Thus ritualized marriage exchange presupposes the nonintegrity of the clan through its explicit recognition of the presence of nonagnates (difference) even as their act of appearance in the ritual (canonized by their contribution) presupposes a sameness in the first instance. The positive reproduction of the clan's integrity/ sameness always presupposes negative performativity as well. A totality's recreation of sameness through the *effacement of difference* erases for the collectivity, that is to say at the level of the social dividual, what everyone knows to be true for the individuals involved, i.e., that they were once bona fide outsiders prior to the ritual construction of a sameness. By a similar act of magic, the positive reproduction of a market's integrity/totality necessarily presupposes the nonexistence of illiquidity and price opacity and the impossibility of systemic counterparty failure. The performativity that silently objectifies the market as a socially imagined totality erases collectively, that is, at the level of the market, what everyone knows to be true for individual funds (that they may "blow up" and become failed counterparties that drain the market of liquidity) and for singular one-off events, crises. What has evolved is a peculiar social epistemology whose defining moment is that the agents involved, in order to create the conditions of profit, impose a form of misrecognition on themselves, bracketing and thus devaluing as singular and episodic (counterparty and market failure) what they know from experience can be collective and systemic.

Exemplifying Performativity

As noted earlier, there are a number of accounts of performativity, especially in the literature on ritual and, more recently, in respect to the derivative markets (Callon 1998; MacKenzie 2006. Their virtues notwithstanding, there is a missing dimension, which is an exploration of the forms of performativity and their constitutive relationships with social practice. Inscribed in our characterization of these theorists is a critique. Its central point is that in order to go beyond the appearance of ritual as operating in respect to already finalized totalities, it is necessary to construct an account of the performativity of practices. Only through such an account is it possible to grasp the dialectic of incorporation and objectification that shapes the reproduction of these totalities. Despite their ethnographic insights, what limits these and other theorists of ritual is that by beginning their analysis at the moment of the already-constituted totality they are prone to look at the effects of a totality's practices and to overlook how the practices produce that totality. It is agreed and indeed proven that sound research requires an objectivist dimension. This is necessary in order to get beyond and to contextualize agents' experiences inasmuch as the participants' "native points of view" tend to fixate on the local, to naturalize social conventions, to be almost exclusively referential, and to emanate from specific positions and perspectives within the social. But there is here a critical "however," for having overcome the limits of agents' primary experience, it is mistaken to declare the analysis complete by turning immediately to how the structure functions (e.g., what a clan or a market does). To the contrary, analysis must transcend and supplement this objectivism by generating an account of how agents' generative schemes are instrumental in reproducing that structure in respect to itself in relation to others. The reason so many analyses are condemned to focusing only on pragmatic performativity is that they have implicitly transmuted the system of objective relations into finished totalities, a move that serves to underwrite the illusion that they are already constituted outside the dynamics of circulation and thus history. It will turn out that there are variegated forms of performativity, that they are frequently inclusive and at times imbricated, and that where they differ is in the relative transparency and participants' (mis)recognition of their objectifications of the social. To give the analysis ground, we theorize this relationship of performativity to practice through an ethnographic example.

Our ethnographic example comes from the Maring people, who live in a remote and rugged terrain in the western highlands of Papua New Guinea. The Maring are divided into twenty clan clusters, each cluster comprised of four or five exogamous, patrilineal clans (anthropological speak for clans that marry out and trace descent through the male line). The most socially central ceremony in Maring society is undoubtedly ritualized marriage exchange, without which clans could not reproduce themselves materially or symbolically. Viewed retrospectively, these exchanges deliberately appear as preordained, riskless, and noncontroversial objectifications of normal social relations. Viewed prospectively, however, the situation looks much different. And much more performative.

The ignition is the agreement by two clans to arrange an intermarriage. The Maring recognize four distinct types of marriage: sister exchange, patrilateral second cross cousin, iterative exchange (characteristically with matrilateral kin in a "sister" clan), and outside transactions (with geographically distant clans). These types are significant in that they determine the character of the compensation, the obligations that are publicly animated as promises, the kind and amount of goods and services that clan members exchange, and the obligations that fall to offspring of the union. There are perfectly aligned unions in which the intermarrying couple fills the precise genealogical slots, but more often than not there is genealogical dissonance such that the respective clans—both internally and with one another—must come to an agreement on the type of marriage that is being consummated. For example, there are numerous negotiated "sister exchanges" that clans arrange between one man's true sister and another man's patrilateral parallel first cousin (a daughter of his father's brother). Such marriage proposals involve risk as they may be contested and ultimately misfire, when typically some fraction with the clan rejects the union by refusing to ratify the classification. What this says is that these negotiations foreground *type-token performativity*: a process of typification in that singular instances are recruited to a recognized type, such that, from a classificatory standpoint, that marriage now appears as an indexical icon—that is, a perfect instantiation—of that type. The key point is that a classification is only as socially real as the valorized acts of typification that instantiate it, just as singular token events/unions become socially real via their typification. The upshot is that analyses and models that reduce the classificatory process to a mechanistic operation that requires no discussion distort and misunderstand the reality in progress.

The marriage typified, among other considerations the participants agreeing on a marriage compensation payment (from the groom's clan to that of his wife) that is always an amount large enough that it can only be collectively assembled, the stage is set for the organization of the ceremony to begin. It is in the process of the ritual's preparation that its totalizing effects start before it commences. This is why the performativity of a ritual has already accomplished much before the ceremony's performance.

A patriclan is a (re)production group that is theoretically composed of all those persons who share a common male ancestor. But it is also a territorial group that practically includes members whose presence is mediated by and the result of the continual circulation of people from other clans. Each ritual marriage exchange is a singularity in that the clan's membership is constantly in flux. So when clan leaders indicate that a ritualized marriage ceremony is to take place, that the clan's women should harvest taro and yams and gather firewood, that the leaders are contributing sacrificial animals and request other's support, the request is constructed so that it embraces (or does not embrace) a husband living on his wife's clan lands, a man residing with his mother's brother, a woman living alongside her in-married sister, a woman who has been adopted by her matrikin, and so on through all the possibilities present by the culturally sanctioned circulatory routes. All of these nonagnatic agents can negotiate whether they can or will contribute labor, food, and sacrificial animals to the bridewealth payment. The act of acting, and having the action accepted, of signaling one's approval by gathering foods or firewood or by donating an animal to the compensation advances the ritual and begins to redefine the totality. When, to give a common and illustrative example, a woman adopted at an early age gathers firewood and taro for the feast, and participates in the ritual, and then recognizes that the men of that clan have become forbidden marriage partners (although, had she remained in her natal patriclan, they might be preferential partners) her "induction" presumes a performative (re)creation of totality. Indeed, when the clans assemble for the ritualized exchange they stand across from one another as totalized entities—the participants who are participating are all equally clan members by virtue of their authentic participation. There is a *constitutive performativity* in that the ritualized exchange presupposes the totality of the clans that are reconstituted through the ritual. There is a reobjectification of the clan as a transformed form of itself. Moreover, the exchange of wealth presupposes and certifies the efficiency of the ritual by transforming its consequences—the reconstitution of these clans, here, now, publicly—into the premise and predicate for further practices. This constitutive performativity produces two embodiments of history. The collectivity appears as an objectification of the ritual as objectified in its clan name, the specifically named territory on which its members have gardened and buried the bones of ancestors, in its record of the clan's exchange relations that also determine the necessity of ritual, and in its narrative accounts of military ventures, consummated treaties, labors, migrations, new settlements, and other foundational fictions of the clan group. The totalizing effects of ritual are also embodied in agents' dispositions, attitudes, generative schemes, motivational structures, and notions of the sense and acceptableness of actions. When, for example, a man who is residing with his wife's clan contributes to a bridewealth payment on behalf of one of its members and then shares in the reciprocal gift, or when, conversely, he remains materially silent when his father's clan seeks to assemble a bridewealth payment, there is a kind of complicity between his social position and his disposition to instantiate or deactivate a specific clan affiliation, a complicity organized offstage by ritual's capacity to foreground totality at the expense of circulation.

The ritual involves a kind of transubstantiation. Within the context of the ritual, every member of the wife-givers' clan shares in the gifts, including women from the wife-takers subclan and clan who have previously married in. And, conversely, when wife-givers' reciprocate a small countergift to their affines, always from pigs nurtured on their clan lands, every member of the wife-taking (sub)clan shares in that pork irrespective of where they originally came from. The subordination of social memory, of what people know, to the construction of a totality can take place because the ritual creates a hierarchy of value that brackets what they remember, the single objective intention of reproducing the group outweighing those aspects of persons that interrelate them to other groups. In so doing, clan members have not forgotten where their wives and in-laws came from. Even less are they enacting a role in which they are pretending to forget. They are entering into the spirit and enframement of value created by the ritual, which, in elevating the values of nurturing, belonging, and groupness, expects of people objectively what they subjectively expect of themselves. By creating a performance that is, in Rappaport's words, "not encoded by the performers" (1999, 24), ritual insures that there will be a close correspondence between the recognized positions and the dispositions of agents to act in a certain way (exemplified by sharing) so as to produce a totality. In another register, because the ritual is concerned to foreground disinterest, to produce connectivity between groups, it creates a temporality-bracketed perspective from which substantially imbricated (sub)clans, (sub)clans that have internalized one another on a continuous basis, appear as autonomous third person collective agents. That is, the groups appear as performatively objectified totalities that can engage in exchange. Constitutive performativity is thus the foundation of the production of the socially imagined totality and thus the logos of ritual as the basic social act.

But it is also the case that due to the power of circulations the matter of clan membership cannot be settled simply by enumerating who is present. There are members who are not present because they are working a faraway job, receiving a foreign education, recuperating in an urban hospital, or living with another group on what is presumably a temporary basis. When the exchanging clans have assembled in the collectively maintained ceremonial theatre, each clan's leader makes a speech in which he first introduces the clan collectively, and then makes a specific point of "calling out" by name all of those persons (plantation workers, politicians, students, etc.) who are absent but nonetheless clan members. There is here a *citational performativity* in which all those named are to be counted as official participants in the ritual marriage exchange, meaning that they are equally responsible for and responsive to the obligations, debts, affiliations, rights, and promises created by the marriage exchange. This citational performativity contains a negative space, in that for a person to be absent *and* excluded from the citation is to be publicly disenfranchised from the clan.

The most visible dimension of performativity, and the one that has to date dominated analytic discussions, is *pragmatic performativity*. This form of performativity is the most transparent and thus most likely to be officially recognized. It can have both repetitive and indexical moments. Repetitively, the continued use of same territorial sites for ritualized exchanges molds the physical landscape so that it bears the trace of past exchanges and is preadapted for forthcoming ones (much in the same way that when, on a university campus, people repeat the same shortcut across the grass, their actions eventually result in a new and recognizable pathway between sidewalks). The obvious aspect of repetitiveness is that by continually realigning a platform—be it spatial, technological, mathematical—with a social practice, they become more adapted to one another (i.e., the path across the grass is more recognizable and easier to manage, which motivates more people to take it).[4] This form of performativity points to syncopation that can evolve between a technological design and the expectations of the agents who use it. The predications of economic models invested with symbolic authority can thus serve as self-actualizing forecasts when the users of a model collectively believe in and use its calculations to organize their actions. MacKenzie (2006) shows this syncopation was the case for the Black-Scholes options pricing model until the unexpected 1987 crisis, after which traders collectively tempered their belief in its accuracy (LiPuma 2014).

The indexical moment stems from the fact that ritual performances are not simply a symbolic representation or expression of some social reality; they are components of the messages they seek to convey. The performative act sets out the conditions and criteria for judging the felicity of the promises or the futures inscribed in the ritual, that is to say, the probability of deliverance. It is one thing for a clan to declare that it can fulfill all of the obligations created by the marriage; it is quite another to demonstrate this indexically by proffering a magisterial compensation payment, assembling a large clan turnout, and then executing the ritual with military-like precision. The clan's size, wealth, and self-regimentation is itself a critical example of it being able to fulfill its obligations. The ritual sacredly promises that the clan will mobilize those resources in the future to fulfill its stated obligations. To put this systemically, ritual's indexical iconic power annuls the risks of circulation by making the intentionality of the agents transparent in that it must be publicly declared as the forthcoming of the relationship. In this way, the ritual seeks to dampen and socialize volatility in order to mitigate the directional risks created by a clan's outstanding vulnerabilities. In another language, ritual is the primary means by which clans create the sociality that allows them to hedge against a host of downside risks (e.g., an increase in population size that allows a clan suffering a shortage of garden land to exploit an affine's borderlands).

Finally, the uptake of any ritualized marriage exchange depends in good part on the discourse or narrative about the ritual that the participants construct and circulate, or occasionally dispute. This induces volatility (to the point of violence) because, and to the degree that, the dispute not only calls this specific ritual into question but implicitly reveals the arbitrariness of the objectifications. Such disputes can spill into violence for good reason culturally: they undermine the groups' permanent and transcendent vision of themselves and diminish the wealth the exchange created. Mostly, however, the depiction of the type-token performativity as cosmologically valorized and thus legitimate as well as an account of its pragmatic performativity in fostering an amplification in the quality and flow of goods and services figure in this narrative. The exchange was a sum-sum game in which the values circulated presently and as futures increases everyone's wealth. The narrative takes it as axiomatic that the typification of the exchange was transparent and indisputable, that the compositions of the clans were the only conceivable compositions, that everyone who was included citationally accepts the full burden of the social responsibilities incurred, and that the community of the excluded excepts and recognizes the results. There is here a *retrospective narrative performativity* founded on the widespread circulation via, especially, the public speeches of its high-status participants, leading to the collective and collectively ratified acceptance of the account. This narrative, which presumably simply explains the success of the ritualized exchange, is actually an instrumental part of its uptake or success because it crystallizes the conditions for future transactions. One feature of this narrative is that it embodies an economical generative scheme, which quasi-magically transforms and canonizes correlations (between a marriage and its outcomes) into positive causations.

It is critical to underline—because this begins to signal the real difference between a capitalist economy and noncapitalist econom*ies*—that the ritual creates wealth through the amplification of sociality. The form of wealth involved is socially and historically specific to that society because the agents exchanged ritually and the objects set in motion will embody the sociality of their makers. A "wealthy" clan is thus a clan whose calculated strategies have resulted in an abundance of sociality, whose existential manifestation is as a stockpile of contingent claims,

that is, an accumulation of claims on others' requital of the socially in-
scripted gifts they have consumed.

Virtually all social practices have some elements of rituality. What
makes ritualized marriage exchange instructive is that it exemplifies a
codified, cosmologically valorized, full-throttle ritual, meaning that its
rituality is explicitly foregrounded such that there is great visibility to
the forms of performativity that generate the objectifications of the social. In contrast, capitalist markets exchange conceals and misrecognizes
these ritualized forms of performativity, but they are no less performative for doing so.

What is a Market Performatively?

We have argued that the annulment of the social is a necessary social
feature of the culture of financial circulation and, with that, the annulment of the rituality that allows the performative constitution of a market. Ironically, the derivative markets above all others are performative,
owing to the fact that the instruments have no use or intrinsic value and
must therefore ultimately refer to an underlying reality that is not a derivative and does not obey a derivative logic. All derivatives, particularly
OTC (over the counter) derivatives, which constitute the vast majority,
are nonexchange traded and thus need not conform to any standardized
design. Exchange-traded derivatives, by contrast, trade the inflexibility
of standardization for the certain alignment of token and type and the
liquidity of each trade's counterparty. The fabrication, pricing, and circulation of OTC instruments must entail the enactment of *type-token
performativity*. The market's makers must typify specific singular derivatives (even if that type is formulated from an admixture of different derivative types). This means further that each act of buying/selling that financial instrument is instrumental in performatively objectifying it as a
specific type of derivative (such as a super senior CDO tranche). Typification is necessary because a market cannot price a singularity or use
it for collateral. No matter how it may look retrospectively, derivatives
are not born with clearly stenciled names or with transparent pricing in-
structions. What is required is an act of classification that defines *this*
token as an instance of *that* type—an act that always presupposes the
power and legitimacy to impose that classification. This is precisely why

and where the reputation, symbolic capital, and financial firepower of the market's market-making institutions come into play. These classifications also shape the mental space of trading, predispose those with a sense of that market to adjust their expectations to the probabilistic assessments of that instrument (e.g., that super senior tranches are bulletproof or that lower tranches have a specific risk/reward profile).

The functionality of the derivative is central. For the derivative to function as a speculative bet, as capital, or as collateral for a loan that leverages a wager depends on the existence of an energetic market. The ontological reason is that, bereft of any use value, the derivative has value if and only if there exists a market for its circulation, a point that the succession of crises has underlined. This raises the question "what is a market?" to a critical problematic in that a market's functionality depends on the willingness of its participants to reproduce a stream of liquidity in the face of uncertain volatility. The standard supposition is that *the market* is an ontologically given well-formed form. But this view does not and cannot explain how the derivative emerged as a form of wealth, how the market for its expansion reproduces itself, or the conditions of failure and the appropriation of the public treasury.

If we critically pose the question *What is a market?* or, more concretely, *What is the derivative market on which these instruments trade?*, the answer is neither simple nor obvious. The market as a social totality or a frame is simultaneously a practical construct, a marketplace that is also the site of work, and a particular kind of "object" constructed by economic theory. This complex multifaceted conception of the market frames the actions of financial firms and participants, the regulatory policies crafted by the Federal Reserve and the Treasury, the picture drawn by the media, and the scientization of the market by finance economics. What all the players have in common is that they share this image of the market, unconditionally; they circulate this image without thinking they are circulating an image, switching fluidly among the various facets, their collective belief influencing their market behavior even as it underwrites their confidence in their interpretations of the behavior of anonymous coparticipants. Syncopation of belief is essential: indeed, the argument that will unfold across the text of our analysis is that the market as a totality is nothing less than an *ontologically real social fiction* that agents quasi-automatically produce through the grace of collective belief[5] and that it is the continually iterated rituality inscribed in the everyday practices of the markets' agents that breathes reality into this fiction.

Read from a social perspective, the centrality of belief is the underlying, unacknowledged theme that appears throughout former Treasury Secretary Paulson's account of the struggle to restore faith in the deeply imperiled credit markets of 2008–2009. Though he recounts his deeds in colorless description, the supposition guiding his actions is that agents' decisions to restart making a market under uncertainty turns on the revival of their collective faith in a market's integrity. Indeed, we now know through the Freedom of Information Act that the Federal Reserve, in collaboration with the Treasury, paid north of one trillion dollars for this outcome (Morgenson and Rosner 2011, 1).

Note that the confluence of the *real* and the *fictional* through the power of collective beliefs, as well as agents' implicit faith in the totality they have instantiated, indicates that markets have a performative aspect. They are defined by a dialectic between rites of self-objectification, large and small and most of all continuous, and the production of a financial habitus that encourages agents to have and maintain faith in a market's integrity. That, for example, agents' objectify liquidity as the normal state of the financial markets goes hand in hand with an ensemble of concepts, dispositions, and positions that normalize their collective faith in the totality or frame. Liquidity is the finance field's representation of sociality, objectified in the notion of the counterparty and the risks posed by those on the other corresponding side of a trade. Termed counterparty risk, it serves to abstract and reify the financial agents whose decision making will, slightly or greatly, now or in the near future, influence the security of securities and thus the collectivities' belief in the market. An examination of what agents actually do demonstrates a constant interplay between the objectification of abstract risk through mathematical modeling (e.g., Black-Scholes) and their attempts to discern what others with the same or similar models are doing. The totality reconstructs itself out of the interplay between overlapping models and the iteration of the models that agents share and attribute to their others or counterparties that comprise the market.[6] There is thus every reason to believe that the market as a social totality lies at the intersection of specific real-time trades and the imaginary community constructed out of everyone's beliefs about, and faith in, what others (counterparties) are doing with respect to similar trades and deals, such as assembling and marketing CDOs. This intersection is technically mediated most significantly by Bloomberg machines, which everyone knows everyone else uses for price discovery. What is outstanding is how the syn-

copated objectification of the local and the totality performatively produces a market (e.g., for credit derivatives) as an instance of *the market*.
Although a/the market appears as the simple aggregation of individual
trades, agents' ability to consummate these individual trades presupposes and thus turns on a faith-based liquidity. Each transaction instan-
tiates and foregrounds the market that it presupposes. This objectification leads to the self-fulfilling because collectively shared prophecy that
a universe of reliable "stranger" counterparties populates a specific market. So long as market agents share and act upon this belief their "religion" will remain intact, that market will remain liquid, and their "collective faith" will remain invisible. The magic of a market is not that it
tricks its participants but that it makes them believe. This is the essence
of the *constitutive performativity* that sustains a derivative market, ultimately composed of nothing else but a circulating ensemble of contingent claims (Ayache 2010). Pricing a portfolio (of CDOs, for example)
on a mark to market basis will, under these conditions, provide a reasonable assessment of a firm's balance sheet. Each successfully executed
transaction reaffirms the group's collective belief in the imagined community of reliable counterparties that it presupposes. Collective belief is
the operative concept insofar as it is virtually impossible in OTC markets to know or verify that the counterparties are reliable or will remain
so over the term of the contract, especially as the speculative ethos that
permeates these markets motivates and incentivizes risky wagers that
engender continually evolving portfolios of what is (despite VAR models) unquantifiable exposure. In essence, the parties who execute a given
trade, as well as those who witness it (typically as an anonymous electronic cipher), will only continue to make a market (e.g., in mortgage obligations) if they "believe" that the only possible reality is that there are
enough liquidity, readily discoverable prices, and solvent counterparties
such that wagers made will invariably be paid. It is this belief, through
the guarantees offered by the government, such as the Troubled Asset
Relief Program (TARP), that Henry Paulson and Ben Bernanke were
trying desperately to restore. They were attempting to reboot the performative impulse that engenders the market as a totality by guaranteeing
the efficacy of the transactions. The idea was that a string of successes
would restore agents' collective faith in the market's integrity. Salvation
thus depended on resurrecting the performative objectification of these
markets as totalities. On this score, the efficient market thesis and the
derivative pricing models it underwrites (Black and Scholes) are blind to

this performative dimension because they reduce a/the market to individual acts of buying and selling.[7]

They cannot thus entertain the question of genesis: What are the conditions for the inculcation of similar beliefs and dispositions, which, in the manner of an orchestra without a conductor, motivate the collectivities' collective faith in a *real* financial market comprised of anonymous agents conditioned to function as reliable predictable counterparties? When we recognize that a market's performativity is the condition of its very existence, the analytical objective changes to illuminating the character of these beliefs and dispositions, how these inculcated beliefs and dispositions performatively objectify financial markets, and how the institutions of finance produced and reproduced them through a regime of work. Economistic definitions of the market, especially those that believe in its inherent efficiency, annul the performativity that brings markets into existence as viable entities. Against this entrenched viewpoint, we would argue that social totalities, such as the derivatives markets, are created performatively by a kind of secular ritualization that links existential events to the social imaginary that is a market. It will turn out that rituality is important because it answers the question of how a collectivity comes to believe that a conceptual object—a nation, an ethnicity, a clan, and a market—is so true, real, and constant, sufficiently permanent and transcendent, that they willingly found their actions, risk their wealth, and, at the point where game theoretics cease to count, predicate their very lives on the integrity of an object, which, having been created at a specific point in historical time through human agency, can also be destroyed through a collective retraction of belief. And we don't have to look farther for an example than the 2008 financial crisis. The evaporation of liquidity that ignited the system's implosion was the result of agents' collective retraction of their faith in the market just as, correlatively, the paralyzing fear of counterparty risk that gripped the market was agents' collective withdrawal of their faith in its participants. Agents can and do disinvest in the investiture of the market.

What makes rituality so important socially is that it allows practices to posit what they effectuate. In this way, rituality creates a performative impulse in which the participants presuppose the realness of the social totality that the event helps to create or effectuate, by assuming that this event—here, now—is simply a replica of previous performances. The performative aspect of the practice is so central because it shapes the illusion that the totality created socially (e.g., the market) is a naturally occurring object. The event summons the participants to believe, to have faith that the totality indexically presupposed by this specific event is as real as the existential lived event itself. There is a cognitive and dispositional obligation to assume, for example, that the efficient market is as real as the trade I have just efficiently made. By this means, the specific trade figurates what it and all of the trades (classified as) like it collectively effectuate. The capacities and dispositions of agents to collectively subscribe to the same understanding (e.g., of the market) without any collective intention does not just occur; it turns on socializing agents through their immersion in the distinctive habitus of the financial field and the hard work of its institutions in inculcating dispositions within the participants (as could be illustrated by their intensive training regimes, which bear more than a passing resemblance to initiation rites). One might note that the economistic depiction of the market is an empirically robust illusion: insofar as the rituality of practices regiments a succession of events that successfully instantiate the market (e.g., the market remains liquid), its social foundations can remain below ground. As long as the rituality of practice brings about the repeated alignment of totality, type, and token, then the act of classification whereby agents typify a token derivative as part of a market totality can remain invisible. As long as this rituality motivates the syncopation of the beliefs and actions of the participants, the market can appear to be entirely formal. As long as rituality produces the collectively shared unquestioned belief that the individual trade I am making now/here is a perfect replica of a known type of trade within a specific effectively perfect market, then that market will appear to reproduce itself naturally, asocially, as a simple progression of the inevitable. This is until, as we witnessed, a crisis of faith in the market ensues, at which time the constitutive power of the social seems to appear from nowhere and remain until the state of emergency subsides.

We observed that the technology of the market registers trades as electronic ciphers between anonymous others. But this is only part of the story, as there is also in train the circulation of information about who is actively participating, important because the players recognize that each institution (e.g., Goldman Sachs) and individual (e.g., John Paulson) is endowed with different quantities of economic and symbolic capital. There is here a kind of citational performativity in that confirmed knowledge, suspicions, hearsay that, for example, Goldman Sachs or Greenlight Capital (a hedge fund) is a major player says much about the potential liquidity and thus the staying power of that market in that it speaks to the relative economic capitalization and longevity of the counterparties. Whether, and to what degree, Goldman Sachs and Greenlight Capital are involved may make a difference as to monetary outcomes—this is a zero-sum game in which the size and power of "the whales" make a difference—but what counts in the production of agents' premise of market liquidity is the collectively shared belief in their participation as sustained by a chain of citations (based presumably on reliable evidence). This is one of the primary reasons that the participants perpetually search for, and critically evaluate, citations on who is making the market.[8] As MacKenzie following Callon points out, a source of *pragmatic performativity* is the fact that financial economics has evolved to become part of the infrastructure of the market such that derivative pricing models exemplified by Black-Scholes-Merton do not just model prices theoretically; they are part of the process of defining them (2006, 15–20). The market is also pragmatically performative in that a directional move (in a currency, for example) can and frequently does motivate an accelerating cycle of wagers that mimic and amplify that directional bet, what is called "momentum trading." These traders, armed with pools of speculative capital, aggressively take positions whose source of profit is the volatility and directional movement that they collectively create (see LiPuma and Koelble 2009). Such performativity also appears sociolinguistically in the way members of the financial field mechanically reproduce a repetitive chain of reference that attaches a specific presumably descriptive name (e.g., the merger arbitrate or credit market) to a specific socially imagined totality and to the chain of definitive events, such as liquidity stops, that are said to characterize the history of the one and the same totality. An endless chain of microacts of citation, circulated through the media, are thus instrumental in iterating a market.

And finally, *retrospective narrative performativity* is an integral dimension of the derivative markets. The participants in the finance field are continually creating and solidifying a narrative about the strategic behavior of the market—a narrative in which the market as a collective agent encodes beliefs and fulfills desires based on its judgments. This includes its anticipation of the future, as when analysts remark that a market declined because it was anticipating an event that had not yet occurred during that recession in prices (e.g., the event being the failure of the European Central Bank to reach an accord on a rescue program for imperiled banks). A distinctive feature of this rear-window narrative is that it engenders a teleology by transforming correlations into causations through the application of a practical logic, which has some of the uptake of a self-fulfilling prophecy in that the circulation and acceptance of a belief may certainly motivate agents to behave in a certain way (e.g., if they collectively believe that the ECB's failure to cut rates will lead to a swoon in prices they may collectively pare their positions) thereby "proving" retrospectively that the correlation was indeed a causation. This narrative continually affirms the typification of the tokens, the totalization of the market, and the integrity of the prices through the personification of the market, including the attribution of intentionality and foresight, which, in turn, bespeaks a teleological arc to its actions.

The Social Mathematics of Black-Scholes

All models sweep dirt under the rug. A good model makes the absence of dirt visible. In this regard, we believe that the Black-Scholes model of options valuation . . . is a model for models: it is clear and robust. Clear because it is based on true engineering; it tells you how to manufacture an option out of stocks and bonds, and what it will cost you under ideal dirt-free circumstances that it defines. The world of markets doesn't exactly match the ideal circumstances Black-Scholes requires, but the model is robust because it allows an intelligent trader to qualitatively adjust for those mismatches.—Emanuel Derman and Paul Wilmott, *The Financial Modelers' Manifesto*

Why is the Black and Scholes formula important socially, especially as the formula applies an abstract mathematical physics formula to the rarified and insulated world of derivatives trading? Our argument for its significance is this: the Black and Scholes model necessarily posits the existence of a/the market as a totality within which it can price the derivative contracts that circulate. The model posits the existence of a specific socially imagined totality, *the market*, in which each market is an instance of the type in that each embodies the essential features of the market, the most important of which is a closed and complete marketplace populated by economically rational agents who have the capacity to instantaneously integrate any new information. Black-Scholes thus posits and envisions the division of the economic from the social. Black-Scholes imagines that the derivative markets, their components (e.g., money), and their agents exist objectively and independently of the social. Technically this stems from the fact that to price derivatives on these terms—in this mathematical manner—it is necessary to exteriorize and reify the social. What makes this necessary is that admission of the social would destroy the conditions for the use of the mathematized model.[9] From a social perspective, the Black-Scholes method must exteriorize structure and desire, setting aside the objective structuring of the financial markets and the cognitive and motivating structures embodied in the agents. This could theoretically portend a mathematics that could encompass the social dimensions of finance and correlatively mathematize as a probabilistic spread the risk of internal systemic devolution (e.g., based on levels of outstanding leverage), the risk posed by the intervention of unforeseeable forces (i.e., black swans), and the risks engendered by the government's securitization of financial markets through the massive (but extremely secret) collection of data on those markets.

But this is only the beginning in that Black-Scholes is an account of the real. So the removal of the social generates an irredeemably real conundrum. This conundrum could be glossed over if Black-Scholes was a purely theoretical solution intended only for theoretical speculation (about which, as in some branches of mathematics, there would be no limit on abstracting from the real world). But derivative pricing is about real people and money, strategically speculating. The problem of the real is that exteriorizing the social removes a derivative market's animating force. The prices generated from within the confines of the mathematics are static, immobile, and determinative, conditions under which there is no incentive to wager on a derivative's forthcoming price. Without the social's generative uncertainty and volatility, market making would be pointless. The market posited by the Black-Scholes formula could not exist if its assumption about the social were an accurate description of financial reality. It's as if one were playing a poker game in which all of the cards were (distributed) dealt face up, rendering betting or bluffing or folding moot since every player knows the outcome in advance. The transaction only occurs when traders have divined and introduced the differences of opinion that allow for a zero-sum contestation over that derivative's forthcoming value. The clockwork of a market is predicated on the extra-model reintroduction of precisely those social aspects that were necessarily excommunicated to constitute the model.

As the epigram from Derman and Wilmott underlines, the mere fact that the Black-Scholes formulation is technically flawed does not mean that it is useless in social practice if the practitioners appreciate the limitations and, through a process of compensation through supplementation, draw in a practical manner on the concepts, experiences, and dispositions instilled in them through their mutual participation in contemporary financial markets to reintegrate the social into the pricing processes. Interestingly, right from their opening paragraphs, Derman and Kani (1994) observe that "by empirically varying the Black-Scholes volatility with [an option's] strike price, traders are implicitly attributing a unique *non-lognormal* distribution" to the option (1, emphasis in original). A *unique non-lognormal distribution* is, of course, what the social would look like from inside the tent of the mathematical formulation. What we will argue, based on our experience and on extensive interviews with derivative traders (from investment banks to hedge funds) is that the abstract formulation has a certain functional necessity in that it fixes the horizon and the space of operations, however provisionally, just as the recalibration process derives in part from the recognition, already present in Black's reflection (2012) on his own device, that the very existence of a derivative market created and recreated by market makers is possible only if volatility is a nonfinite stochastic process. This is a mathematical way of saying (with a discernable smile) that the door to the social is thrown open because what motivates the participants to use the model and recalibrate derivative prices is exterior to the model yet constitutive of the market. A Black-Scholes pricing outcome provides a benchmark that allows the participants to turn the contestability of future value into a contest based on their variable apperception of what important socially deserves to be discounted. What Black appreciated, exemplified in his justly famous yet commonly misconstrued article "Noise" (first published in 1986), is that the mathematics of the Black-Scholes model is the negative imprint of the social just as the sociality of the market is the positive print of the qualitative dimensions of the mathematics, that is, its founding suppositions.

The use of Black-Scholes problematizes the relationship between the model and the market. What lie in between and are constitutive of this relationship are participants' trading practices, which thus presuppose and require a theorization of practice. From the trader's practice, the model and the market do not stand in opposition to one another, nor is there a directional sequencing from model to market. Their practice does not presume there is a contradiction between model and market or that the behavior of the market falsifies the formulation; rather, for practitioners the categories unfold as a *spread* phenomenon—a spread between technical rigor and pragmatic play that they negotiate through a reflexive series of adjustments. Traders use their immersion in the worldview of the habitus of finance to reintroduce the sociality externalized by the Black-Scholes model, making what appear to them to be intuitively reasonable recalibrations. The spread names the mental device traders use to reconcile the model's externalization and removal of the social with the ensemble of social determinants presented by the market. In this space of practice, there is no opposition or contradiction between technical rigor and pragmatic play because they are both mutually imbricated aspects of derivatives pricing. The dispositions and affect of traders serve to incorporate the practice of logic into the logic of practice: the mathematized result into existential decision making under uncertainty. From the purview of the trader in the act of trading, neither the structure nor the event are apparent, only his body (rift with anxiety, pressured, and hypervigilant) serving as the interpolator of the spread between the model's abstract price and its pragmatic recalibration. To appreciate how traders can negotiate this spread, using the model's results as the horizon for reintroducing the social that the model exteriorizes, it is necessary to grasp the equation in its abstract economistic form and then deconstruct the equation so that what is social again becomes visible.

An illustration that is also a pillar of the Black-Scholes pricing model is the notion of arbitrage. The Black-Scholes model contains an argument about hedging that depends on the nonarbitrage provision. This is critical to the model because a price's platform is set by and calculated from an instrument's "risk neutral" valuation. The argument posits a nonmathematical parameter that guarantees that the interior space of a derivative's market is immune from any and all socioeconomic differentiations that would alter the pricing of a derivative. Thus the same derivative cannot simultaneously have one price on the Tokyo exchange and another on the New York exchange, nor can two identical instruments have different prices on the same exchange. On these grounds, the abstracted economic model presumes that one can hedge a derivative with the underliers to generate a perfectly risk-free instrument. For this artificial instrument to accurately mimic the derivative, the market in question must be complete in that prices are singularities. As Bailey (2001) explains in *The Economics of Financial Markets,* this entails that no security can have more than one price (called *the law of one price* in finance economics). The *law* is secured through the axiom that markets by virtue of their constitutive principles eschew arbitrage such that the existence of singular or state prices precludes arbitrage.[10] The key supposition is that for a market to be sufficiently efficient to allow such hedging, arbitrage must be impossible. So one of the foundational suppositions of Black-Scholes is that the very possibility of a market depends on the nonexistence of arbitrage, complemented by the secondary supposition that should arbitrage opportunities materialize (due to market anomalies) the spread between prices would be instantaneously closed.

Note the peculiar logic to the co-occurrence of the abstract and pragmatic. The presentation and closure of the arbitrage presupposes the failure, the end, due to "excess" volatility, of the market within which the opportunity arose in the first place. The occasion of arbitrage can only thus occur within a market that cannot exist as such because a market's existence is inseparable from the null set of arbitrage possibilities. The notion that closure occurs instantaneously, whether ever empirically true that it is not, is irrelevant since the disavowal has already removed the (healing) power of time. The relative length of a timeless interval that cannot exist is a meaningless measure. Nonetheless, for the Black-Scholes formula the nonexistence of what exists is critical to the formation of the state prices that underwrite the argument about hedging upon which the analysis ultimately rests. Ironically, this move is archetypical of the economistic tradition in finance that Fischer Black took pains to distance himself from, for it consists in recognizing that the possibility of arbitrage is always present, that the nonarbitrage clause needs to be a critical supposition only on the condition that arbitrage is an ever-present possibility in the financial markets. But in the name of a tractable mathematics it inserts an idealized perfectly homogeneous space that banishes arbitrage to a timeless exteriority where it can no longer do what it actually often does: inflect derivative pricing. Thus conceived, analysis can now no longer interrogate how arbitrage inflects the structuration of the markets. The model thus excludes what it recognizes as a possibility for every market transaction. And it does this by valorizing an immediate simultaneity—the instantaneous eradication of two prices for the identical security—that lies exterior to the concept of the market that it posits. To put this another way, the fact that the real world is saturated with arbitrage opportunities reveals why spreads are so ubiquitous.[11]

A Left-Handed Equation

Solving the Black-Scholes equation involves what mathematicians refer to as backwardation. For the equation, this means that it is necessary to specify the payoff at expiration and then work backwards in time to determine present values. This backwards regression from the future to the present derives from the fact that Black-Scholes, like a percentage of people, is left handed (i.e., there is a zero to the right of the equal sign). For equations, at least, this is important in that when applied to things social, such as trading derivatives, left-handed equations have specific consequences, in the critical sense that their satisfaction entails exteriorizing the social practices and circumstances of the circulation of derivatives in the real world. To begin with, the equation's calculus works if and only if the terminal payoff is foreordained; that is, the payoff must be a riskless event in several senses. First, the value of money must be constant in that inflation or deflation would change the calculation. In real-world trading, this is either insignificant because the temporal interval is relatively short or, in the case of longer-term contract, traders take this possibility into consideration in respect to their overall price calculation. In other words, the future price of money is an enshadowed variable in which traders use their understanding of the world's political economy (e.g., Federal Reserve and ECB monetary policies) to assess inflationary trends. Second, the payoff must adhere to a finalism in which the initiation of a contract determines its final outcome. There cannot, accordingly, be any possibility whatever that a counterparty (e.g., Lehman Brothers) defaults on the payoff. The formula assumes that the participant's evaluation of their counterparties will never influence the pricing process. In practice, these can be very critical determinations, especially when evaluating OTC derivatives. Traders take into consideration the fact that a solvent counterparty may rapidly become insolvent, and they use their sense of the market and knowledge (or lack thereof) of the counterparty in question to price this uncertainty into what they are willing to pay for a derivative. Again, we see that the theoretical model that allows backwardation is eminently different from the prospective character of practice.

Black-Scholes Viewed Theoretically and as Social Practice

The godfather of modern mathematical statistics, Andrei Kolmogorov,[12] laid out the architecture for constructing an abstract space of events where the action, such as pricing derivatives, would occur. Now, as alluded to earlier, analysts could deal with the flaws and failings of Black-Scholes by adding missing variables to enrich the space. That said, including other plausible variables, like whipsaws in volatility, oscillations in market liquidity, the effects of (changing) supply and demand, distortions to the risk free rate, the solvency of the counterparties, the persistence of arbitrage opportunities, and more would soon render the Black-Scholes equation far too complex to be tractable or useful in practice.[13] Given traders' mathematical limitations—they are after all recruited and rewarded because they excel at trading, not computation—and the fact that the realities of the market usually mock the model and occasionally explode its usefulness, real-world finance has opted for a Black-Scholes model with the smallest number of variables or unknowns.

Our ethnography of trading indicates that, for traders, their trading practices are coherent and meaningful not only because they lead to the creation of repeatedly profitable strategies but because they are readily mastered and manageable. So what appears socially is that practice leans towards an economy of practice whose aims are its own, not those of finance math. What is more, traders have from their experience every reason to subscribe to the virtues of their economy. There is an important distinction between precision and accuracy, such that greater precision does not inherently produce greater accuracy. Adding "improvements" to Black-Scholes presumably results in greater theoretical precision at the cost of increasing complexity. But, and here is the double-sided conundrum, not only does it make the Black-Scholes formula more difficult to master and manage practically, it does not result in greater accuracy if the new inputs don't do what they mathematically cannot do: encompass the social and its strictly sociological modes of regimenting practice. This is why attempts to tweak Black-Scholes to make it consistent with the socially induced "mispricings" of volatility that characterize and thus *make* a derivative market add several coats of complexity but fail to improve the model's accuracy[14] and why traders gravitate toward the simplest model possible.

Black-Scholes as Theory and Practice

The Black and Scholes formula exists in a polychromatic space, a space that agents interpolate from what are the four cardinal directions of its (re)production and use. These various interpolations, which are all in their own way constitutive of the production of a derivative market, depend on what the users of the formula believe that it does and, more foundationally and critically, on what is happening socially beneath transactions whose appearance is that of a pure calculation. This deep sociality is important because the reproduction of the market and the success of the formula depend on a sociality that is so exteriorized that it is unrecognized as such.

The first interpolation of Black-Scholes is as a scientific, mathematized theory of how derivatives work and can be priced. As noted, this account is unsound theoretically because parameters constitutive of the object—from supply and demand to the market itself—are bracketed as a condition of the production of the mathematized account. And it is unsound empirically in that real market transactions almost invariably violate some of the founding principles, such as two derivatives with the same underlier having different volatilities. Notwithstanding these serious problems—which would in physics would lead to the abandonment of the paradigm—finance economists feel compelled to affirm and uphold the scientific truthfulness of this account because any recognition of its theoretical and empirical failings would undermine the suppositions that undergird the discipline. That is, they are socially motivated, and understandably so given the awards and rewards that have become attached to this position, to cling to an objectivist account of objectification in which mathematical axioms give rise to financial theorems. This interpolation is also social in its construction of the object of knowledge. Specifically, it constitutes a financial market as a homogeneous structure populated by agents whose forms of rationality are purely cognitive, singular, and identical to the mathematized (asocial) rationality by which the economist constructs that space as an object of contemplation staged from an Archimedean view from nowhere. The deep social moment is that finance economists transplant into the market the principles of their relation to it, leading them to conceive the market as a pregiven totality intended for cognition alone, in which all transactions are reduced to axiom-driven utility maximization. Unfortunately, this bears no relationship whatsoever to the real world of derivative pricing and therefore to the reproduction of these markets, which explains why neoclassical economics cannot begin to explain the 2008 financial crisis.

One thinks here of books such as *Liquidity and Crises* (Allen et al. 2011) whose purpose is to address the fact that an "important reason for the global impact of the 2007 financial crisis is massive illiquidity in combination with an extreme exposure of economically and politically relevant parties to liquidity needs and market conditions" (3). This gesture toward the real world notwithstanding, the articles cannot escape their intellectual heritage. Accordingly they leverage formulations such as a "decline in the supply of liquidity" (Allen and Gale 2011, 112), "aggregate liquidity risk" (Bhattacharya and Gale 2011), the misbehavior of the value of money (as in "the value of money is not well behaved") (Allen et al. 2011, 11), and a plethora of other terms and noun phrases that treat concrete social relations as though they were abstract objects. From a social standpoint, four methodological tropes lie at the epicenter of finance economics:

1. Concrete social relations are transformed into abstract objects (e.g., liquidity), which are then imputed to possess a life of their own

2. These abstract objects then interact with abstract general agents constructed by bracketing the specific social and economic characteristics of the concrete agents. In *Liquidity and Crisis*, the abstract agent, "financial intermediaries," encompasses institutions that are fundamentally dissimilar and had extraordinary different relations to the market's construction of liquidity. The abstract agent, financial intermediary, encompasses institutions as dissimilar as investment banks like Goldman Sachs and Morgan Stanley, nonbank banks like GE Capital, and hedge funds such as Soros Investment, Vanguard Mutual Funds, the Baton Rouge Community Savings Bank, and the California State Pension Fund.

3. The concrete agents that comprise the abstract agent are posited as behaving uniformly in respect to the abstract objects, because they all behave as economically rational, utility-maximizing entities in a hypostatized economy.

4. This allows for the production of imaginary ethnography in which an author will declare, for example, that some financial intermediary faced with a given circumstance (e.g., increased risk) will invariably behave in a certain manner (e.g., implement hedging strategies). Historically speaking, this is sometimes

so, sometimes not, as the crisis of 2008 illustrated, which begs the question of what actually determines their behavior.

Twenty-six articles and seven hundred pages later, the reader of *Liquidity and Crisis* is not one centimeter closer to understanding what about liquidity was instrumental in creating a real-world crisis. Not once in all 707 pages is Goldman Sachs, Bear Stearns, AIG, Morgan Stanley, Lehman Brothers, or Fannie Mae even given so much as a mention. There is no mention of the speculatively driven trading in CMOs and CDSs. Also conspicuously absent is any mention of the political power of the financial sector to inflect regulatory regimes, voter perceptions, and government responses to the crisis. The volume exemplifies how the presupposition of a formalized space-time entails that the agents and institutions within that space-time be similarly objectified and disembodied.

The second moment of Black-Scholes is that it allows for the objectification of the market as a totality. No matter for what purpose it is used or how the equation is solved, its construction posits, as pregiven and inalienable fact, a closed and complete market. That is essentially a self-referential totality. But the objectification is more than theoretical. The Black-Scholes model is an award-winning representation—circulated globally through the Euro-American financial media—that the economy is separate from other forms of social life and that the market is its own independent collective agent. The social ontology is that the model's representation of the market is the totality that, subjected to real-world forces, becomes deformed. Nonetheless, to believe in the market is to believe in the ontology of the model's suppositions in that collective participation in any market in which the counterparties are anonymous only makes sense if the agents believe that there is price discovery, only unusual counterparty defaults, continuing liquidity in that there is a quorum of players and enough sufficiently speculative capital, and regulatory tolerance toward that market (here, now, for the foreseeable future). In other words, the Black-Scholes formulation does two things socially: it is a mathematical representation of the market as a natural perduring type, and it is part of the solution to the construction of a social form that circulates excess capital via the financialization of life. Central to the project of capitalism is to make all markets, even derivative markets, which are not only the most contemporary of financial inventions but also synthetic, appear natural to those who encounter them. That these markets can be modeled mathematically—using the tools we use for nature—helps them to assume the aura of self-evident facticity. What is so interesting about Black-Scholes is less that it is an essentialist reading of the present than that it is a central ideological cog in the real relations of the (re)production of the conflation between economic categories of practice and analytical categories.

The third direction of Black-Scholes is as a communal tool. Where the model assumes every token is a perfect exemplar of the type, traders know better, so they operate on a different model on the implicit understanding that markets have a protean character. Every derivative market and every trade is irredeemably particular, yet they are also general and discursive. Accordingly, traders think of Black-Scholes in what we may characterize as a modular form, essentially, the doubled idea that Black-Scholes is universally applicable though invariably in need of contextual refinement. In this respect, it mirrors the doubled character of the market as simultaneously universal yet granular in its capacity to price even the most exotic singular abstract risk-driven derivative. Our ethnography underlines that traders have an inherently sophisticated grasp of markets, although their contexts of practice never call upon them to use this understanding more than as the implicitly unspoken ground of practice. For them, each derivatives market is a multiform and differentiated axis of circulation to which certain generative schemes, such as Black-Scholes, may apply. Each market is an arena of monetary but also symbolic struggle in that grasping all of those things that lie beyond the Black-Scholes formula is simultaneously the source of profit and a public commentary about oneself. And more, all markets are interfunctionally dependent in that pricing in one market may well be radically interdependent with other markets. On the ground, traders can use Black-Scholes as a modular form integrated in more general generative schemes for pricing. That is, Black-Scholes intersects with the generative schemes for the inclusion of the social, allowing for the creation of a spread that serves as the ground of the speculative wager. It thus comes to serve as a departure point because there has evolved a deeply inculcated consensus on the utility of Black-Scholes, meaning that the founding concepts are easy to understand, the model's faults, which reside mostly in its underlying assumptions (e.g., no counterparty risk, perfect price discovery) are common knowledge (e.g., discovering a derivative's price often requires a combination of economic insights and social maneuvering), and traders have learned how to discount what the model dismisses or omits. At the molecular level, traders know every derivative is different in some respect (especially volatility), so they don't organize their calculation to each feature of the contract. Rather, they assume that while no two derivatives or combinations thereof are ever entirely alike in all possible respects, they are sufficiently alike in key respects to allow an approximation of price. Based on traders' practical knowledge, they take account of and incorporate into their generative schemes for pricing an expectation of volatility that, while inconsistent with the theoretical mathematization of the market, is consistent with their more practical calculus of their reality.

The final and most critical dimension is the social practice of pricing and trading derivatives. In contrast to the usual scholastic portrait, which arises from an only implicit, conceptually mushy notion of practice, the pricing of derivatives flows from the habitus of the market's participants (a habitus that encompasses the collective supposition of a derivative market's totality), the notion that the mathematization of the Black-Scholes formula imbues it with legitimacy, and the shared belief that it is a communal or collective tool that creates the common ground for pricing. The economy of pricing takes place at the intersection of the objective structure of a market at a specific point in time—the players, the participating institutions, the derivative instruments, the Black-Scholes model—and the embodied dispositions and generative schemes of traders. It is these incorporated dispositions and schemes, visibly articulated as players' sense of the game, that allows them to begin with the Black-Scholes pricing formula as a launching point to recalibrate a derivative's price, founded on the common understanding that there is always an element of contingency and indeterminacy yet also a recognizable necessity in that traders can use their knowledge and intuitions to decipher that derivative's "correct" price, its forthcoming value at expiration, thus moving them to jointly "pull the trigger" and consummate the bet.[15] To fathom why traders continue to use the Black-Scholes formulation—despite its well-documented theoretical flaws and empirical failings—it is necessary to appreciate that a mathematical logic unfolding in a perfect world (the complete market) is, for traders, only a first approximation of a practical logic unfolding in a social universe. Because an agent's habitus is the product of a confrontation with a market defined by irregular regularities, it can produce through reasonable adjustments a wager adapted to the probable volatility of the market. At an existential level, the price of a derivative stems from agents' recognition of conditional cues to which they are predisposed to react due to their indoctrination in, and experience of, that specific market. The basis of these reactions may encompass, but also extend far beyond and sometimes owe little to, rational calculation. The market as a social fact owes its practical coherence and continuity in the face of volatility, illiquidity, and counterparty failures to the reality that it is the product of practices that are coherent practically in that the participants can recalibrate them to the objective state of the market (e.g., a terrorist attack or a hedge fund collapse) and are manageable because they are parsimonious. On these grounds, it is easy to see how useful the Black-Scholes formula is practically: adaptable, economical, mutually shared, and robust.

When we have put aside the objectivist account of objectification, amplified and exemplified by the mathematization of the finance market, the question of the market as a capitalist production, in which the circulation of capital is the worksite of struggle among competing participants, remains. The question is whether analysis can account for derivative markets by developing an approach that considers the systemic dimension of these capitalist capital markets, the family resemblance among different markets brought about by use and adaptation of reflecting modular forms and generative schemes, and the space for the incorporation of all those things social that motivate agents to collectively reproduce the market as a totality. The genius and scandal of the Black and Scholes formula is that it is instrumental on all these levels.

Conclusion

We have expressly framed the questions bracketed by both neoclassical and Marxist approaches of how markets are realized as collective agents and how the markets sustain themselves as such. The critical ground is that *a market enacted as a continuous set of transactions functions (remains liquid) because its agents presuppose the market as a (imagined) totality, even as the existence of that totality depends on the continuity of those transactions.* Speaking to the relationship between collectivity and totality requires a theorization that is specifically social and that illuminates the generative structure by which financial markets accomplish this. Based on a theorization of the evidence, we argue that the objectifications of these derivative markets turn on forms of performativity that direct and harness the inherent rituality embodied in social practices.

While rituality may seem far removed and remote from the world of finance, rituality in its modern secular form is, on our understanding, the hidden constitutive dimension of the innovation and (re)production of financial markets, including the derivatives markets. This analytical focus requires that we historicize the concept of the market by illuminating the sociospecific and historically imperative character of modern derivatives markets, critically the forms of performativity these markets embody and motivate. There is too much at stake to leave the financial field to theories that bracket the social. Our aim at the present conjuncture has to be to develop theories and methods that can adequately grasp a social whose arc is moving away from the social that reigned during the salad days of production-centered capitalism, a transformative social that is emerging in the context of the restructuring of the relationship between production and circulation, in ways whose dynamic lies in how new forms of detachment involve new dimensions of connectivity. Our argument is that an understanding of the relationship between performativity and objectification and of how the technical production of the spread through the wealth-generating pricing mechanism of Black-Scholes is open to a sociality that it must bracket if it is to maintain its internal dynamism, or dynamic replication that shows the hedging strategies of rituality to lie at the heart of what was itself once bracketed as the economic, is a first step in that direction.

CHAPTER THREE

From Primitives to Derivatives

Benjamin Lee, The New School

In this chapter[1] we continue the "social reading of the derivative" that Appadurai and LiPuma initiated in their chapters and also begin our "derivative reading of the social" with an interpretation of Marx's surplus value as a value arbitrage. Appadurai and LiPuma introduced two concepts in our "social reading of the derivative": dividuality and performativity, which can be seen as contributing to an alternative account of subjectivity than that of the standard belief-desire model presupposed by contemporary economics and finance. We extend those accounts to Weber's analysis of the spirit of capitalism, and our reworking of Marx's account of relative surplus value allows us to see the internal connections between subjectivity and capital—one of the goals of the Frankfurt School's project, with its almost obsessive concern with the connections between commodity fetishism and culture—and rework them in the face of derivative capitalism's focus on uncertainty and volatility. The notion of the dividual is meant to contrast with the "possessive individual" decision maker that is at the heart of modern economics and finance. It draws upon a rich anthropological tradition going back at least to Marcel Mauss, whose work on the gift and exchange was meant to give an alternative to the "possessive individualism" of the Hobbesian contract model of society and was the starting point for Lévi-Strauss, Bourdieu, and Derrida on the nature of the gift. Mauss's legacy sees persons as formed by their gift/exchange relationships; instead of individual autonomous agents exchanging alienable objects such as commodities and money, people are connected by social relations of shared substance and conduct that are manifested in precognitive embodied sensibilities and practices, what Bourdieu called *habitus*, a term also used by Aristotle, Aquinas, Weber, and Merleau-Ponty.

Donald MacKenzie and Michel Callon had already extended Austin's analysis of speech acts to show the performative dimensions of the Black-Scholes formula in options trading and pricing. Its anthropological extension to ritual was meant to capture dimensions of affect, motivation, and embodiment, which are not captured by MacKenzie and Callon's work and the belief-desire model of agency dominant in economics and finance. Instead, the reanimation of notions such as aura, charisma, spirit, habitus, and ethos in a Weberian reading of the development of the "spirit" of finance capitalism provides us with an account of the subjectivity needed to support the "nonlinear but directional" historical dynamic of relative surplus value's exploration of the uncertainty of social innovation.

Despite the general acknowledgement that they are among our greatest accounts of capitalism, Max Weber's *The Protestant Ethic and the Spirit of Capitalism* and Karl Marx's *Capital* sometimes seem to be like ships passing in the night. They appear to be on different trajectories, with Weber exploring the spirit or ethos of capitalism while Marx articulates its structural dynamics. Yet the 2007–8 financial crisis would seem to be due to some combination of the rise of a "speculative ethos" and the structural conditions that made derivative speculation possible, suggesting that there is a continuing relationship between ethos and capital that undergirds the development of finance capitalism. In this chapter, we use three concepts—performativity, arbitrage, and uncertainty—to build an internal connection between Weber's notion of ethic and spirit and Marx's analysis of capital, the parameters of which remain in play in finance capitalism. We connect the idea of performativity, used by Appadurai and LiPuma in their social reading of the derivative, to that of arbitrage, which will be developed by Meister and Martin in their derivative reading of the social. Uncertainty is a concept that is shared by both readings; it has achieved contemporary prominence due to the growing interest in volatility, especially as it relates to "fat-tailed" and "black swan" events such as 9/11, the 2008 crash, or Hurricane Katrina; uncertainty and volatility have become the new mantras of "postrisk" societies, but their mutual exploration by Weber and Marx initiates a trajectory that continues in the present.

Performativity and arbitrage turn out to have an internal connection. Arbitrage is a mispricing that allows a riskless profit—a gift or "free

lunch"—and when arbitrage opportunities appear they rapidly close because they are quickly exploited. The nonarbitrage principle is a standard
presupposition of most financial pricing models and is a kind of negative
performativity—instead of the creative self-reference of explicit performatives, the appearance of an arbitrage difference is self-referentially
self-cancelling. Marx's account of relative surplus value is also a value
arbitrage—technological innovation produces a discrepancy between
the average labor time for producing a commodity and that needed for
the innovation; the capitalist pockets the difference. This value arbitrage
sets up a dynamic of the creative destruction of value, which manifests
itself in the tendency of the rate of profit to fall, a directionality that can
be offset by countertendencies such as decreases in the cost of constant
capital, increased unemployment, or foreign competition. Martin's chapter shows how the hedging of these countertendencies creates the spread
dynamics out of which finance capitalism will develop.

Weber's account of the development of the spirit of capitalism starts
from a very different angle, that of the supersession of ritual magic in
Catholicism by a Calvinist ascetic ethic in which the motivating force
is the uncertainty of God's greatest gift—salvation. While Marx's discovery was to locate the source of the dynamic of capitalism in the
logic of relative surplus value, Weber was concerned with explaining
why capitalism developed first in Protestant Europe rather than among
Catholic monks, Jewish businessmen, or Chinese merchants. What was
special about the Calvinist motivational structure that would give birth
to someone like Benjamin Franklin, Weber's paragon of the spirit of
capitalism?

Our answer will lie in the existential uncertainty of God's gift of salvation. Drawing from Derrida's argument about the impossibility of the
gift, we will argue that the "impossibility" of that gift creates an existential uncertainty that can never be grounded or resolved, thereby producing the intensity of the Calvinist experience that made it so unique
in Weber's eyes. With the retreat of the Calvinist God as a motivating
factor, what remains is an inward and reflective subjectivity whose infinite open-endedness can be measured by the temporality of money—in
Benjamin Franklin's words, "time is money," which has a "prolific, generating nature" that "can beget money, and its offspring can beget more,
and so on." This type of "objectified" subjectivity will develop in its full
form in the rise of the modern novel and be the basis for a new kind of
consciousness produced by print capitalism, that of "we, the people" de-

scribed by Benedict Anderson in his *Imagined Communities* (2006); it is a subjectivity that is in tune with the logic of surplus value and distinguishes Marx's miser ("the capitalist gone mad") from the capitalist ("the rational miser").

Models and Reality

The Weberian account of the rise of capitalist subjectivity at the heart of our social reading of the derivative runs counter to the assumptions about the relationship between models and reality presupposed by much of contemporary finance and raises challenges to the dominant "belief-desire" model of economics and decision theory. The formal languages of mathematics and science are supposed to be independent of what they represent and logically extensional—terms that refer to the same things can be substituted for one another without a change in truth value in the expressions they are part of. But as the philosopher Gottlob Frege pointed out, such substitutions fail in the propositional contexts introduced by verbs of speaking, thinking, and feeling—"Oedipus wanted to marry Jocasta" could be true, but "Oedipus wanted to marry his mother" is false because Oedipus didn't know that Jocasta = his mother. Contexts in which substitution of coreferring terms fail to preserve truth value are logically intensional and include quotation, reporting speech, performatives, intentionality, and modality (Frege 1980). The importance of the intension/extension distinction is that phenomena that the natural sciences describe and explain are treated as *extensional* whereas finance depends upon peoples' expectations and motivations, which are logically *intensional*.

In the case of pricing models such as Black-Scholes, model and reality are represented by the relationship between theoretical and market prices for options. The theoretical prices are modeled by "tree diagrams" ("binomial trees") that map the movement of prices over time in ways suggestive of actual price movements; there are several examples in Derman's chapter, which share a common structure. From a given state of the world at time t_0, one can imagine the various possible states of the world in succeeding time periods $1, 2, 3 \ldots n$. Each state transition has a probability of occurrence and the state of the world at t_1 consists of all the possible state prices at t_1 and the associated probabilities of their transition from t_0. The result is a branching tree diagram with

t_0 as the initial node; at t_1, each state is also the locus of a tree diagram ad infinitum.

The basic idea is that you can map the possible prices of a derivative as states of the market at a given time. Any market price will look like an instance of the one of the possible state prices at a given time within the model. A particular market price thus looks like an instantiation of the theoretical values given by the model. Taking market prices as the starting point for the construction of risk-neutral valuations or state prices give the illusion that all price movements can be mapped in a probabilistic space of which the actual market price is a mere instantiation of one of the state prices of the model. Agents make calculations in accordance with their beliefs and desires (the so-called "belief-desire" model is also commonly used in decision theory) and then decide to buy and sell assets at the various price points given by the model; agents have a transparent "grasp" of the prices given by the model. Because the market price appears to be a transparent token instantiation of the type level state price, it looks like the model is directly instantiated in reality without the need for any indexical or performative calibration. To the extent that the market price does not exactly map the price predicted within the model—the discrepancy is often characterized as due to "friction"—some of the conditions of the model aren't satisfied, for example, lack of liquidity or presence of arbitrage opportunities.

Two of our coauthors in this volume, Emanuel Derman and Elie Ayache, share a healthy skepticism about the use of such models in finance, with Derman drawing upon his experience as one of the first quants building models for pricing options and Ayache from his practical experience as a derivatives trader. When Derman first arrived at Goldman Sachs, he believed that the goal was to create a "physics of finance"; when he returns to academia some two decades later he thinks such attempts are misguided: "there are no genuine theories in finance" (2011, 193). Rather financial models are "collection(s) of parallel thought universes," which should be used "like a fiction reader or a really great pretender, to temporarily suspend disbelief, and then push it as far as possible" (2004, 269).

The temptation is to make analogies with physics and engineering and elevate what Derman calls a model to the status of an explanatory theory. Finance is based upon expectations about risk and uncertainty that are logically intensional, which are then regimented and translated into extensional mathematics. Derman takes the equational identity at the heart of replication and interprets it as setting up a metaphor, an analogy that allows one to "describe one thing relative to something else." Metaphors often take the linguistic form of an equational identity or metasemantic definition—"The world *is* a stage"—that asserts the identity of two things known to be different so that one can notice a point of relevance; metaphors play with extensional definitions to bring out the intensionality of meaning. Pricing models rely upon expectations about the future; replication is one of the points where the intensionality of intentionality gets translated into the extensionality of mathematical finance, giving the appearance of a "physics of finance" even when the foundations are intentional and intensional.

While Derman criticizes what he sees as a misunderstanding of the analogical dimension of models in finance, Ayache criticizes the assumptions of financial models by focusing on the event of market making and trading. He uses the work of Alain Badiou, Quentin Meillassoux, and Jorge Borges to develop a "theory" of "necessary contingency," "backwards narrativity," and dynamic replication to develop an alternative to the "physics of finance" approach. Ayache (2007) uses a story by Borges, "Pierre Menard, Author of the *Quixote*," to highlight the tension between stochastically given "possible (price) worlds" and the social reality of writing. Borges's short story is about a twentieth-century French writer who is trying to write a word-for-word recreation of some chapters of Cervantes's *Don Quixote*. Given the passage of time, and the differences in Menard's and Cervantes's native languages and cultural backgrounds, the narrator makes the case that the re-creation is perhaps more creative than the original. The original *Don Quixote* is to its (re)writing as stochastically described possible worlds are to the act of trading or tree diagrams of theoretical price movements are to the flow of market prices.

> If you believe in the metaphysics of possibility and probability, where everything is framed in identified states of the world, and so on, then Pierre Menard is doing nothing, totally nothing. Yet by reading Borges, you are really led to believe it is possible that Pierre Menard has done something original; and the key thing to me is that what Pierre Menard has done is to *write* two chapters. . . . So, he really needed the material medium, the writing itself, in order to produce something that, when you read it, you say well, although it's the same—it has the same identity as Cervantes's novel—it is materially a new work. And although my main object is the markets and finance, al-

though that's important and I identify the medium of contingency as the market in my specific case, in the end its generalization is also *writing*. (Ayache, 2011, 24)

Ayache develops his approach in two stages: first a critique, then an alternative. The critique draws upon Badiou's argument that a "true contingent event" is not part of any set; the event is the set that is a member of itself and "creates the possibilities that led to it," what Nassim Taleb (2007) calls "backwards narrativity." For example, a "black swan" event is one that is unimaginable before it occurs; when it occurs, then there is a reconstruction of the chain of possibilities that lead to the event and "explain" it. In this "backwards narrativity," there is no way to build a tree diagram with probabilistic transitions between possible states of the world—since the possibilities postdate the effect or result, there can't be any prior probabilities for the occurrence of the event, thereby making the event unmodelable.

If the stochastic modeling of possibility does not apply to trading, if a "physics of finance" is not possible, what is the alternative? Based upon his experience as a developer of option pricing software and as a trader, Ayache argues that traders grapple with the contingency of events through "dynamic replication" in which they run Black-Scholes backwards to compute "implied volatilities." It is at this point that Derman and Ayache's accounts overlap, as Derman is one of the pioneers in developing implied volatility trees. Starting from his experience as a physicist, Derman sees the inadequacy of financial models as due to a kind of overreaching—making claims for robustness and explanatory power that belie the complexity of socially generated risk. Ayache starts from the reality of the market—the making of prices—and insists that understanding trading as a kind of writing leads to an "ontology of exchange."

Both Derman and Ayache are critical of the "physics of finance" viewpoint that is dominant in finance, with Derman starting from a critique of the ways models are understood and Ayache insisting upon the fundamental irreducibility of the event of trading to any formal statistical model. They converge around the indispensability of Black-Scholes and the importance of what is called the "implied volatility smile," but for reasons that go against the grain of many of their colleagues.

The "smile" is an anomaly for the "physics of finance" model that many in finance believe in. There are five variables that determine the value of a call option in Black-Scholes: stock price, strike price, volatility, time to expiration, and short-term (risk-free) interest rate, of which four are easily observed; the fifth is volatility, which when plugged in will yield the option price. In finance, volatility is uncertainty about the size of price changes in an asset, and is the standard deviation (the square root of the variance) of those price movements. In calculating the option price, usually some version of historical volatility is used. On the other hand, since there are observed market prices for option transactions, one can compute what is called the "implied volatility" of the stock by inverting the formula and then inputting the market price of the option, the option's expiration date and strike price, and the risk-free interest rate. Inputting the market prices for options at different expirations and strike prices will result in different implied volatilities for the stock, thereby violating the constant volatility assumption of Black-Scholes; implied volatilities should be independent of expiration dates and strike prices, but since the crash of 1987, implied volatility has varied as a function of strike price and expiration date. According to Black-Scholes, since volatility is constant, the volatility surface should be smooth and flat, but since 1987 the actual volatility surface looks more like a "wave" (see diagrams in Derman's chapter, this volume).

In response to the appearance of the smile, Derman and others proposed to run Black-Scholes backwards. Instead of using volatility to calculate the price of the option, why not start with the market price of the option and then calculate the (implied) volatility that would "explain" the market price? The imputation of implied volatility is the "backwards narrativity" used to make the model "real," to make it work in the world, and is that which grips the trader at the level of embodied sensibility and habitus; the whole process of dynamic replication is the constant updating of the model by "reality," by calculating a new implied volatility for each market price (traders watch real-time implied volatilities stream by on the top of the Bloomberg machines that almost all traders use). The backwards calculation of implied volatility provides the presupposed framework for hedging one's position and making future trades, whose prices are then used to recalibrate the model by calculating a new implied volatility. Ayache describes the process of derivative pricing as a sequence: dynamic replication > theoretical pricing > observation of empirical option prices > calibration of model to option prices > recalibration (2008, 42).

Instead of abandoning a model "falsified" by the data, the use of Black-Scholes has increased to the point where it could be said to be a crucial element in the "worldview" of finance; there are no real rivals except models that are formally equivalent such as binomial trees. Ayache, even while insisting on the irreducibility of the event to formal models such as Black-Scholes, will argue that dynamic replication at the heart of the Black-Scholes model is the only way to enter or face the volatility smile, which he opines is "the reality of options markets" (Ayache 2008, 37). And Derman will write: "I would say that Black-Scholes is the language in which we try to express its own internal inadequacies, like Wittgenstein's attempt with ordinary language. You cannot get away from it yet" (2014, personal communication).

What would explain the enduring belief in finance in a model widely known to be continuously falsified by the very data it purports to explain? A close reading of Ayache's *The Blank Swan* and Derman's *Models.Behaving.Badly.* would uncover references to God, writing, and uncertainty that suggest that the ordinary functioning of derivatives touches upon larger issues that are almost existential in their import—trading options are all about confronting volatility and uncertainty in ways that resemble a big-wave surfer or high-stakes poker player rather than the belief-desire calculations of rational actors:

> Through the dynamic delta-hedging and the anxiety that it generates (Will I execute it right? When to rebalance it, etc.), the market-maker penetrated the market. He penetrated its volatility and he could now feel it in his guts. In a word, he became a *dynamic trader.* He now understood—not conceptually, but through his senses, through his body—the inexorability of time decay, the pains and joys of convexity. (Ayache 2008, 36–37)

The Performativity of Finance

The interface between the volatility smile and Black-Scholes is also the starting point for Donald MacKenzie and Michel Callon's elaboration of a performative approach to finance, which also suggests a way of connecting the existential issues that Derman and Ayache hint at with the internal workings of quantitative finance. In a pathbreaking historical reconstruction of the discovery, use, and popularization of the Black-Scholes equation for pricing options, MacKenzie (2006) shows that shortly after the publication of Black-Scholes and the founding of the Chicago Options Exchange in 1973, there was an initial "spread" between the theoretical volatilities predicted by Black-Scholes and the actual market volatilities, but as the formula became the standard way to price options, the spread narrowed so that by the mid-1980s the volatility surface was relatively flat, indicating only minor discrepancies between implied and realized volatilities—the constant volatility assumption of Black-Scholes seemed to be confirmed by the actual market prices. MacKenzie argues that the use of Black-Scholes made some of the theoretical conditions presupposed by Black-Scholes "real in practice"—lowered transaction costs, greater liquidity, fewer arbitrage opportunities, a phenomenon he and Callon, drawing from John Austin's work on speech acts, have called "performative" (MacKenzie 2006; Callon 2010). After the crash of 1987, this relationship broke down and the "smile" appears, which continues till this day.

The performativity of finance thesis argues that finance is to some degree created by the models that it uses. It's not like physics or other natural sciences in which model and reality are seen as independent; there is a constructivist moment in finance, especially around the use of Black-Scholes, that would seem to complement Derman and Ayache's speculations on the relation between model and event; Ayache even goes so far as to postulate what might be called a "retrospective performativity" to finance as part of the process by which we create a "stochastic narrative" for the movement of option prices.

MacKenzie and Callon use performativity to question the claim that economics is a science and that physics is an appropriate model for finance. Coming out of a background in science studies, the idea of performativity allows them to develop alternative social science approaches to the claims of economics and finance to be both scientific and yet also capable of handling uncertainty and risk. Yet perhaps it is this background that makes them reluctant to push their performativity thesis further, beyond the claims about models and reality, to the existential dimensions that Derman and Ayache hint at.

In Search of the Existential: The Performativity of Ritual

Those existential dimensions are highlighted in the anthropological study of ritual, in which performativity plays a key role, especially as developed by Stanley Tambiah, Michael Silverstein, and Roy Rappaport, which in turn has connections to the work of thinkers as diverse as Erving Goffman, Clifford Geertz, and Judith Butler, not to speak of a distinctively French line of thought that includes Pierre Bourdieu, Jacques Derrida, and Jean-Luc Marion. Rituals are also concerned with the relation between model and event in which the ritual event is a "microcosmic" instantiation of a "macrocosmic" model; the ritual event creates an instance of what it represents in representing it, much like a linguistic performative that creates what it refers to (Austin himself repeatedly makes the connection between performativity and ritual). But as the Appadurai and LiPuma chapters show, ritual performativity is closely tied to issues at the heart of derivative finance such as uncertainty, liquidity, and arbitrage.

Austin's work on performativity (1962) kicked off a cottage industry in what was called "speech act" theory in linguistics and literary studies. It soon became clear in work such as John Searle's *Speech Acts* (1969) that performatives combined a propositional component with a "force" component, which was subdivided into "illocutionary" and "perlocutionary"; most of the attention focused on the illocutionary component (glossed as what was done "in" saying something), although Stanley Cavell, one of the earliest "ordinary language philosophers" and a student of Austin, has recently been exploring the perlocutionary dimensions of speech acts (what is done "by" saying something) in his work on "passionate utterances and performatives" (2006).

The peculiarity of performatives from a propositional and logical standpoint is that they create what they refer to "in" referring to it, thus undoing the independence between language and reality that science and mathematics presuppose; they undermine the boundaries between the extensional and intensional. The illocutionary force of a performative is what differentiates it from other speech acts, what makes the utterance of "I will be there tomorrow" in a particular context a promise, report, statement, or even a threat while the perlocutionary focuses on what is done "by" speaking. By using the term "force" to apply to both the illocutionary and perlocutionary dimensions of speech acts, Austin clearly signaled that he was in the realm of moods and affects, including sincerity, truthfulness, consensus, and dissent. Since almost all of his examples of explicit performatives are ritual actions (christenings, bequeathals, marriages, etc.), the embedding of linguistic performativity within ritual action connected performativity to areas normally investigated by anthropologists (Austin 1962). This was the insight that drove Appadurai and LiPuma to extend performativity to issues such as Durkheim's "collective effervescence," Mauss's discussions of *hau* and *mana*, Weber's "charisma," or even Walter Benjamin's "aura."

At the same time, the intensionality of performative verbs of speaking connected them to other verbs of feeling (I am afraid that . . .) and thinking (I believe that . . .) and modal contexts such as possibility and necessity, all of which can take propositional complements (I believe *that* . . . , it is possible *that* . . .). The philosopher Zeno Vendler (1972) has investigated Austin's typology of explicit performative verbs and discovered that there is almost a complete correspondence between categories of performatives and mental activity (i.e., "discover," "decide," "infer") and mental state verbs ("know," "believe," "hope"), leading him to conclude that "almost anything that can be said can be thought, while anything that can be thought can be said" (Lee 1989, 211). This interlocking intensional and intentional system of speaking, thinking, and feeling comprises the linguistic infrastructure of the "belief-desire" model of subjectivity presupposed by economic and game theoretic models of agentive behavior. In this primarily cognitive model of decision making, beliefs and desires are seen as having different "directions of fit" that work together to produce an action. Beliefs are seen as having a representation-to-world direction of fit, while desires transform the world to fit the representation ("I desire that . . ."); actions are the result of people weighing their beliefs and desires and then choosing accordingly, usually subject to some constraints such as utility maximization.

MacKenzie and Callon's adoption of Barnesian performativity focuses on the creative self-referential properties of performatives—more specifically, the "direction of fit" between theoretical option prices given by Black-Scholes and their market prices, which converge until Black Monday, 1987, and afterwards have tended to diverge. They argue for a performative effect of Black-Scholes as the prices converge and a counterperformativity after 1987, which would support a creative and constructivist approach to finance. Relying upon Barnes's account of performativity, they do not discuss the illocutionary component of speech acts. Yet the illocutionary component, which distinguishes what type of performative act is being performed, is crucial for creative self-reference because it is what is named and created by the use of the explicit performative and also taps into affective and motivational registers that play an important role in their ritual functioning. Much of our work focuses on putting the "spirit" back into the machine of finance by exploring the "force" dimension of financial practices. At the same time, it's not a recourse to the "animal spirits" of behavioral finance but rather a set of concepts that wind their way through the anthropology of ritual and exchange into the ideas of creative destruction at the heart of Schumpeter's and Marx's accounts of capitalism.

In their chapters, Appadurai and LiPuma introduce some of the features of ritual performativity, especially the retrospective or backwards performativity of rituals (also captured in Ayache's idea of the backwards narrativity of options trading), and their staging of the types of uncertainty they are designed to resolve. The staging of uncertainty also introduces a play dimension into ritual, a fact noted by Huizinga in his classic work on play, *Homo Ludens* (1971). Ritual performances are shot through with playful exaggerations of normative behavior. Groups may become hyperaggressive, challenging and insulting counterpart groups almost to the point of real insult; some rituals may even invert the status of groups (Bakhtin's carnival) only to have the ritual process restore the equilibrium by transforming the marginalized into the normatively acceptable. It does this by determining the nature and membership of the relevant social groups, which involves selecting out of the myriad relationships created by everyday activities some subset that will be seen as the "embodiment" of those groups (i.e., "eagle clan" or "turtle totem"). In many cases this will involve going beyond the ideal norms of group membership to incorporate "fictive kin" (for example, a family without a son might "adopt" the male child of a patrilineal relative); the processes of social circulation and exchange produce the "excess" that ritual exchanges will play with and represent. Ritual plays with the normative by exceeding it, as in the famous example of Trobriand cricket where the Trobrianders took the colonial game of cricket and converted it into a ritualized parody of warfare. The model becomes real in ritual only by exceeding it; the reality depicted in ritual is a stylized and playful evocation of reality. Play, in the sense of behavior that exceeds the norm by "playing with it," is a constitutive component of ritual exchange in that it incorporates new social relationships and their concomitant claims and obligations into the ritualized value hierarchy of society.

The Gift of Arbitrage

If the origins of capitalism lie in the uncertainty of the gift of salvation, then the origins of finance could be said to lie in the gift of arbitrage.

In the financial literature, arbitrage is represented as a form of "negative performativity": the representation of a difference leads to the self-referential cancellation of that difference. The example usually given to introduce the issue of arbitrage is that of an asset that has two prices; one could make a riskless instantaneous profit if one could simultaneously buy the asset at the lower price and sell it at the higher one. However, the presence of arbitrage opportunities leads to their self-cancellation as people take advantage of the spread and it closes.

Arbitrage works so as to performatively close the spread between prices, to bring the market back into alignment with the model. The opening up of the spread is the "play of excess" that produces the pricing inefficiencies and noise that trading depends upon—a difference that is turned into a profit by buying short and selling long. It differs from the "normal" way of making a profit only in the collapsing of the time interval; by buying and selling simultaneously one guarantees a riskless profit, the "free lunch," or gift, of arbitrage. The mathematical models of arbitrage wipe out the ritual/play dimensions of arbitrage, which reappear in the rhetoric of free gifts and lunches but reemerge in full force with all their religious overtones in financial crises where the "normal" interplay between noise, information, and liquidity becomes disengaged by the return of the existential through the fat tails of crisis.

The absence of arbitrage opportunities is taken as a presupposition of most financial models. The nonarbitrage principle is generally spoken of as the "fundamental theorem of finance," and Modigliani and Miller's use of arbitrage arguments have become a standard "proof" procedure in financial engineering. The nonarbitrage principle acts like the principle of extensionality in logic: it determines what assets are "equivalent" and can be interchanged for one another—how to "replicate" assets. The development of the nonarbitrage principle will give birth to the capital asset pricing model (CAPM) and the Black-Scholes equations, which in turn will lead to the development of efficient market models, risk-neutral valuations, state prices, and martingales, all of which are at the heart of contemporary finance; Derman's derivation of Black-Scholes from the nonarbitrage principle highlights its fundamental importance across contemporary finance. These discoveries interlock to create a totalized vision of a market where asset pricings no longer depend on the risk preferences of individuals (i.e., "risk-neutral valuations") but are located in an idealized mathematical/statistical space of possible asset prices and their movements (martingales, implied volatility trees, state prices, etc.). The view of an abstract social totality purged of individual risk and imperfections (no arbitrage opportunities) is reminiscent of religion—as one of the traders we interviewed said, "Black-Scholes is God"—and arbitrage opportunities are often spoken of as free gifts given by chance or even God, like finding a twenty dollar bill on the sidewalk.[2]

Playing with Uncertainty: Frank Knight and Fischer Black

While the details of ritual performativity seem a long way from the formal mathematics of derivative pricing, both Derman and Ayache will raise questions about the status of models and their relation to the events they are supposed to represent, which will be the starting point for Callon and MacKenzie's performativity thesis. But while MacKenzie focuses on the relation between theoretical and actual option prices, ritual performativity suggests a deeper connection between uncertainty, play, and ritual that rests upon complex socially constituted motivational structures that are caught in the collective "force" behind ritual activity. Although some of these connections are now being explored by the recent turn to "animal spirits" and behavioral economics, it is Frank Knight and Fischer Black, mediated by the anthropologist Clifford Geertz, who in their own ways see the internal connections between economic behavior, ritual, play, and uncertainty.

Frank Knight and Fischer Black were founding figures in economics and finance in the United States. Knight was a founder of the Chicago School of economics, while Fischer Black was not only a codeveloper of the Black-Scholes options pricing formula and the dominant asset pricing model, the capital asset pricing model (CAPM), but also one of the first financial analysts to move from the academy to investment backing; Robert Rubin brought him to Goldman Sachs to introduce modern techniques of quantitative finance and change its trading ethos.

Although Black moved to the University of Chicago shortly before Knight died, there is no indication that they met or that Black had read Knight closely. Clifford Geertz, one of Black's favorite teachers at Harvard, was also at Chicago, but it's not clear if they ever met before Geertz left for Princeton. Geertz had a development anthropology background and would later publish an article in the *American Economic Review* about information and pricing in the *souk* or bazaar, drawing upon then-cutting edge work by George Akerlof, Kenneth Arrow, Michael Spence, and George Stigler to give an account of pricing in "inefficient markets" (1978); he also shared with Knight a deep interest in Max Weber. Yet they all shared a deep concern for the role of uncertainty in economic processes, and several of Knight's basic economic theses are also presuppositions of Black's work. Both Knight and Black started with an abstract and idealized notion of economics and finance based upon utility maximization and perfect competition; but in both cases, instead of seeing these models as imperfect approximations to reality, they saw a more complicated relation between model and reality in which uncertainty played a crucial role.

Knight is generally credited with introducing the distinction between uncertainty and risk into economics. In *Risk, Uncertainty, and Profit,* Knight distinguishes between risk and true uncertainty. Risk is measurable uncertainty, unknown outcomes for which there are known distributions of outcomes either via a priori calculation or statistical enumeration, and uncertainty involves unknown outcomes that lack such ex ante probability distributions. Knight insisted that there was a qualitative difference between uncertainty and risk and that utility maximization only applied to the latter, in which there were calculable probabilities, and not the former, which included catastrophic singularities and situations "in which one's whole fortune (or his life) were at stake" (Knight 2002, 234).

Knight also made a distinction between static and dynamic analyses of the economy that would foreshadow a similar distinction made by von Neumann and Morgenstern in their theory of games.[3] Static economics was a science like physics that built upon "abstraction and analysis" (von Neumann and Morgenstern 1944) to construct idealized economic models based upon equilibrium and utility maximization; the goal of a scientific economics was to uncover the unchanging realities of economic activity. Such models might have only a tangential relation to actual economic practices, which were always undergoing change and therefore subject to uncertainty. There was an "impassable gulf" between the equilibrium systems posited by static analyses and the working of the real economy. Dynamic analyses would have to leave the idealized world of static equilibrium models and embrace the historical study of institutions, including legal, moral, and political systems, which is why Knight found the work of Max Weber so attractive.

Theoretical analysis must start from the conception of a "perfectly competitive" economy organized through a system of theoretically ideal markets. Here all profit (and loss, negative profit) is excluded. Such ideal or "frictionless" conditions would make all costs equal to selling prices, the whole value-product being distributed among those who supply the various productive services. The prerequisite is errorless foresight of future conditions in all business decisions.

Omniscient direction becomes identical with automatic adjustment to conditions. If a particular entrepreneur had perfect foresight, he would never incur a loss; and if his competitors had it, he would never make a gain. This condition is a necessary hypothesis, though absurd if taken as realistic. (Knight 1999b, 348)

The link between static and dynamic systems was the entrepreneur. One of the problems with static analyses of perfect competition and equilibrium was that the motivation for profit seemed to disappear; a similar problem arises in Black's account of trading—in financial markets, if noise is eliminated, liquidity disappears and there is no motivation to trade. Knight moves beyond a static model of the economic system and its techniques of risk management and introduces the problem of uncertainty. Since all economic systems are subject to change and change introduced uncertainty, it was the role of the entrepreneur to face uncertainty and profit from it: "Profit arises out of the inherent, absolute unpredictability of things, out of the sheer, brute fact that the results of human activity cannot be anticipated and then only in so far as even a probability calculation in regard to them is impossible and meaningless" (Knight 1999b, 311). Entrepreneurs are participants in a competitive game to take advantage of uncertainty; this competition provides the missing piece in static models, profit, which creates the dynamic that drives capitalist economic systems. The motivation for businessmen and entrepreneurs is not reducible to anything rational but instead "is the desire to excel, to win at a game, the biggest and most fascinating game yet invented, not excepting even statecraft and war" (Knight 2002, 360), in which success depends upon one's "ability to play, effort, and luck" (Knight 1999a, 79). Competitive game playing under radical uncertainty turns out to be the engine of the real economy!

Black certainly understood the role of models in physics and mathematics—he had been a physics major at Harvard and then entered its PhD program before turning to applied mathematics. He was also briefly a social relations major, and his favorite undergraduate professors were the psychologist Jerome Bruner, the anthropologist Clifford

Geertz, and the philosopher Willard Quine, who was also on his PhD committee and whose work on logic and language was the inspiration for his thesis, which was on machine translation.[4]

During the fifty or so years that separated Knight's first work on uncertainty from Black's development of CAPM, the fundamental nature of finance had changed—the axiomatization of expected utility by von Neumann and Morgenstern, Harry Markowitz's portfolio theory, and the nonarbitrage arguments of Modigliani and Miller had transformed the nature of quantitative finance in which Black would play a pioneering role. His own interest in finance came after his dissertation when he worked as a computer analyst at Arthur Little and met one of the codiscoverers of CAPM, Jack Treynor, who would become a lifelong mentor and colleague. While always acknowledging his debt to Treynor, Black also transformed CAPM to fit the ongoing discussion of arbitrage, equilibrium dynamics, and efficient markets. Throughout his career he would move back and forth between the academy and finance, and it was on December 30, 1985, that Fischer Black, the vice president of trading and arbitrage at Goldman, Sachs & Co., would make a now-classic presidential address of the American Finance Association on "Noise."

Drawing upon his extensive experience with traders and trading (his first office was right next to the trading floor of Goldman Sachs), Black's talk inverted several of the verities presupposed by financial theorists, particularly the relation between what he called "noise" and "information" trading. Efficient market theory, as developed by Eugene Fama and his Chicago associates, was a theory of how the market's processing of information determined prices of assets such as stocks. Drawing upon the distinction between noise and information developed by Shannon and Weaver, which was part of the intellectual background for his dissertation, Black added Quine's work on the indeterminacy of reference and translation to fashion a unique interpretation of the role of uncertainty in financial and economic processes.

In addition to the standard use of arbitrage theory and rational expectations (utility maximization) characteristic of asset pricing models such as CAPM, Black's address made a distinction between noise and information. Noise, which consists of the various forms of social uncertainty, "makes our observations imperfect," including keeping "us from knowing the expected return on a stock or portfolio" (2012, 529), and would be part of Knight's dynamic economics. Trading on information would be trading on the basis of accurate valuations (calculated with an appropriate model such as CAPM), suitably tweaked as information came in from the markets, which would be part of Knight's realm of static equilibrium models.

When Black moved to Goldman Sachs, traders used two strategies to discover trading opportunities: technical trading that looked for trends and patterns in price movements, or company- and economy-level research. From Black's perspective these were noise-trading strategies, and it was his responsibility to bring in information trading based upon the latest developments in quantitative finance—options pricing, efficient markets, and CAPM. But unlike most quantitatively based traders who saw almost an existential gap between the idealized asset prices of equilibrium models and the economic realities they faced, Black saw a dynamic relation between noise and information: "Noise makes financial markets possible, but also makes them imperfect" (2012, 530). But it is precisely these imperfections that make people want to trade and provide the necessary liquidity to price assets; without such pricing, there would be no motivation to trade and thus no markets. But if liquidity depends upon the presence of noise trading, then the counterintuitive conclusion is that "what's needed for a liquid market causes prices to be less efficient" (Black 2012, 532). Efficiency and liquidity part company. The very things that efficient markets marginalize as the source of inefficiencies (noise or uncertainty) turn out to be those that make possible the existence of trading and markets in the first place.

For Black, it is noise trading that provides the crucial link between uncertainty, liquidity, and efficiency. For Knight, it was the entrepreneur's confronting uncertainty that provided the motivation for profit missing in static equilibrium models of the economy. Where they differed is the nature of the empirical validation for their models. While for Knight the ultimate empirical test for economic models would be the kind of historical and comparative research that Weber conducted, for Black it was the ability of the model to make money.

People trade thinking they are trading on information, but they can never be sure; there will always be ambiguity about who is an information trader and who is a noise trader. Each trader will assume that other traders think they are trading on information. Yet in a given trade someone will be wrong in the trade (i.e., trading on noise) and each trader will be motivated to trade only if he believes he has information that is different from his counterparties. If traders believe that they have special information, they will also believe that others may have their own special information, so everyone will have a motivation not to trade because they will be unsure whether their information is really correct. If people hesitate to trade then there will not be sufficient liquidity to determine asset prices. Black argues that there is a kind of "misrecognition" at the heart of finance: noise traders think they are trading on information even though they are just trading on noise; to the extent that there is noise trading, information trading will increase because there will be more opportunities for information traders to make money. However, there is always an ex ante uncertainty whether one is trading on information or noise that is only resolved after the trade by seeing who makes money; discovering the information trader is always a retrospective act that depends on the success of the trade in making money.

Black then points out that the more noise trading there is, the more opportunity there is to observe prices (i.e., the greater the liquidity of the market). Noise trading "prices in" noise into asset prices and thus creates opportunities for information traders to make money. But since the increase in information trading is because there is more noise in the prices, asset prices do not become more efficient as information trading increases. Instead, that which increases liquidity (noise trading) decreases price efficiency!

Whereas Black could be said to update and refine Knight's distinction between statics and dynamics and their relation to uncertainty and apply it to an information-processing model of financial markets, he limits his account of how people handle uncertainty to speculation, animal spirits, and a sense of play—"perhaps they just like to trade" (Black 2012, 531). Knight, however had a very different view on the motivational sources for economic activity. His view that business was a competitive game rested upon his belief that economics had a fundamentally misguided theory of human motivation. In their rush to be scientific, static models of the economy treat wants and desires as facts, not as "values" or "oughts" whose "intrinsic nature . . . [is] . . . to grow and change" and are therefore "not amenable to scientific description or logical manipulation" (Knight 1999a, 41). In his "Ethics and the Economic Interpretation" he argues against what he takes to be the dominant view of human motivation presupposed by economics:

> Economics has always treated desires or motives as facts, of a character susceptible to statement in propositions, and sufficiently stable during the period of the activity, which they prompt to be treated as causes of that activity

in a scientific sense. It has thus viewed life as a process of satisfying desires. (Knight 1999a, 42)

Instead, Knight maintains that wants are inherently unstable and change, especially since what the individual "wants is not satisfactions for the wants which he has, but more, and better wants" (1999a, 42), foreshadowing the contemporary philosophical discussion of second-order desires but moving it from the realm of discussions of free will and akrasia to economic behavior. Echoing Weber's notion of "value-rationality," Knight writes that

> Wants and the activity which they motivate constantly look forward to new and "higher," more evolved and enlightened wants and these function as ends and motives of action beyond the objective to which desire is momentarily directed. The "object" in the narrow sense of the present want is provisional; it is as much a means to a new want as end to the old one, and all intelligently conscious activity is directed forward, onward, upward, indefinitely. Life is not fundamentally a striving for ends, for satisfactions, but rather for bases for further striving; desire is more fundamental to conduct than is achievement, or perhaps better, the true achievement is the refinement and elevation of the plane of desire, the cultivation of taste. And let us reiterate that all this is true *to the person acting*, not simply to the outsider, philosophizing after the event. (Knight 1999a, 43)

The upshot of this line of thinking is not only to call for a larger theory of human motivation but that even within the domain of economic processes, the notion of what is now known as "interest" is inadequate: "Economic activity is *at the same time* a means of want-satisfaction, an agency for want- and character-formation, a field of creative self-expression, and a competitive sport" (Knight 1999a, 66). In perhaps an even more astounding conclusion for the economist who is considered one of the founding fathers of the Chicago School of economics, he connects the dynamic analysis of economic activity to play and ritual.

> We have also pointed out that economic life, in the meaning ordinarily understood, really has much of the character of play. It is a mixture of solitaire and competition and also "ritual" but attention may be here confined to competitive play. The ethics of play or sport is a topic strangely neglected by moral

philosophers, even modern free society, and is virtually ignored in all discussion under religious auspices. (1999b, 301–2)

The play impulse is not a supplementary feature of the dynamic aspects of economic life, but in a discussion that foreshadows the contemporary discussion of "flow," it turns out that play is an essential counterpart to work and the source of (charismatic) leadership.

> Perhaps we can say that in play the objective usually follows so closely upon the activity that the two are naturally thought of as a unit, or that the result occupies the attention so fully as to exclude the effort from consciousness altogether, while in work they are contrasted and the activity is presented to the mind as a means, over against the end. At least, the feeling tone of play can often be imparted to work more or less voluntarily by fixing attention upon the objective, thus crowding the effort out of consciousness. The power to induce this shift of attention in other persons seems to be an important factor in leadership. (Knight 1999a, 79)

Although Knight had a lifelong interest in these issues, they surface in his writings on ethics and liberalism and have generally been overlooked by economists. Knight devoted his technical writings to the elaboration of the static dimensions of the economy, whereas understanding the relations among play, work, uncertainty, and entrepreneurship would demand a different methodology than that adopted from the "static" analyses of the natural sciences.

Knight's lifelong fascination with Max Weber would intersect with this interest in historical dynamics; he would argue that the study of real economic processes requires Weberian-style historical research on how social institutions change. Such work would entail "an interpretive study (*verstehende Wissenschaft*) which . . . would need to go far beyond any possible boundaries of economics and should include the humanities as well as the entire field of the social disciplines" (Knight 1999a, 303).

In discussing the origins of capitalism, Knight maintains that Weber is the "only one who really deals with causes or approaches the material from the angle which alone can yield an answer to such questions, that is, the angle of comparative history in the broad sense" (Knight 1999a, xiii). Knight always regretted that he did not carry out such systematic comparative-historical research; toward the end of his career, when asked by a former student if he would have done anything different, he replied, "There has been the work of one man whom I have greatly admired. If I were to start out again, I would build upon his ideas. I am referring of course to Max Weber" (Schweitzer 1975, 279). Like most of their colleagues, Knight and Black had a deep commitment to formal equilibrium models based upon perfect competition and utility maximization. But from the onset of their academic careers each of them also had experiences that would make dealing with uncertainty a fundamental part of their thinking, rather than something simply to be managed (i.e., "risk management") or marginalized. For Knight, it was his deep interest in Weber; his first graduate degree was in German studies, and he attended Weber's seminar at Heidelberg. For Black, it was probably a combination of his Harvard education, with its eclectic mix of psychology, anthropology, linguistics, physics, and mathematics, and his practical experience working at financial institutions such as Arthur Little and Goldman Sachs. The upshot is that they both posit an internal connection between static and dynamic economics or noise and information rather than the more standard attitude among their colleagues of refining models so that they simply get closer and closer to an independent external reality.

Although both recognized the importance of uncertainty for economics and finance, neither conducted empirical research into its sources or development. For Black, noise and uncertainty could take many forms, from "style and technology" to government policy, "a diversified array of unrelated causal elements," as he put it in his noise paper. For Knight, his forays into entrepreneurial motivation were probably his attempt to reformulate Weber's hypothesis about the religious origins of capitalism, but he never developed the kind of social institutional framework that Weber's comparative-historical work provided.

Knight argues that the entrepreneur is the engine of capitalism because he faces uncertainty and takes the risk of failure even as he bets on innovation. On this point, he seems to differ from his great intellectual inspiration, Max Weber, who ascribes the origins of capitalism to religious motivation. Although Knight had reservations about the religious origins of Western capitalism, Weber's *Protestant Ethic and the Spirit of Capitalism* is probably the most dramatic argument for the structuring role that uncertainty plays in the development of capitalism. Weber's account shows how an existential version of decision making under uncertainty—in principle the Calvinist believer can never know if he is destined for salvation or damnation—transforms the relations among ritual, work, and play so as to create a rationalized work ethic that will be the foundation for Western capitalism.

The importance of Knightian uncertainty is that it expands the notion of decision making under uncertainty beyond the confines of standard decision theoretic approaches coming from game theory and rational choice.[5] In normal cases of strategic interaction, utility maximization might be a good idealization of the psychological processes involved; but as the stakes rise and personal identification makes the instance into a singularity (how many times in one's life can one's life, career, or fortune be at stake?), the possibility of a qualitative break with the norms of strategic rationality increase. This qualitative transformation highlights the difference between Knightian uncertainty and standard approaches to decision making under uncertainty; it pushes us into the realm of Weber's account of the existential crisis of the Calvinist believer and even Kierkegaard's leap of faith and the teleological suspension of the ethical.

Most commentators on Weber interpret his sociology of religion as showing how an increasing rationalization eventually leads to the development of capitalism. In this line of thinking, *The Protestant Ethic and the Spirit of Capitalism* represents a historically specific transition between a ritual- and magic-based Catholicism and the capitalist "iron-cage" of instrumental rationality. By placing it in the context of the comparative studies of religion that come after *The Protestant Ethic* (Weber first lectured on the Protestant ethic in 1897), there is a tendency to overlook the radical nature of Weber's thesis. Weber argues that capitalism exists in many societies, and so do many of the institutional prerequisites such as double-entry bookkeeping. What is unique is the Protestant ethic and its rationalization of work in the face of uncertainty. At its core there is the fundamental uncertainty of salvation, an existential gap, which no "ex ante" calculations can bridge, and it is this existential crisis that provides the motivation for the rationalization of work—the systemization of instrumental rationality arises out of the confrontation with true Knightian uncertainty; nothing you can do can affect the outcome and there are no calculable probabilities of salvation. This version of decision making under uncertainty involves the whole person; his rationality, his capacities for enjoyment, work, embodied sensibilities, and salvation—the uncertainty of salvation rationalizes work by seeing it as a "calling" directed by God.

Modern finance can be seen as an elaboration of a nonexistential version of "decision making under uncertainty." The first great breakthrough is von Neumann and Morgenstern's axiomatization of expected utility, which leads directly to Markowitz's development of portfolio theory, where the goal is to create optimal portfolios that maximize return while minimizing risk. The key components in Markowitz's theory are the mean and variance of a portfolio. The mean is simply the weighted average of the returns per some fixed time period for the stocks in the portfolio, while the variance is the weighted sum of the squares of the deviations from the mean. The mean is a central tendency while the variance measures the "spread" of prices around the mean and is considered to be a measure of the volatility or riskiness of a portfolio. CAPM develops directly out of portfolio theory—the Sharpe version of CAPM (for which Sharpe developed the "Sharpe ratio" that Derman uses to derive Black-Scholes) not only presupposes von Neumann-Morgenstern expected utility but directly follows from assuming that everyone follows the principles of portfolio theory in constructing their portfolios. From CAPM it's just a short step to Black-Scholes whether via Black's CAPM derivation, Merton's continuous time version, or Derman's Sharpe ratio formulation.

Derman's derivation of Black-Scholes elegantly combines some of the basic principles of contemporary finance. The overall framework is that of arbitrage as expressed in the *law of one price* or the *principle of riskless arbitrage*, which state that "any two securities with identical future payoffs, no matter how the future turns out, should have identical current prices" (Derman, this volume). If they don't have identical current prices, then an arbitrage opportunity would exist by buying the lower priced and selling the higher-priced asset. Derman implements this principle by equating the Sharpe ratios of the option and the corresponding stock, which is a simple way of expressing Black's idea that holding an option gives one direct exposure to the risk and volatility of the underlying stock. He then applies three commonly used financial practices from portfolio theory—dilution, diversification, and hedging—to strip out different types of risk to get to create a delta-hedged or risk-neutral portfolio consisting of the option and a delta proportion of shorted stock (in the case of a call option). The price of the option can then be calculated by using the risk-free interest rate to discount the value of the stock-option portfolio to the present.

Derman's account shows how theoretical pricing models are constructed in finance by transforming as much as possible uncertainty into manageable risk ("risk-neutral" valuations and the "risk-free" interest rate). Black's argument in "Noise" is that uncertainty provides the motivation to trade, so that trading presupposes what the pricing models exclude: uncertainty, which is also captured by the implied volatility smile, which measures the deviancies of market-priced volatilities from the constant volatility presupposed by Black-Scholes. Yet the marginalization of uncertainty seems to be at the heart of the development of economics and finance; it appears in Knight in the form of social innovation by entrepreneurs and as existential or extreme fat-tailed anomalies in the mathematics of expected utility. Uncertainty is also a key component of ritual; rituals can be seen as the performative staging (play) of social uncertainty so as to manage it (Appadurai, this volume). At the same time, ritualized exchanges are also the source of social wealth in precapitalist societies, suggesting that there may be some connection between wealth generation, ritual, play, and uncertainty in the long path from primitives to derivatives.

Playing with Fat Tails: The Balinese Cockfight

One way of interpreting the anomalies to von Neumann and Morgenstern is that expected utility and values like status are relatively interconvertible in ordinary circumstances but part company in extreme situations. But Weber's Calvinist example suggests something even more radical: the fat-tailed extreme and uncertain event "gives meaning" to the everyday and is the source of the "wealth of societies." It's the existential uncertainty of salvation that motivates the Calvinist creation of capitalist wealth.

These themes come together in an unlikely example: Clifford Geertz's account of "deep play" in the Balinese cockfight (1977). While the discussion around Geertz's article has focused on the implications of its celebration of "social action as text," much less has been said about its critique of expected utility and formal economics. Indeed, the theoretical thrust of the article is to explore the Weberian distinction between "instrumental" and "value" rationalities as encapsulated in the betting patterns, which are presented in almost painstaking detail. It is the interplay between the center and side bets that is both the analytic and rhetorical pivot of the paper; right after describing the social mechanics of betting, Geertz indents and highlights the part of the text that describes the dynamics of deep play.

Given its centrality in the essay, it is surprising that there is virtually no commentary on the betting pattern. Yet the section entitled "Playing with Fire" breaks with the previous two-thirds of the essay by opening with an explicit critique of expected utility (more specifically, "marginal disutility") with three direct references to Bentham's utilitarianism and a reworking of Weber's distinction between instrumental and value rationality: "And as (to follow Weber rather than Bentham) the imposition of meaning on life is the major end and primary condition of human existence, that access of significance more than compensates for the economic costs involved" (Geertz 1977, 434). At the heart of Weber's sociology of religion is the distinction between instrumental and value rationality. Instrumental rationality is directed toward people and objects in the world and treats them as means toward ends, which are "rationally pursued and calculated." There is a long, complex history to the development of instrumental rationality that would have to go back at least to Hirschman's distinction between passions and interests and the rise of utilitarian thought; the axiomatization of expected utility by von Neumann and Morgenstern would provide the mathematical tools for distinguishing risk and return, which would lay the foundation for both quantitative finance and game theory. Value rationality involves actions that are pursued for religious, ethical, or aesthetic reasons as ultimate ends in themselves, independent of purely practical considerations; it touches upon issues of charisma, ritual, magic, and uncertainty, all of which figure in Weber's famous account of the Calvinist origins of the spirit of capitalism.

In "Deep Play" the tension between instrumental and value rationality is represented by the spread between the odds offered by the center and side bets. The center bet "makes the game" by defining its "center of gravity" (Geertz 1977, 430). The individually placed side bets are pragmatic and instrumental assessments of the relative strength of the cocks, working like "a stock exchange on . . . the curb" (ibid., 426). The opposition between "status gambling" and "money gambling" instantiated by center and side bets draws upon and motivates a series of tensions: cross-contextual versus situational, collective versus individual, deep versus shallow. The drama of deep play occurs when high status equals oppose each other: the higher the status and more equal the opposed groups are, the deeper the identification of cock and man, the finer the cocks involved, the more the spread between center and side odds collapses, and the greater the "liquidity" of betting. Unlike economic rationality, which seeks to manage risk by minimizing it, deep play seeks to maximize uncertainty by embedding the instrumental rationality of betting (particularly the side bets) within the value rationality of the Balinese (ultimate) concern with status. In the Balinese cockfight, the drive for meaning requires a maximal confrontation with uncertainty, which grounds the values of everyday life and social interaction.

When von Neumann and Morgenstern published *A Theory of Games and Economic Behavior*, it was quickly pointed out that there were several exceptions to their axioms of expected utility such as when one's life, reputation, or wealth were at stake. As Luce and Raiffa (1989) demonstrated in their classic exposition of game theory, *Games and Decisions*, someone would not be considered irrational if he rejected a lottery in which the choices were a highly probable large payoff (say 99.9 percent chance of $10,000) versus a low probability of death (0.1 percent chance of death—note the use of betting as a way of differentiating risk and return); the marginal disutility of death, infamy, or total bankruptcy is simply too great.

Yet as Geertz points out, deep play is possible because in ordinary life (and ordinary cockfights) the Balinese do value money. But it is in the situations of deep play when money becomes the measure of something beyond the utility of money as the universal means, an index of the things that money can't buy—"a status bloodbath," to use Goffman's term (Geertz 1977, 436). As repeatedly retold by high-stakes poker players, in the great side games at the World Series of Poker where only the best can play, the chips represent more than money and become a measure of how one stands in the eyes of one's peers. You can buy chips, but you have to earn your reputation.

Indeed, deep play can be read as a commentary upon von Neumann and Morgenstern that emphasizes the importance of the fat-tail and antifragile convexity in which it is the extraordinary that gives meaning and liquidity to the ordinary and everyday. Using the very idiom of betting at the heart of the formal accounts of expected utility—indeed, betting is performative, thereby invoking ritual as well as uncertainty—Geertz shows how economic utility is embedded in what ritual performativity addresses: the existential dimensions of Balinese life.

> It is in large part because the marginal disutility of loss is so great at the higher levels of betting that to engage in such betting is to lay one's public self, allusively and metaphorically, through the medium of one's cock, on the line. And though to a Benthamite this might seem merely to increase the irrationality of the enterprise that much further, to the Balinese what it mainly increases is the meaningfulness of it all. (Geertz 1977, 434)

This dynamic is directly reflected in betting patterns:

> The higher the individual bets center and outside, the shorter the outside bet odds will tend to be, and the more betting there will be over-all.
>   The less an economic and the more a "status" view of gaming will be involved, and the "solider" the citizens who will be gaming. (Ibid., 441)

Geertz's Balinese cockfight brings together in one dynamic example ritual, play, and uncertainty. The tension between center and side bets reflect the immersion of the ritual order (the center bets, which are always even odds) as an immanent potential into the everyday (side bets are off odds calculated according to the relative strengths of the cocks). Competition between the highest status groups produces a staging of uncertainty that reveals the values presupposed and enacted by the ritual. It is deep play that produces the greatest social liquidity, the involvement of the whole community in a collective risk taking under maximum uncertainty.

Geertz also notes something interesting about deep play: the economic gains and losses cancel out over the long run, and no real changes of status occur through cockfights. His interpretation is that the cockfight is the Balinese version of Macbeth, a "kind of sentimental education" (1977, 449) that reveals their existential concerns to themselves. But another interpretation suggests itself. Deep play stages uncertainty by pitting high-status groups in equal competition. The betting and social liquidity are at their heights and the even center and side odds reflect the volatility of the competition and a situation in which directional risks have been neutralized, a kind of Balinese delta hedge. It doesn't seem to matter whichever side actually wins (the transfers of wealth equalize over time and no statuses really change), and in deep play the ritualized cockfight looks increasingly like the staging of uncertainty so that the Balinese could enjoy the resulting volatility by putting their money where their cocks are, like the "big swinging dicks" of Wall Street. In an inversion of Weber's Calvinists, the Balinese indulge themselves by ritually staging uncertainty so that they can enjoy the social volatilities of engaging a simulacrum of the existential issues that structure their everyday lives. The cycle of cockfights effectively hedges away extreme monetary gains or losses in order to access and dynamically replicate the volatility of meaning. Instead of being the Balinese Macbeth, perhaps the cockfight is their version of the VIX (Volatility Index).

Derrida's Gift

Geertz's analysis of the Balinese conflict raises the stakes by insisting that the search for meaning frames the search for money, that what money can't buy is the key to the "forces" that motivate economic activity. In everyday activity, the existential dimensions are backgrounded, but in certain ritual and play situations, they are brought to the forefront, and the oscillation between the foregrounding and backgrounding of the existential is the "spread" out of which both social and economic wealth is generated. The Balinese cockfight is an example of Appadurai's "ritual staging of uncertainty"—the constitution of meaning by socially framing uncertainty so as to enjoy the ensuing volatility. The interplay between center and side bets indexes the shifting relations between value and instrumental rationalities. Geertz portrays his village as both traditional and part of a larger money economy, a mix between the dividualism that Appadurai and LiPuma describe and the individualism that will develop with the rise and spread of capitalism.

Weber's account in the *Protestant Ethic and the Spirit of Capitalism* examines the shifting of this balance in the development of the inward-facing subjectivity of Western capitalism. He suggests that the spirit or "force" of capitalism is also the result of a search for meaning, that of God's gift of grace. But we will show that an existential gift of the sort that Weber describes produces a special dynamic of its own, one that ties it to the question of the "gift" that founds modern finance: arbitrage. Adapting an argument first developed by Jacques Derrida in *Given Time*, his rumination on Mauss's *The Gift*, it's the impossibility of God's gift that makes the Calvinist ethos so unique (1992).

Derrida opens his discussion of Mauss with the same question that Mauss raises in the first page of *The Gift*: "What force is there in the thing given which compels the recipient to make a return?" (Mauss 1967, 1) In anthropology the answer to this question has focused on Mauss's analysis of the Maori concept of *hau*, which has evoked extended commentaries by Lévi-Strauss, Marshall Sahlins, and David Graeber, just to name a few of the better-known names. In Sahlins's analysis, *hau* is a principle of fertility, which compels any excess produced by the gift to be returned to its origin and maintained as a source for future "fecundity." It is the Maori term for their ideology of wealth production (Sahlins, 1972). Derrida insists that Mauss's great breakthrough is to recognize what we might call the dividuality of the gift and locates the force of return not in the agents of the gift but in the gift object:

> Here is, it seems the most interesting idea, the great guiding thread of *The Gift:* for those who participate in the experience of the gift and countergift, the requirement of restitution "at term," at the delayed "due date," the requirement of the circulatory difference is *inscribed in the thing itself* that is given or exchanged. Before it is a contract, an intentional gesture of individual or collective subjects, the movement of gift/countergift is a *force* (a "virtue of the thing given," says Mauss), a property immanent to the thing or in any case apprehended as such by the donors and donees. Moved by a mysterious force, the thing itself demands gift *and* restitution, it requires therefore "time," "term," "delay," "interval" of temporization, the becoming–temporization of temporalization, the animation of a neutral and homogeneous time by the desire of the gift and the restitution. Differance, which (is) nothing, is (in) the thing itself. It is (given) in the thing itself. It (is) the thing itself. It, differance, the thing (itself). It, without anything other. Itself, nothing. (Derrida 1992, 40)

The key insights in Derrida's analysis are that (1) the interval of time constitutive of the gift/countergift relation is "*inscribed in the thing itself*"; (2) giving is a "*force*" "immanent to the thing"; (3) it predates contract or any "intentional gesture" of either "individual or collective subjects;" (4) it is a "force" that animates the return and not the intentionality of the givers/receivers. Twisting Derrida to our purposes, a central insight of Mauss's *Gift,* which was written as an alternative to Hobbes's social contract, is to introduce what Appadurai and LiPuma have characterized as *dividuality* into the precontract, prelinguistic, and nonintentional level of social being.

If Mauss's *Gift* is a pre-Hobbesian account of dividuality, then it is the performativity of the social contract that transforms dividuals into individuals and passions into interests, paving the way for the rational maximizers of expected utility. In Derrida's account, the pathway to economic man passes through the portal of the impossibility of the gift. His argument is that the linguistic structure of "A gives B to C" in Indo-European builds upon a level of social being that it cannot analyze—the "givenness" of the being of language.[6] His language in describing what we are calling the "dividual" dimensions of the gift is deliberately qualified and temporizing:

> If there is gift, the *given* of the gift (*that which* one gives, *that which* is given, the gift as given thing or act of donation), must not come back to the giving (let us not already say to the subject, to the donor). It must not circulate, it must not be exchanged, it must not in any case be exhausted, as a gift, by the process of exchange, by the point of departure. (Derrida 1992, 7)

This description would also fit Bourdieu's and Mauss's accounts of the gift, except that the references to agency are more qualified ("let us not already say to the subject, to the donor") and the point of view of narration is that of the gift, not any of its subjects or agents. There is also an implicit negation of the original given of the gift by the fact that it cannot be reciprocated, that there can be no countergift in response to the gift.

Derrida then raises the question "Why and how *can I think that the gift is the impossible?*" (ibid., 10) and, as if recognizing the linguistic specificity of the "*I*" of his question, moves very carefully to language, with five qualifications in the space of two pages: "in our logic and our language" (ibid.), "our common language or logic" (11), "according to our common language and logic" (11), "our language or in a few familiar languages" (12), "in certain languages, for example in French" (12). As if agreeing with Benveniste (1973) on the Indo-European specificity of his claim, Derrida argues that it is the three place predicate structure of "A gives B to C" that imposes a semantic interpretation—"someone wants or desires, someone intends-to-give something to someone"—which, when combined with the idea that gifts cannot be reciprocated, leads to the negation/cancellation of the intention behind the gift. This structure is an immanent potential within the semantics of giving in "our common language and logic."

Derrida's impossibility of the gift thesis rests upon this particular structure in Indo-European languages in which there is a subject-dominated intentionality that motivates the gift.

> In our logic and our language we say it thus: someone wants or desires, someone *intends-to-give* something to someone. Already the complexity of the formula appears formidable. It supposes a subject and a verb, a constituted subject, which can also be a collective, for example, a group, a community, a nation, a clan, a tribe—in any case, a subject identical to itself and conscious of its identity, indeed seeking through the gesture of the gift to constitute its own unity and, precisely, to get its own identity recognized so that that identity comes back to it, so that it can reappropriate its identity: as its property.
> (1992, 10–11)

Derrida's analysis of the gift is reminiscent of the analysis of meaning proposed by Paul Grice, a philosopher of language and colleague of Austin. Grice (1957) proposed that someone "means" something by an utterance if and only if he intends to produce a response in his audience by means of their recognition of his intention to produce that response. This self-referential subject-based intention actually maps the intentionality of the gift, which in the above description requires not only an intention to give something as a gift, but for that very intention to be recognized "so that that identity comes back to it" (Derrida 1992, 11), Derrida's argument is that the gift can have no meaning because any intention to give the gift results in its cancellation—"*At the limit, the gift as gift ought not appear as gift to either the donee or to the donor*" (ibid., 14).

If, as Derrida intimates, we can identify at a preintentional level a protoform of the gift as something that is given but not reciprocated—"the *given* of the gift (*that which* one gives, *that* which is given, the gift as given thing or as act of donation) must not come back to the giving (let us not already say to the subject, to the donor)" (ibid., 7)—then to make that dividualized preintentional act of giving into an intentional object (A intends to give B to C) is to render it impossible. To intend to give something as a gift is to intend something as that which cannot be reciprocated; if the mutual recognition of that intention by the donee and donor is a condition of the meaningfulness of that action then recognizing that intention would also be to recognize its non-reciprocity, which would be a contradiction. The intention to give something as a gift to someone cannot be recognized by either the donor or the donee because the condition of the gift that it not be reciprocated cancels out the reciprocity of intentionality that would make it meaningful; the gift is thus meaningless. But this indexical self-referentiality is also the condition of performativity—intending something as a gift triggers a negative performativity that self-referentially cancels the gift. But if meaning is based upon a self-referential recognition of intention, then gifts have no meaning, are meaningless, and hence unthinkable; "true" gifts exceed the phenomenology of intentionality.

Derrida seems to imply that there are two notions of the gift that are in tension with one another. The first is a dividualized notion of the gift that rests upon the pragmatics of giving and receiving that are built into the social relationships in which the exchange is embedded. The second is that of the semantics of the gift created by thinking about exchange through the lens of our language of intentionality (also outlined in our earlier discussion of Vendler's work on performativity) in which people make intentional decisions about gift giving; this level of consciousness about agentive subjectivity produces a semantic paradox about the gift that questions its very intelligibility. At the dividualized, pragmatic level gift giving is embodied and unreflective; at the level of individual reflective thought, the notion of the gift becomes semantically self-contradictory.

In the subsequent debate with Jean Luc-Marion, it became apparent that the "aporia" of the gift could be tied to the idea of God, who transcends the limits of human understanding. But this juxtaposition of an all-knowing and all-powerful God, an existentially significant gift, and the limitations of human subjectivity maps perfectly Weber's description of the Calvinist predicament. In orthodox Calvinist doctrine, it would be blasphemous for insignificant and depraved individuals to know or understand an all-knowing and all-powerful God's intentions, especially those surrounding his greatest gifts, those of grace and salvation. The true gift cannot be even known as a gift by either giver or recipient and must remain totally uncertain in its destiny. It is the uncertainty around the gift of salvation that gives meaning to the daily asceticism of the Calvinist true believer and that, according to Weber, is the spirit or "force" that motivates the development of capitalism.

Existential Uncertainty and the Origins of Capitalism

Weber was the inspiration for Geertz's analysis of the Balinese cock-fight with its interplay between what Weber and the Frankfurt School would have called "value" and "instrumental" rationalities. In every-day circumstances, pragmatic instrumental rationalities carry the day, but in special occasions "deep play" reveals the fundamental structures of meaning that govern the quotidian and is a paradigmatic example of what Appadurai called the "ritual staging of uncertainty." Weber's ac-count of the origins of the ethos of capitalism introduces a new level of complexity by combining what might be called "decision making un-der existential uncertainty" and the question of the ontological status of God's gift of grace and salvation. Like the Balinese cockfight, monetary success is subsumed by the search for meaning. The uncertainty of sal-vation intersects with the ineffability of the gift to inaugurate an inward exploration of a potentially endless subjectivity, which will be the basis for the spirit of capitalism embodied in Weber's paragon thereof, Benja-min Franklin; this spirit is a secularized and monetized subjectivity that is completely in tune with the acquisitive and competitive logic of Marx's account of relative surplus value.

Weber's argument in *The Protestant Ethic and the Spirit of Capital-ism* proceeds through four phases. The first is that of Catholic magic and ritual in which dividualized relationships based upon the doctrine of transubstantiation and the ritual of the Eucharist unite the Catho-lic community around a shared substance (bread and wine as Christ's body and blood) and code for conduct, including the ritual magic of con-fession. The second is the Calvinist elimination of ritual magic, which produces an existential uncertainty about salvation that gives birth to a lifetime ascetic search for this worldly success for the glory of God. With the decline of an overarching religious motivation, the inward as-cetic turn is transformed into the spirit of capitalism in which the pursuit of this worldly monetary success becomes an end in itself. The last stage is where Benjamin Franklin's more upbeat spirit of capitalism is super-seded by Weber's famous "iron-cage" of modernity in which instrumen-tal rationality has replaced value rationality at both the social and indi-vidual levels.

The Protestant Ethic and the Spirit of Capitalism can then been seen as an account of how a religious worldview that grapples with existential uncertainty creates a protocapitalist ethos that replaces what might be called a dividualized system of religious belief based upon ritual magic. The lynch pin is the gift of grace, which in Catholicism is tied to the ritual of confession; in Calvinism, God's grace is both uncertain and ineffable, yet is supposed to give meaning to man's existence. Weber gives a vivid portrayal of how existential uncertainty and the ineffability of the gift produce the inward subjectivity of the modern capitalist individual. If Hobbes's social contract presupposes self-interested decision-making individuals, then the ritual magic of transubstantiation and deathbed confession in Catholicism presupposes dividual subjects. The radical uncertainty of the true fat-tailed event (i.e., God's bestowal of grace and salvation) places the Calvinist believer in a situation of *individual* existential anxiety and loneliness, which is only increased by his inability to fathom God's motivations. It is the combination of existential uncertainty and semantic incomprehensibility that paves the way for the development of the modern individual subject, which is encapsulated in the belief-desire model of agency at the heart of modern economics and finance.

Weber describes the situation of the individual Calvinist believer as one of existential loneliness and meaninglessness, which locks the Calvinist true believer into his own subjectivity and paves the way for the development of the possessive individual of modern capitalism. It is out of this emotional crisis that he has to create some system of meaning that can guide his actions. The solution is a life of "constant reflection" and working for the glory of God, a Cartesian performative self-monitoring ("I think there I am" is a quintessential performative) in which existential anxiety is transformed into forward-looking motivation. A gambling strategy of "playing for position" stretches the immediate situation into that of a long-term confrontation with volatility whereby existential uncertainty is transformed into manageable risks. The Calvinist believer becomes what in poker parlance is known as a "grinder," grinding away for God's glory. With the rise of secularism and the removal of God, the grinder becomes the incarnation of the modern possessive individual who then becomes the rational decision maker of finance capitalism.

Weber saw the Calvinist uncertainty principle as a transition between Catholicism and the spirit of capitalism, between a past in which "good works" were framed by ritual magic and a future in which the work of making money could be seen as an end in itself in an increasingly secularized world. Indeed, the downfall of magic and ritual inaugurated by

Protestantism is part of a disenchantment of the world that is integral to
the development of secularism and the full flowering of capitalism. For
the Catholic, the magic of confession guarantees salvation; instead of uncertainty, the risk of sinning is managed by priestly absolution and individual penance. For the Calvinist, the lack of any magical means to salvation makes the uncertainty of predestination an existential dilemma
that leads to a lifelong ethical transformation. For the secular capitalist,
the removal of the connection between work and salvation meant that
all risks confronted at work were to be rationally managed on their own
terms without religious connotations.

Weber's account of the Protestant ethic is built around what might be
called decision making under existential uncertainty. It shows how an
extreme, fat-tailed, and uncertain event—the possibility of being saved—
gives meaning to the norms that govern everyday life. As the origin of
the "spirit of capitalism," it also marks the emergence of a rationally oriented individual decision maker (whom Weber described as locked into
loneliness) from the magical ritualism of Catholicism, whose dividual dimensions are revealed in the doctrines of transubstantiation and confession. Yet even as the Calvinist was making his own subjectivity the
self-referential object of a "constant reflection" with the performative intensity of "Descartes's *cogito ergo sum*," the intentionality of God's gift
of grace became increasingly unknowable; as the Calvinist believer became more self-reflexively aware of his own intentionality, he could not
imagine God's intentionality as an extension of his own because of his
depraved and unworthy state. The uncertainty of grace, man's deprav-
ity, and the inscrutability of God's motivations engendered "a feeling of
unprecedented inner loneliness *of the single individual*" (my emphasis,
Weber 1992, 60).

On the surface, the Weberian Calvinist leads a life of rationalized
productive work for the glory of God, and his this-worldly success is
the sign of his certainty of grace. But the religious foundation for this-
worldly asceticism lay in an existential crisis caused by the ultimate uncertainty of predestination. The Calvinist could only act as if he had
grace, which required him to ask, "Am I one of the elect?," a question for
which there was in principle no sure answer but would "sooner or later
have arisen for every believer and have forced all other interests into the
background. And how can I be sure of this state of grace?" (ibid., 65).
The contrast could not be sharper with the Catholic, for whom "the absolution of his Church was a compensation for his own imperfection"

and "the priest was a magician who performed the miracle of transubstantiation, and who held the key to eternal life in his hand" (71).

In no area was the contrast between Catholic and Calvinist clearer than that of work. The "very human Catholic cycle of sin, repentance, atonement, relief, and followed by renewed sin" (70) meant that good works and duties remained a series of *isolated* actions that were not "combined into a unified system" (71). Without such recourse to priestly absolution of sins, the Calvinist sees every action as a potential sign of one's commitment to God and life on earth as a means to the higher end of increasing God's glory on earth. The resultant constant monitoring of behavior leads to the ascetic and rational cultivation of one's life and work toward God's will in the form of a "calling," a "task set by God" (Weber 1992, 45).

In the Calvinist variant of the Protestant ethic there is a rationalization of work and life plans as means to securing certainty of grace. In the spirit of capitalism, the link between work and salvation is broken, leaving a rationalized ascetic work ethic to develop on its own terms in an increasingly secularized world. Weber's example of the spirit of capitalism is a passage by Benjamin Franklin, which, in contrast to Calvinist attitudes toward work, is all the more striking for its "being free from all direct relationship to religion" (ibid., 14) and its insistence upon an ethic in which a duty to increase one's capital was "combined with the strict avoidance of all spontaneous enjoyment of life . . ." (18). Modern capitalism breaks the connection between work and religion and presupposes the spirit of capitalism as an "ethically-oriented maxim for the organization of life" in which exists "the idea of a duty of the individual toward the increase of his capital, which is assumed to be an end in itself" (16). At the same time, it is precisely this "frame of mind" as a dominant ethos of a society that "would both in ancient times and in the Middle Ages have been proscribed as the lowest sort of avarice and an attitude entirely lacking in self-respect" (21).

Since the Calvinist church could not guarantee salvation to anyone, it provided the believer with the next best thing: a route to feeling certain of salvation. The goal was to live a Christian life dedicated to increasing the glory of God. God has chosen a select few to be blessed, but no one in the community of the faithful knows who the chosen are, and even more, no one can do anything worldly that will guarantee salvation (as compared to Catholic confession). There is no purpose in trying to effect salvation, for nothing can redeem those "foreknown to damnation"

(Taylor 1989, 228). Everyone knows that some of the faithful are blessed, but they do not and cannot know who they are. Believers live in a state of radical uncertainty, creating an inner-worldly existence of loneliness and desperation. The agonizing existential dilemma becomes "How can I attain certainty as to my status as one of the chosen?" The move from a state of nature to a state of grace entailed a wholesale transformation in the meaning of one's life. Good works become the signs of salvation but never, as a matter of unimpeachable doctrine, the means to salvation. And, in this race to confirm a salvation that no one, even those predestined to be regenerate, could cognitively verify, believers competed to demonstrate God's glory and find signs of salvation. The more I succeed over others, by gathering earthly riches that I do not succumb to, the more I appropriate the world through unceasing labor while renouncing its fruits in God's name, the more I can believe and can affirm that I might be one of the elect.

Only the select have grace, and God worked through their success to fulfill his plan. Having grace meant that God was working through you to produce authentic good works according to his plan and in so doing to increase his glory; to the extent that the individual could feel God working within him to produce good works for the glory of God, he could achieve certainty of grace. The combination of this worldly success and the feeling of internal transformation provided the Calvinist with the closest he could be to certainty of salvation. Without resource to ritual magic and uncertain of God's grace and motivations, the Calvinist believer is locked into his own subjectivity and experiences a deep existential loneliness; there is no dividualized ritual magic of transubstantiation and deathbed confession that can mollify his anxiety. The escape is to throw one's self into working for the glory of God by transforming anxiety into forward-looking motivation.

The Protestant ethic leaves its imprint on modern capitalism in its commitment to a rationalized and ascetic work ethic. Weber emphasizes that the particular combination in Calvinism of this worldly activity and the notion of a calling played a crucial role in the development of the capitalist spirit in which the pursuit of worldly goods is an end in itself. In Calvinism, such activity is a means to the higher end of salvation. But the peculiar structure of Calvinist angst leads to the rationalization of work as part of a larger process of the retreat of magic and religion and a concomitant rationalization and disenchantment of the world; the ascetic attitude leaves its imprint in the positive valorization of hard

work and sobriety and negative attitudes toward gambling and speculation, which found their contemporary resonance in the regulatory debates over whether trading options was a form of gambling. In the Calvinist version of decision making under uncertainty, the ultimate values
that structure work and life expectations are religious.

The decline of religiosity is what characterizes Weber's description
of that paragon of the capitalist spirit, Benjamin Franklin. Franklin was
a successful practitioner of print capitalism, which Benedict Anderson
would later call the first global capitalism with the book as the first truly
global commodity. *The Protestant Ethic*'s long opening quotation from
Franklin is free from any direct references to God or religion and instead represents the capitalist as one who is aware of the opportunity
cost of time and money. Time and credit are both money, which should
be properly invested because *money is of the prolific generating nature . . . Money can beget money, and its offspring can beget more, and so
on.* Any time or money not used for the systematic pursuit of "profit for
its own sake" was not merely wasteful but represented a lost opportunity
to make more money. Franklin's image of life as a constantly updateable
profit and loss ledger replaces the Calvinist obsession with diaries, which
were invariably recordings of sins and omissions tinged with an aura of
despair as believers looked for signs of election or reprobation in their
lives. Compared to the Calvinist, Franklin represents a completely monetized subjectivity in which the passage of time was measured by the unfolding of interest, a preparation for the "empty, homogenous time" that
Walter Benjamin will attribute to modernity.

For Weber, the decline of magic and ritual begins a historical descent
into the "iron cage" of modern bureaucracy and rationality. The decline
of the Protestant ethic is at least in part due to "secularizing influence
of wealth" (Weber 1992, 118), slowly "giving way to utilitarian worldli-
ness" (ibid., 119). Secularization breaks the tight link between work and
salvation; the pursuit of worldly goods and profit is free to pursue its
own course of development. Unlike his account of Calvinism, there is no
elaboration of a new internal dynamic linking secularism and the nature
of work, just the fading away of religious influence.

In his famously pessimistic conclusion to *The Protestant Ethic and
the Spirit of Capitalism,* Weber portrays a grim picture of an unfettered
capitalism without any transcendent values. With the Protestant ethic,
ascetic rationalism moved out of "monastic cells into everyday life" (Weber 1992, 123), unleashing the very economic powers that will make it

increasingly irrelevant. Calling modern capitalism "the last stage of this cultural development," Weber envisages a world of "specialists without spirit, sensualists without heart; this nullity imagines that it has attained a level of civilization never before achieved" (ibid., 124).

Weber does not attribute to modern capitalism any particular ethical framework beyond a ruthless utilitarianism. He sees religion and secularism as basically opposed, with the moral compass provided by the former lost as the latter rises. What remains is the mantle of ascetic rationalism: "The ideal type of the capitalist entrepreneur, as it has been represented even in Germany . . . avoids ostentation and unnecessary expenditure, as well as conscious enjoyment of his power, and is embarrassed by the outward signs of the social recognition which he receives" (ibd., 33).

In his characterization of what might be called the "extreme capitalism" of his time, Weber gives us a hint of where the capitalist spirit might go as secularization digs deeper: "In the field of its highest development, in the United States, the pursuit of wealth, stripped of its religious and ethical meaning, tends to become associated with purely mundane passions, which often actually give it the character of sport" (1992, 124). Since any further discussion of the development of the spirit of capitalism "brings us to the world of judgments of value and of faith" (ibid., 124), Weber concludes with a call for the historical study of worldly asceticism from its medieval beginnings to "its dissolution into pure utilitarianism" (ibid., 125).

The Performativity of *Capital*

If play and ritual performativity lie at the heart of Mauss's account of gift-based societies, arbitrage could be said to lie at the heart of finance capitalism. If there is a performative dimension to arbitrage, then the extension of performativity to ritual and play suggests that the social origins of arbitrage may antedate its full-fledged form in contemporary finance. Randy Martin's and Robert Meister's chapters in this volume suggest that the origins of derivative finance lie in Marx's account of capital, particularly relative surplus value and the countertendencies to the falling rate of profit in volume 3 of *Capital*. The question then arises whether performativity and arbitrage play any role in Marx's mature work on capital.

Our answer is that in volume 1 of *Capital*, Marx systematically constructs capital (more specifically value) as a performative subject and that the full realization of the performative dimension of capital is in the arbitrage structure of relative surplus value. In his self-avowed inversion of Hegel's dialectic, Marx uses Hegel's example of the Absolute Idea, the pronoun "I," as his model for the self-valorizing properties of capital. As pointed out by the French linguist Emile Benveniste, the first person pronoun "I" shares the self-referential and indexically creative properties of explicit performatives: "*I* refers to the act of individual discourse in which it is pronounced and by this it designates the speaker" (Benveniste 1973, 226).[7]

In subsequent analyses, Benveniste showed how a linguistic performative combined different levels of abstraction ranging from the indexicality of the first person pronoun to the metaindexicality of the performative verb of speaking such that its utterance creates an instance of what the verb refers to. The philosopher Charles Sanders Peirce even gave a nonlinguistic example of a performative: drawing a map of a beach on the sand of that very beach; the map would contain a representation of itself on the beach and in the map there would be another map ad infinitum—what Peirce would call an "indexical-icon," a sign that represented that which it was a part of. Marx builds a similar structure of abstraction out of his money dialectic and valorization process, eventually leading to the fully performative nature of relative surplus value. All these examples—explicit performatives, the first person pronoun, Peirce's indexical-icon, rituals, and Marx's surplus value—share a semiotic component in which a process of representing something as an instance or token of an abstract type creates an instance of that type; the indexical specification of a token as an instance of a metaindexical type ("I *hereby* promise . . .") creates a token of that type. The indexical/metaindexical structure is particularly salient in linguistic performatives because of their grammatical patterning. In the explicit performative "I hereby promise to leave," the nonindexical level is signaled by the metalinguistic verb and its unmarked nonprogressive aspect, while the indexical elements include the first person pronoun, the present tense, and the temporal demonstrative "hereby." The utterance of a linguistic performative classifies the ongoing indexical speech event as a token instance of a speech act type named by the performative verb and in so classifying brings about some of the conditions that made the utterance true or a successful instance of the type. For example, if one of the conditions of successfully promising is that the speaker represents herself as intending to do what is promised, then uttering "I hereby promise . . ." makes it true that she has promised—an example of the backwards or retro-performativity that Appadurai, LiPuma, and Ayache describe in this volume.

It was the unique ability to combine the indexical and nonindexical that made Hegel turn to the first person pronoun in his formulation of "the Absolute Idea":

> By the term "I" I mean myself, a single and altogether determinate person. And yet I really utter nothing peculiar to myself, for everyone else is an "I" or "Ego," and when I call myself "I," though I indubitably mean the single person myself, I express a thorough universal. (1969, 38)

In the opening sections of *Capital*, Marx famously inverts Hegel's dialectic by replacing Hegel's thought with labor as the immanent identical subject-object. The money dialectic in the very first chapter of *Capital* builds up a movement from concrete to abstract labor time that is mediated by the various forms of money, which is the counterpart to the indexical/metaindexical hierarchy at the heart of linguistic performativity. The production of any particular commodity occurs in a specific time and place, with specific subjects and resources, and with a determinate expenditure of concrete labor time. The abstract labor time immanent in the production of any commodity is not realized until there is exchange; it is only through confrontation with another commodity that a given commodity's exchange value is realized.

In the simple form of value, the equivalence is with another object and is local and contextually specific, and the nonindexical equivalence is merely immanent. In the total form of value, the value of a particular commodity is expressed in terms of "innumerable" other commodities; value is a general form of social mediation but not yet represented as such. In the general form, commodities represent themselves in a single commodity, which functions as the universal equivalent and represents abstract labor time as a general form of social mediation. The money form is simply the selection, by custom, of a commodity that has direct and universal exchangeability, such as gold. Exchange value ultimately becomes the socially necessary labor time needed to produce the commodity, a society-wide abstraction of labor time whose quantitative and qualitative dimensions are realized through the mediation of exchange by money. With the development of surplus value, the immanent performativity of the commodity is realized in a sociohistorically specific form: capital.

The crucial moment in the development of capital is when labor power becomes a commodity; this will make possible the production of surplus value. Like any commodity, the value of labor power is the socially necessary labor time needed to produce it.

> The value of labour power is determined, as in the case of every other commodity, by the labour time necessary for production, and consequently also the reproduction, of this special article. So far as it has value, it represents no more than a definite quantity of the average labour of society incorporated in it. . . . the value of labour power is the value of the means of subsistence necessary for the maintenance of the labourer. (Marx 1976, 274)

Since labor is the only commodity whose use value can produce more value, the possibility of "surplus value" arises when the value produced by labor is more than value needed to produce labor. If the amount of value necessary for the reproduction of the laborers (in the form of the necessities of life such as food, housing, etc.) is less than the value embodied in the commodities produced by them, then surplus value is created. The key historical moment is the commodification of labor power. This condition presupposes both a market for labor and a contract model of exchange.

> . . . labour-power can only appear on the market as a commodity only if, and in so far as, its possessor, the individual whose labour-power it is, offers it for sale or sells it as a commodity. In order that its possessor may sell it as a commodity, he must have it at his disposal, he must be the free proprietor of his own labour-capacity, hence of his person. He and the owner of money meet in the market, and enter into relations with each other on a footing of equality as owners of commodities, with the sole difference that one is buyer, the other seller; both are therefore equal in the eyes of law. (Marx 1976, 271)

Like any other commodity, labor power is produced to be consumed, but unlike any other commodity, its consumption also produces value. The capitalist buys commodities, including labor power, and uses them to produce commodities that he then sells for a profit that represents the surplus value added by him.

The money owner buys everything necessary for this process, such as raw material, in the market, and pays the full price for it. The process of the consumption of labour power is at the same time the production process of commodities and of surplus value. The consumption of labour power is completed, as in the case of every other commodity, outside the market or the sphere of circulation. (ibid., 279)

Marx then identifies two forms of surplus value that the capitalist can appropriate. Absolute surplus value can be increased by lengthening the working day or employing more people, but perhaps the most important way of increasing surplus value that is under the control of individual capitalists is through technological innovations that increase the productivity of labor ("relative surplus value"), thereby producing a dialectical dynamic that Postone describes as a "treadmill effect" particular to capitalism.

Increasing productivity results in more value produced per unit of time until this level of productivity becomes generalized across the economy by the spread of the innovation; at that point, the magnitude of value derived in that time period, because of its abstract and general temporal determination, will fall back to its previous level. The cycle of productivity gains, followed by a return to the pre-existing level of value formation, compel even those producers who had resisted adopting these new methods to do so. (Postone 1996, 290)

If the society-wide amount of labor time expended in production is held roughly constant, this treadmill effect of competitive productivity produces an increasing disparity between value—in the form of abstract labor time—and material and monetary wealth, a contradiction that intensifies as capital expands. Capitalism is a social totality that is in constant motion, destroying itself in creating and expanding itself. Capital is the performative analog to Hegel's "Absolute Idea":

Hegel:
But in the Idea of absolute cognition the Notion has become the Idea's own content. The Idea is itself the pure Notion that has itself for subject matter and which, in running itself as subject matter through the totality of its determinations, develops itself into the whole of its reality, into the system of

the science [of logic], and concludes by apprehending this process of comprehending itself, thereby superseding its standing as content and subject matter and cognizing the Notion of the science. (Hegel 1969, 843)

Marx:

It [value] is constantly changing from one form into the other without becoming lost in the movement; it thus transforms itself into an *automatic subject* . . . . In truth, however, value is here the *subject* of a process in which, while constantly assuming the form in turn of money and of commodities, it changes its own magnitude . . . and thus valorizes itself. . . . For the movement in the course of which it adds surplus-value is its own movement, its valorization is therefore self-valorization. . . . Value suddenly presents itself as a *self-moving substance* which passes through a process of its own, and for which the commodity and money are both mere forms. (Marx, amended translation by Postone 1996, 75)

With the creation of surplus value, changes in productivity produce an abstract social totality in which productive innovations reset levels of productivity in the treadmill structure of competitive capitalism. Marx draws a picture of a society whose economy is driven by changes in productivity. Innovations have a duplex value structure, what might be called a value arbitrage. While selling at the norm, they profit to the degree of increased productivity; the commodity has two values, one that is the socially necessary average labor time to produce the commodity, the other the reduction in labor time produced by the innovation. Since the innovative commodity is sold at the socially average price, the capitalist innovator is paid at the rate of the socially necessary labor time but pays at the lower rate, thereby pocketing the difference. Unlike absolute surplus value, which is linear, relative surplus value produces an asymmetric upside, which has what is called "convexity." Like financial arbitrage, the innovation soon spreads, the arbitrage spread closes, and the value level is reset—Marx's version of the creative destruction of innovation in which innovation mines uncertainty and serves the role of play in creating the spread that produces value, which the negative performativity of arbitrage then harvests and closes.

The arbitrage dynamic creates what Moishe Postone has called a "treadmill" effect, which continually resets the standard of productivity so that standard levels of socially necessary labor time are continuously redetermined as insufficient. The productive innovation will appear as an arbitrageable "deviancy" that allows the innovator a momentary advantage to amass surplus value. As the innovation spreads, the socially necessary average is reset; at this later time, what was deviant now becomes the norm, and the previous average becomes the exception and eventually obsolete. The norm becomes deviant, the deviancy becomes the norm; capitalism is an arbitrage-driven performative chiasmus continually in motion.

Innovation is the "play" that opens the spread between the values of the commodity and its innovation; as soon as the innovation is successful, others adopt it, and the ensuing negative performativity closes the spread at a new (lowered) value setting. This dynamic has a directionality in the increases in productivity and sets up a nonlinear but directional historical process. Each commodity is not simply an indexical-icon of the totality of value at a given moment, but also either a presupposition of a standard destined to become obsolete or a creative innovation destined to become a new presupposed standard. Commodities, under the conditions of the production of relative surplus value, become indexical-icons of the performative process itself; the creative destruction of innovation drives society and imparts its nonlinear but directional arbitrage dynamic to history that will be captured by the development of derivative finance; its realization will be the delta hedging and dynamic replication built into derivative trading by Black-Scholes.

Marxist theories of subjectivity have been heavily influenced by the analysis of fetishism that occurs in the opening section of *Capital*. Volume 1 of *Capital* is written as an immanent critique and thus starts with the commodity form of the contemporary capitalism of Marx's time and reconstructs its forms of appearance starting from the simple form of exchange value, through the money dialectic, and then value in the form of absolute and relative surplus value. Immediately after his presentation of the money dialectic, Marx describes an earlier stage of exchange that produces the "reciprocal isolation and foreignness" (1976, 182) needed for people to treat each other as independent and objects as alienable, which are conditions presupposed by the simple form of value. He notes that the "exchange of commodities begins where communities have their boundaries, at their points of contact with other communities, or with members of the latter" and "does not exist for the members of a primitive community of natural origin" (ibid.) except at the margins of society; once the exchange of commodities starts, it then moves inward and the evolution of the money form produces the possessive individual who can objectify himself and others as they buy and sell commodities.

We can reconstruct in the first four chapters of volume 1 of *Capital* at least four phases in Marx's development of subjectivity: (1) nonalienable exchange in "primitive" communities; (2) alienable relationships of barter and exchange; (3) fetishized relationships mediated by the money form; and (4) the miser as the "capitalist gone mad" and the capitalist as "the rational miser." If we rework these phases in light of Appadurai's and LiPuma's discussions in the preceding chapters, nonalienable exchange corresponds to the ritualized gift exchanges that Mauss describes in *The Gift*. Mauss's argument was that precapitalist and pre-Hobbesian man was embedded in relationships of gift/countergift that were his answer to Hobbes's "war against all," which would lead to the creation of a social contract that would replace or supersede the gift. This suggests an alignment between gift societies and what Appadurai and LiPuma have called "dividualism"—the fundamental social relationships that constitute dividuals are gift/countergift relationships, which are also the source of wealth in these societies. The performativity of the contract "objectifies" the dividualized gift relationship into an exchange of alienable objects between decision-making individuals—which is Derrida's point in his long commentary on the gift, with his additional insight into how the structure of Indo-European languages surreptitiously inserts the language of intentionality and agency into the description of gift exchange.[8]

Since the seeds of the fetish already exist in the simple form of value or exchange value, the successive forms of value ("total," "general," and the "money-form") represent successive stages in the development of an objectified social totality mediated by value (abstract labor time), which eventually becomes measured by money and price. The transformation of the precapitalist dividual into the self-maximizing possessive individual of capitalism is part of the process described by the development of the money form and capital. The objectification of labor time through the development of money leads to people seeing price as a quasi-natural property of commodities that is independent of their direct actions. People are not related by direct social relations but through the production and exchange of commodities ("material relations between people"), and commodities seem to circulate and move by themselves ("social relations between things"). This fetish quality of money is not so much false consciousness as a necessary misrecognition around which the development of capitalism depends. Since value is only created through production, the social contract model is the ideological expression of exchange. For Marx, circulation is a necessary moment in the realization of value since no commodity can express its value in itself, but instead needs an equivalent form (either another commodity or money) to express its value.

Objectification is literally the "thingification" (*Verdinglichung*) of social relationships, which in capitalism is expressed by seeing social relationships in terms of the relations between commodities. The origins of objectification and the fetish are in the simple form of value, and the money dialectic describes how a particular property that can be used to establish equivalences between objects (the abstract labor time needed to produce them) becomes a general property of the social totality in which commodity exchange is embedded, eventuating in the development of value as the performative subject of capitalism. Capital is the performative objectification of labor time, and each commodity is an indexical-icon of the larger social totality of which it is a part, a token instance of a type defined by the abstract labor time needed to produce it.

A similar process of performative objectification can be seen in the development of narrative subjectivity in which a narrating subject describes the speech, thoughts, and feelings of other subjects. Narration thus uses the full armature of verbs of speaking, thinking, and feeling, including performatives, mental act, and mental state verbs, to report on the subjectivities of self and others in a variety of linguistic genres, including diaries, journals, and novels. Vendler notes that the auxiliaries used with performatives include "make," "give," and "issue," whereas the mental state verbs share "have" ("to have a belief") and a large number of other alternatives; mental act verbs draw from both sets. The propositional complements of these intentional and intensional verbs encode "thoughts" that can be treated like alienable objects that are communicated and exchanged between people.

> Man lives in two environments, in two worlds: as a "body," and "extended thing," he is among objects and events in the physical, spatio-temporal universe: as a "mind," a "thinking thing," he lives and communes with objects of a different kind, which he also perceives, acquires, holds, and offers in various ways to other citizens, to other minds. (Vendler 1972, 34)

The alienability of thoughts is part of an "objectification of subjectivity" that turns thoughts into objects (a "fetishism of consciousness"), which can then be transmitted and exchanged between communicating agents. This alienability is also presupposed by Descartes's cogito, which Weber repeatedly invokes in *The Protestant Ethic* to describe the ideal of a continuous and potentially infinite (or at least lifelong) personal self-monitoring that would be the basis for ascetic self-disciplining. But the cogito is also the starting point for a larger objectification of subjectivity that starts with the performativity of thinking and speaking: "We must come to the definite conclusion that this proposition: I am, I exist [ego sum, ego existo] is necessarily true each time I *pronounce* it, or mentally conceive it" (Descartes, my emphasis, 1984, 150). Thinking or uttering "I am" is necessarily true because uttering the pronoun "I" creates the speaking subject of the discourse to whom the predicate "am" or "exist" can then truthfully apply.

The performativity of speaking and thinking anchors a larger picture of subjectivity that radiates from this core and includes all verbs of speaking, feeling, and thinking that take propositional complements, including performatives, mental activity, and mental state verbs. Our linguistic ideology describes the structure of communication as transitive and alienable: one can think a thought, judge it to be true or false, and then transmit that thought to others. Not only are thoughts and propositions alienable objects that can be grasped, transmitted, and exchanged with other thinking subjects, but the there is also an objectification or "thingification" of the subjects: I become "aware that I am, I think, I am a thinking *thing*" (Descartes, my emphasis, 1984, 327).

The retreat of ritual magic and the existential uncertainty and loneliness of the Calvinist predicament move the performativity of ritual inside the subject. The ensuing performative "objectification of subjectivity" produces a narrative consciousness that creates an inward-oriented subjectivity that sees itself as limited only by itself; this new narrative subjectivity is expressed in the explosion of spiritual diaries that were running records of moral consciousness as Calvinists searched for signs of election and reprobation in their daily lives. In his remarkable account of Nehemiah Wallington, a Puritan lathe worker, Paul Seaver caught the creation of an internalized "meta-subjectivity" who thought that his sole purpose and function was to show how God's providence worked in the world; self-examination and the glorification of God would go hand in hand: "I glorify God by self-examination and judgment of myself. As it is also God's command to examine myself, and also in examining myself I see much of God, which doth abound much to the glory of God" (Seaver 1985, 6). As the money-mediated production for exchange expands, the Calvinist impulse begins to transform into the spirit of the secular capitalist and the contract ideology grows from an economic metaphor to that for the creation of civil society supported by a self-regulating market. Seen from another angle, the contract model of exchange interacts with the money fetish and the objectification of labor time to create a model of a self-regulating social totality created by the contractualized exchange relations of its individual participants. Thus civil society is seen as performatively autochthonous, even though its origins lie in the performative construction of capital. Completing Marx's analyses of the fetishes of circulation, the contract model becomes the socially necessary misrecognition that makes people think that the origins of the market and society lie in circulation, rather than in production; it is this form of contract-based performativity that gives rise to Marx's famous invocation of "freedom, equality, property, and Bentham," which characterize the market ideology in which labor becomes a commodity. Performativity is seen as located in the contract and circulation, not in capital and production, but this misrecognition is a constitutive element of capitalism.

Once labor power becomes a commodity, it begins the valorization process that leads to the creation of the self-positing performative subject of capitalism, surplus value, which occurs in two forms: absolute and relative, which create two very different types of subjectivity. The logic of absolute surplus value is that of a linear and directional accumulation—the more abstract labor time expended, the more wealth (in the form of value) accumulated, which produces the subjectivity of the miser, "the capitalist gone mad." But relative surplus value is a nonlinear and directional dynamic, which resets itself in the process of creating and destroying itself. The miser is not in tune with the logic of relative surplus value. By holding on to his wealth, he potentially devalues it as the technological innovation resets the socially necessary labor time needed to produce commodities.

The only way to keep up with the logic of capitalism is to constantly reinvest your capital—the "ceaseless augmentation of value . . . is achieved by the more acute capitalist by means of throwing his money again and again into circulation" (Marx 1976, 254). Marx even uses the same reproductive metaphor of "offspring" as Franklin: "By virtue of being value, it has acquired the occult ability to add value to itself. It brings forth living offspring, or at least lays golden eggs" (ibid., 255). The circulation of capital becomes "an end in itself" that is "limitless" (253). Benjamin Franklin becomes the perfect embodiment of the spirit of capitalism as the "rational miser" in whom the religious motivations of the Calvinist have been "routinized" and dissipated and who recognizes the opportunity cost of time and the value of credit by constantly reinvesting his capital.

Implications

If Marx can be said to give an "objective" account of capital, Weber's emphasis on ethic and spirit can be seen as providing an account of the kind of subjectivity needed to support its functioning. Both would probably agree that the Benjamin Franklin passages in *The Protestant Ethic* capture the capitalist spirit of the limitless self-reproducing and self-expanding quality of money and the constant need to throw one's money back into circulation, to continuously reinvest one's capital. But less noticed is the role that uncertainty plays for both Weber and Marx. For Weber, the capitalist spirit develops out of the Calvinists' existential confrontation with uncertainty; for Marx, that spirit will lie in the capitalist as a "rational miser" who confronts the uncertainty and volatility of the arbitrage dynamic of relative surplus value. Relative surplus value makes the uncertainty of innovation a systemic organizing principle of capitalism, ironically confirming Knight's insight that the entrepreneur's search for innovation is the source for profit that makes the capitalist economic system "dynamic."

Relative surplus value creates a "spread" between the socially constituted average amount of time needed to produce a commodity and the new average introduced by the innovation. If successful, the innovation will eventually spread and become the new norm setter; there is a constant opening and closing of the spread, which constitutes the historical dynamic and directionality of production-centered capitalism as a constant oscillation between the play and shock of the new and its routinization as it destroys the old. Instead of dampening volatility, capitalism thrives on it.

While uncertainty has played a crucial role in the development of modern finance, the implications of volatility weren't clear until the discovery of the Black-Scholes formula, in which volatility replaces expected return as the key parameter in calculating the value of an option. Derman's chapter demonstrates that the breakthrough of Black-Scholes is to show how to access volatility by neutralizing directional risk through "dilution, diversification, and hedging." Black-Scholes implements a particular type of hedging called "delta hedging" to calculate the price of an option. If the hedge is properly implemented, it is possible to make money with an option regardless of which direction the underlier (i.e., the stock) moves as long as there is sufficient volatility to overcome time decay. The formal expression of the delta hedge is the Black-Scholes differential equation, in which volatility replaces expected return as the key component in calculating the price of options; the practical implementation has been the use of implied volatility to deal with the "volatility smile." Of course, the technology that grew out Black-Scholes has become increasingly complex, but the idea of hedging away risk to access volatility continues to play a key role in derivative finance, as in the continued use of implied volatility and the rise of the VIX (the Volatility Index).

The subjectivity associated with derivative capitalism has been made famous in the portrayals of greed, speculation, and excess in movies like Oliver Stone's *Wall Street*, Martin Scorsese's *The Wolf of Wall Street*, and Michael Lewis's classic *Liar's Poker*, which he wrote as a warning to his readers but which has been taken instead as a how-to-do-it book. Ayache has emphasized the embodied emotional component of market making as they surf the volatility wave ("he could now feel it in his guts"), while Caitlin Zaloom (2006) captures the emotional tightrope traders on the Chicago Board of Trade experienced as they navigated the "flow" of volatility on the trading floor. In his chapter in this volume, Wosnitzer returns to Geertz and the Balinese cockfight to describe the dance of status and money that motivates traders to "risk together" as they manipulate the "zone of arbitrage," the bid-ask spread. At the very end of his chapter about perhaps the most controversial aspect of contemporary finance, proprietary trading, Wosnitzer writes:

> The structure of the ritual trade is arbitrage, where the trader—and sales person—are simultaneously "going short" and "going long" through the combinations of social and economic attributes available for circulation and exchange. In this "work of arbitrage," the structure of the speculative ethos

emerges, rendering the process of speculation in this particular way as the means by which the self might experience success. While it is a truism that profit in the market emerges as the modern-day equivalent of god's grace, there is more to it than just that which is meaningful. It is the trade itself, the process by which it happens, that provides the trader with a sense of mastery and transcendence over the radical uncertainty that is the market. (270, this volume)

Although Marx builds the uncertainty and volatility of innovation into the arbitrage dynamic of relative surplus value, Marxist theories of subjectivity have been heavily influenced by the Frankfurt School's analyses of the fetish, alienation, and reification in which uncertainty does not play an explicit role. However, there is another line of thought initiated by the social philosopher Georg Simmel that describes the development of a "buffered" subjectivity in response to the volatility of urban life; its further elaboration can be seen in Walter Benjamin's work on the flâneur. Simmel derives some of the qualities of this urban subjectivity from the abstract properties of money as a form of "stranger mediation," but he makes no further connections between money and capital. But if arbitrage, uncertainty, and volatility are at the heart of both production-centered capitalism and derivative finance, then perhaps there is an alternative trajectory by which we can connect the Calvinist ascetic to the "big swinging dicks" of Wall Street.

The affinity of traders for extreme sports, gambling, and risk taking in general are expressions of the intimate connections between feelings of identity, self-worth, and economic success. Like Geertz's Balinese cockfight, meaning is created out of the battles for money and status, with a constant updating of literal and figurative "credit" reports. But the Calvinist predicament underlines the tension between a subjectivity created by the performative monitoring of behavior across a lifetime in which the ultimate outcome is uncertain and the embodied sensibilities that motivate it. Weber graphically describes the loneliness at the heart of these swings of emotion; the Calvinist experiences the full force of the volatility brought about by existential uncertainty. At an epistemic level, the Calvinist *knows* that no matter what he does there is no assurance that he will be saved, but this-worldly success in the "holding environment" of church and community can make him feel when things are going well as if he was "the instrument of God" working in the "zone" where aspirations and abilities seem to be in a productive tension. But this feeling is short lived—as soon as he steps back and reflects upon his feelings the epistemic uncertainty of salvation undoes his confidence and the cycle begins again.

The existential nature of God's gift of grace places the Calvinist believer in an impossible situation of continually undermining the momentary confidence he gets in his own this-worldly success, which is a sign of divine favor but can never guarantee it. The spread between uncertainty and certainty is always kept open, and there is no way to manage "risks" in this world so as to guarantee salvation in the next. The Calvinist cannot stop his ceaseless accumulation for the glory of God because the meaninglessness of the activity guarantees that there can never be a solution to his predicament; since he can't know anything about God's intentions, the search for meaning is potentially endless, and his existential dilemma cast across a lifetime of potentially ineffective good works creates a situation whose intensity far exceeds that of the faithful Catholic or this-worldly Confucian.

Locked into his individual subjectivity and constantly scrutinizing his behavior in a performative Cartesian manner knowing that ultimately nothing can guarantee him salvation, he can only do his best to place himself among those who succeed for the glory of God in the hope that he will be one of the chosen from the "finalists." The key is not to make money or succeed at any particular moment but to build up spiritual "credit" over a lifetime of good works, like a good poker player nursing his bankroll and knowing how important it is to stay in the game until the end even if he can't guarantee that he'll be the last person standing at the "final table." Emotionally, the important thing is not to go "tilt" in any particular situation but instead have the discipline to speculate with a view for the long term.

But the ascent of capitalism also means the concomitant loss of the religious impulse, so that by the time of Benjamin Franklin, what remains is the compulsiveness about money and "wasting time" without the Calvinist's existential anxiety. The Calvinist internalizes the immanent spirit of capitalism as an internalized dynamic replication in the face of volatility, harvesting profits for the glory of God. With the retreat of religion as a motivating force, the capitalist becomes a rational miser who constantly reinvests his own capital and exposes himself to the volatility of competitive capitalism as a disciplined speculator.

Lurking beneath this Protestant ethic is an existential moment that parallels that uncovered in high-stakes poker, especially Texas no-limit hold 'em, the game of choice among traders and speculators; the analogy reminds us that despite the seeming contrast between Calvinist asceticism and the "masters of the universe" of Wall Street, there is a common hedging strategy of how to face the volatility that uncertainty unleashes. The key here is not to focus on winning a single hand but to adopt a winning strategy across games, which allows one to be among the last men standing at the end. In the face of radical uncertainty about his prospects for salvation, the individual goes "all in" and makes the maximum possible bet: that of his life or reputation in order to place himself in the best position to be saved even though there is absolutely no guarantee that his actions will succeed.

The inner-worldly ascetic bets the social and material rewards that he has in hand against a future outcome over which he may gain insight but not control. In the language of game theory, which poker has adopted albeit in a more colloquial argot, the Calvinist stance toward the world is based on a kind of "position playing under existential uncertainty." The stance is that this is the best I can do given what others have done, and the more certain I am that I have honored God, the more certain I can feel that I am destined for salvation, even if I can never *know* it. There is always the possibility that even if I play life's hand to the best of my abilities, having faithfully followed Calvin's admonition to sacrifice myself to God, I may ultimately face the same damnation as the unregenerate sinners whose immoral lives insult God.

The echo here is the poker player refrain after a "bad beat"—that though he lost in the end, he played the best he could given his cards, the odds, and the circumstances. Here the gambling analogy is useful once again. If it's an all or nothing (salvation or damnation) game, then your strategy has to be to stay in the game until the very end; you don't want to be knocked out before the final turn. Since you can't know if you'll ultimately win, the turn of the cards being in principle unknowable, you play to position yourself to be one of the finalists when the cards are played at the end and the winner(s) determined. Playing the best you can entails maximizing your chances of being a finalist and provides you the psychological feeling that you've done the best you can and, all things being equal, your effort is as good as anyone else's. The rest is the luck of the draw. And the way to play one's best is to do the best one can as far as performing good works, for even though it can't guarantee winning, it guarantees that you've done your best given your cards, and if you remain until the end, you could be one of the chosen.

At an existential level, the Calvinist pioneering capitalists were making the ultimate speculation[9]—by investing their very subjectivity in a hand whose outcome was doctrinally unknowable. Because the intentions of God are unknown, the passage from our worldly existence into the afterlife is a game in which the stakes are so large and the risk of damnation so terrifying that the believer's speculation must be the wager of going *all in* with one's life. Under these existential values, ascetically sacrificing one's life to God is the only ecclesiastically conceivable *hedging* strategy in the face of truly radical and existential uncertainty.

While the speculator and the believer both face uncertainty, they approach this from different directions. The speculator calculates and embraces risk by compressing time to the moment of taking a specific position and making a bet, whereas the believer hedges risk by spreading it across a lifetime of good works. The difference between no-limit hold 'em and Weber's paradox underscores that radical uncertainty—the understanding that the situation contains mortal risks—produces a family resemblance that links uncertainty, risk, and the trajectory of agents' hopes and fears into an existential bind in which the final move is truly a leap of faith. On the one hand, the notions that a regenerate moral life will allow for salvation or that mathematizing a financial derivative will illuminate its risk profile rest on the idea that decision making under uncertainty requires rational calculation both in terms of purpose and value. On the other hand, the rationality of salvation or the nonarbitrage principle seem to be constantly undermined by the social reality of the uncertainties and volatilities of everyday life.

The ritual solution for the tension between social ideal and social reality is to use the "force" of the former to turn the latter into an instance of it. But the existential uncertainty of salvation in Weber's *Protestant Ethic* produces a new historical dynamic in which feelings of loneliness, anxiety, and existential uncertainty create in the Calvinist true believer an internalized individual subjectivity that will be the basis for the possessive individualism of the modern capitalist subject. The "inward turn" of the Calvinist true believer breaks the bonds of dividuality, and the uncertainty over salvation stretched over a lifetime effectively locks the true believer into a potentially limitless internal subjectivity. As he updates his "credit" with God in the face of the volatilities of everyday life and the vicissitudes of his calling, he turns his life into a running account or profit-loss ledger, constantly trying to maneuver himself into the position of those who might receive God's grace as he avoids going "tilt" in any particular situation.

The inward turn establishes a potentially limitless subjectivity, which breaks the embodied dividualized social relations created by ritual practice and creates a subjectivity that supports the belief-desire model of intentionality at the heart of derivative finance. With the decline of an overtly religious motivation, the capitalist-as-Benjamin-Franklin begins to measure the temporality of that inward subjectivity with that of money, so that the subjectivity produced is now a monetized subjectivity, which prepares the way for both the arbitrage logic of relative surplus value and the nonarbitrage logic of contemporary finance.

PART II

CHAPTER FOUR

Liquidity

Robert Meister, University of California, Santa Cruz

P revious chapters show how the idea of optionality used since 1973 to value financial derivatives has a broader epistemic and affective significance. We have seen the role of both models and traders in the pricing of contingent claims and how the ability to price these claims is embedded in broader forms of technology and sociality. From there we have explored the mode of pricing derivatives as a cultural logic that extends beyond financial markets themselves to other forms of life in twenty-first century capitalism in much the way that the cultural logic of commoditization was said to work in the early twentieth century, and we have looked backwards to so-called "primitive" societies to see how the logic of hedging, which is essential to the pricing of financial options today, is also essential to understanding the performative role of gifts and rituals as hedges against uncertainty about whether the future of the seemingly natural order will be like its past. A central premise of this book is that what we here call the option form of value, encompassing both the intertemporal and the interpersonal dimensions of social life, both includes and surpasses the commodity form of value that describes the interpersonal exchange of things among persons at a fixed moment in time.

In this chapter we move on to consider the political implications of considering the option (and more specifically the hedge) alongside the commodity as the kernel of value in capitalism, both now and from the beginning. We thus follow in the footsteps of Karl Marx, who analyzed capitalism as generalized version of the commodity form extending even to human labor power, which is also subject to the discipline of monetary payment as a condition of access to the means of subsistence. Here we ask whether a project like Marx's can be reimagined for the twenty-first century so as to encompass the social production of financial assets, such as debt instruments and options. Do recent theorizations of the valuation of these instruments allow us an understanding of the role of capital within capitalism that supplements the understanding Marx gained from reading Smith's and Ricardo's explorations of the valuation of wage goods in terms of labor time?

No less important, however, are the political questions that drove Marx's analysis. He saw the extension of the commodity form into all aspects of life as heightening the conflict between wage laborers and those who live off profits and accumulated wealth around the question of what proportion of national income should be available for the purchase of consumer goods. This would be for Marx a question that involved both direct power at the point of production and that also implicated the role of the democratic power of the state. Our overarching question is whether we finally get capitalism only when (if?) the financial system itself becomes a focus of democratic demands and a site of class struggle. What follows from the ways in which both production and the state must be financed? And to the extent that consumption, and even unemployment, must also be financed, what is the role of debt and credit instruments as a site of political resistance?

This chapter thus extends our discussion of derivatives to politics as we know it today. To accomplish this we must connect, as Marx did, the hegemonic character of capitalist thought with the technological and social conditions of its emergence.

A good place to start is with Timothy Mitchell's provocative recent book arguing that the potential for resisting capitalism in Marx's lifetime arose not from the emergent general form of commodity production as such, but rather from the technosocial conditions surrounding the transition from wood to coal as a source of energy. These conditions allowed the growth of large-scale industry, but in a way that for a century gave organized workers an unusual degree of power to subvert the power being exercised over them by, essentially, blocking the extraction and transportation of coal (Mitchell 2011).

The core claim of this new perspective is that individual miners, isolated at the coalface, occupied a "chokepoint" at the beginning of the industrial supply chain. By coordinating their actions horizontally, rather than obeying orders transmitted vertically from the surface, they could eventually bring all industrial production based on coal and steam power to a halt. Railway workers occupied further chokepoints down the line and could have more immediate effects by refusing to move coal from the mines to the factories. If factory workers, those working in the steel mills for instance, were then to join such a strike (rather than demanding military seizure of the mines and railroads), there would be a general strike that an elected government might not have either the legitimacy or security resources to suppress.

The possibility of a general strike gaining democratic legitimacy in this way had the potential to subvert the electoral technologies that legitimated the state itself. Elections are normally used to manufacture popular consent for the deployment of security forces so as to isolate subversives from their potential social base and drive down the cost of political repression. But the state's increased reliance on electoral technologies to accomplish this in the era of coal was vulnerable to horizontal coordination of voters outside the polling place around the question of whether an elected government would use military force against popular assemblages in the event of a general strike. In practice this issue rarely presented itself, but the longer term results of a linkage between the right to strike (which had material effects) and the right to vote (which had legitimating effects) was the opening for the class compromise over government economic policy that is now, often nostalgically, associated with a Fordist regime of high wages backed up by a welfare state regime of non-wage transfer payments that did not put jobless workers in debt.

One possible conclusion from this line of thought is that the transition from coal to oil by the mid-twentieth century defeated the historically specific assemblage of political and social forces that briefly democratized the industrial West. The reason is that oil workers were proportionally fewer than coal miners and could not exercise the kind of outsize leverage that coal miners had over production. This left the power to wreck a domestic economy to individual terrorists who could blow up a pipeline without either needing or receiving organized popular support. The more effective chokepoints of oil-based production were in the hands of the oil companies and, by the 1970s, in the hands of oil-producing states that were able through OPEC to control prices.

The social and institutional sources of democracy, in this account, look very different from those we have been used to. However disorienting this perspective may appear, it has the virtue of linking the roles of both sabotage and legitimation in defining modes of democratic

resistance to capitalism. This means that to be effective a democratizing movement must have the threat potential of a strike that occupies
and takes control of vital chokepoints, but that to be democratic such
a movement must have the communicative potential to build or occupy
public spaces whether these are physical or virtual. To achieve success
it becomes imperative to overcome the tensions inherent in the differences between the forms of expressive and embodied occupation a given
technosocial mode of production makes possible and effective.

One tactical question today is whether symbolic reoccupations of
public space can be joined to forms of collective action in the privately
regulated spaces that people already occupy but do not effectively control. Is it possible, for example, that power, transportation, national security, and internet-based industries could be made inoperable by those
with hands-on power to control significant nodal points on their respective grids?

A larger strategic question is whether the powers of internal sabotage
that our oil-based financial system makes available to key actors create
the potential for democratizing it from within. Put more starkly, what
is the relation between the securities industry and the security industry,
given the multiple points at which the entire financial system is vulnerable to illiquidity as a consequence of disruptive events that could be coordinated horizontally in ways that resist command from above?

The argument of this chapter is that we need to extend this materialist
analysis of the political potential of coal- and oil-based technologies of
production to the global technologies of financial accumulation that enable the current energy-extraction system to exist.

Let us start with the question as to whether, and to what extent, the
crucial period of 1971 to 1973, corresponding to the birth of financialization, represents a new phase in the oil-based regime of global governance. The Bretton Woods agreement, concluded in 1943, required that
oil be priced and purchased in dollars. This mechanism linked how much
oil would be produced to how many dollars (and dollar-denominated
credit instruments) must be pumped into global circulation to keep the
oil flowing. In the 1950s and 1960s the European banks issued what were
essentially credits in the form of Eurodollars that could be used to purchase oil because they were valued at par with US currency.

By 1971 the glut of Eurodollars in the petroleum market caused the
United States to repudiate its obligation under Bretton Woods to re-

deem dollars in nondomestic circulation with gold. This meant that henceforward dollars were only redeemable with dollars and that the ability of newly empowered oil states to pump out more oil without a fall in prices was directly tied to the ability to pump out more dollars (now seen as credit money) without reducing the value of the dollar as a unit in which the value of financial assets can be accumulated. By the early 1970s prominent economists perceived a "trilemma" in which nations could not simultaneously maintain fixed exchange rates, capital mobility, and the monetary autonomy needed to control the double-digit inflation that was then occurring (Triffin 1960; Mundell 1960, 2000; Amato and Fantacci 2012a).

"Whipping inflation" (the monetary crises) while repricing oil (the energy crisis) required the creation of new financial instruments, essentially options, that could *store* value in a highly liquid form in the sense of being easily convertible into actual *funds*. These new financial instruments would eventually change the meaning and use of money (the conversion of assets into funds) as it had been previously understood. I refer here to the emergence around 1973 of a new technology for creating liquid assets, based on the Black-Scholes-Merton (BSM) formula for pricing call options. This technology specifically assumes an abundance ("nonscarcity") of publicly and privately created debt vehicles that are "risk free" in the limited sense that bonds issued by one branch of government (the Treasury) are ultimately backed by the ability of another branch of government (the Fed) to issue the currency (dollars) in which they are redeemable. The fact that US taxes are also *collected* in dollars means that the US government can *repay* its bonds with revenues raised from taxpayers whose spendable income would thereby decline.

The alternative is for the Fed, here acting as the Treasury's agent, to *repurchase* these bonds by issuing new dollars that do not come from taxes. Such an always-possible public-sector swap of debt for dollars resembles a private-sector swap of debt for equity in that the value of the dollar/equity could go down due to inflation/dilution.[1] This dilution effect on spending power is why taxpayers/shareholders are often willing to pay their creditors ahead of other demands—an economic motivation that is far from universal or self-evident (Reinhart and Rogoff 2009). But it is the ever-present alternative of monetizing government debt rather than repaying it that makes it possible to view the growth of government debt as a supply of safe collateral (and thus a store of value) whether or not it is used to fund public spending beyond what current tax revenues will support. Government entities—that can both tax and borrow—are now being put under pressure to spend less (austerity) so that they can borrow more, so as to fulfill the need of the private sector for "safe" (i.e., tax-backed) collateral in sufficient quantities to allow all riskier (non-tax-backed) credit to be priced.

I won't dwell further on the link between the return on safe securities (US government bonds) and the supply of base money (US dollars) that makes those bonds the best—that is, most "liquid"—collateral for the global financing of everything, including oil (Singh and Stella 2012; Gourinchas and Jeanne 2012). For now, I'll just say that BSM implicitly built upon ways in which optionality attached to "dollars" gave oil its *financial* "liquidity" to describe the direct manufacture of options, beginning with calls and puts, that shared properties with money (because they could be continuously priced) but that could also be used to hedge the price of *both* oil and dollars in a way that allowed the dollar price of oil to rise without lowering the value of the dollar itself. If the inflationary impact of a trade deficit in oil could be hedged during an era of seeming overabundance, this was attributable not only to the monopoly power of oil producers but also to an emerging financial system that can assign a bankable present value of oil reserves as dollar-denominated assets that have not been sold (liquidated) on the spot market.

The bottom line is that by the 1970s the price of liquid *carbon* could be controlled only because there were new ways to manufacture liquidity in the global financial system through the expanded use of options.[2] This left the central banks with the task of controlling inflation while creating enough base money to maintain the liquidity of markets in these new financial instruments so that asset prices could rise in relation to the value of goods and services without an offsetting decline in the value of the currency in which the assets were denominated.[3]

This conception of liquidity creation explains why, as early as the 1970s, standard textbooks on finance (such as Brealey and Myers 2003) used oil reserves as an illustration of how the option not to produce makes it possible to treat oil itself as a financial asset in which wealth is stored, and not merely as a revenue-producing commodity. According to the BSM options pricing formula, a proven oil reserve becomes exponentially more valuable to its holder as oil prices become more volatile. If the volatility of oil is what is priced in the financial assets market, then it is clear that volatility can be manufactured and managed in political ways. Oil shocks are political manipulations in that they can be used to control prices that have never been determined by an automatic market mechanism in which supply rises to meet demand.

From 1971 to 1973 we had the "energy crisis," the "monetary crisis," the "inflation crisis," "the democratic overload," and the "environmental crisis" as sources of volatility (Hacker and Pierson 2010; Crozier, Huntington, and Watanuki 1975; Meadows 1972). But as volatility (the measurement of spreads around a mean) became the analytical tool for extracting financial value from all these crises, we also got the BSM formula that allowed us to predict option prices from the merely "historical" volatility of the underlying price. We could then calculate what future volatility is "implied" by a market price that differs from the formula's prediction (Derman and Kani 1994; Derman, this volume). What follows from this is the Chicago Board of Options Exchange, the ability to hedge currency risk, and the growing dominance of the financial sector in what is now called the "real economy." This new concept and technology of financial liquidity explains globalization in the form of chronic trade deficits that do not lead to currency devaluation as they would have under the gold standard. This is why Nixon's decision to default on the gold standard led directly to his opening to China and the chronic trade deficits that ensued.

By the 1990s the ability to manufacture fully hedged, dollar-denominated assets in which capital could be accumulated allowed for a world economy in which persistent trade deficits and trade surpluses could simply be financed rather than eliminated. This is the phenomenon that we commonly refer to as "globalization" when we want to stress its effect on the shifting spatial location of production. It is also—and just as importantly—a regime of financialization, which is what we call it when we want to stress its effect in creating vehicles of capital accumulation that are not necessarily investments in expanded production.

The essential point is that the globalization of production required globalization of financial markets—free flow of capital in a way that can offset trade deficits. This lifting of capital controls (the state-imposed requirements for domestic reinvestment that monetary economists call "financial repression") was connected to increased repression of the "inflationary" political pressures for high public spending characteristic of the welfare state during the late Bretton Woods era. In addition to keeping inflation low, the new job of the central banks was to supply enough money to keep liquidity high in the market for safe collateral in which asset value can be stored (Blinder 1998). Beginning in the 1980s, growth in the dollar value of markets in purely financial assets had been effectively decoupled from growth in the dollar value of GDP, and by the 1990s it would exceed the rate of GDP growth by an ever-growing margin.

I indicated earlier that this new world of liquidity in both energy and finance changed the use and meaning of money, and having introduced the concept of financialization, I am in a better position to say why. Standard texts in economics say that money is a measure of value, a store of value, and a medium of exchange. What finance textbooks add is that in capital asset markets the particularity of money is also a measure of the gap between the liquidity (or price) of an asset and its liquidation value (the monetizability of required collateral)—a gap that can be continuously measured by engaging in a market for options that sets a price on the risk of default.

Put crudely, liquidity is the property that financial assets have when they can be priced without being turned into money by stripping off all or some of this credit risk through an options market. An asset's liquidation value is the cash that a lender could get out of it by selling the collateral in the event of nonperformance on the expected revenue stream. The expected liquidation value of an asset, for example in bankruptcy, is generally less than its mark-to-market price as a performing asset, which is why secured lenders almost always require borrowers to post a capital cushion, or take a "haircut," as the margin on pledged collateral that may have to be sold into a falling market (Gorton and Metrick 2010a; Kaminska 2011b). When liquidations become widespread, the value of collateral collapses much faster than the value of the debt that it is liquidated to repay (Minsky 1986). This is because there isn't, and couldn't be, enough currency in the world to liquidate all assets or, put differently, to repay all debts if they were simultaneously called (Amato and Fantacci 2012b). Collateral is itself, as we shall see, the principal store of the surplus value that precipitates out of the production process Marx describes.

What has been said thus far is merely a restatement of what Irving Fisher called the "debt-deflation spiral," what Keynesians call "the liquidity trap," and what Hyman Minsky called the problem of "validating" (and thus pricing) the overhang of past debt. They all tell us that to avoid depression a central bank must supply enough currency (or base money) to prevent financial assets, and especially credit instruments, from being liquidated all at once.

Marxist economists would add that preserving the liquidity of debt (postponing its liquidation) is all about accumulation. How large is this accumulation? In the United States alone the value of total credit market debt (TCMD, as reported by the Federal Reserve), the financial assets that along with cash, equities, and real estate constitute a minimal measure of accumulated national wealth, is now about four times the dollar value of US GDP[4]. And, since one person's debt is someone else's asset, the total volume of high-quality debt (plus cash, equities, and real estate) is roughly equivalent to the volume of bankable collateral that can be used to store value.

As long as debt (and other collateral) remains liquid it does not have to be called, in which case massive asset disaccumulation by means of monetization is avoided. But of course the most highly liquid collateral is easily rehypothecated—this happens all the time in the overnight repo market—so the velocity of collateralization and the extent of cross-collateralization is also a factor (Singh and Stella 2012; Riles 2011). For present purposes, we can say that the amount of stored or accumulated wealth is substantially more than the sum of global credit market debt (ca. four times GDP) but substantially less than the global notional value of all outstanding derivative positions based on this cross-collateralization, which has been estimated to exceed seventeen times the GDP.

Marx could not, however, grasp (for reasons explained below) how the production of liquidity in general is the emergent problem addressed by a system of capitalist finance that lacked "safe" collateral as a store of value. Throughout *Capital*, he discussed the issue of liquidity as a "realization problem" in regard to the expected return on an investment in producer goods (will you realize your "cost-price"?) and as a validation problem in regard to the expected repayment of a loan (will the collateral be called because of fear of default?). Modern finance theory shows how risks based on the carrying costs of producer goods and the nonperformance of loans can be hedged, and even fully-hedged if one is willing to sacrifice returns.

To own a hedge is, by definition, to own an asset in which capital accumulation is locked in (fully or partially) for a period of time. If, as BSM suggests, it is also possible to produce and sell new assets by means of hedging existing assets (and thus without assuming the underlying risk), then we would seem to have a capitalist mode of producing financial assets that parallels the capitalist mode of producing of commodities. The most important question is not whether this financial mode of production solves the problem of smoothing out the business cycle caused by Marx's investment realization and debt-validation problems better than the Keynesian tax state. We now recognize that the state stands behind many of these financial products, which are really contracts, as the counterparty of last resort.

The important question to answer is whether the technologies for making and pricing financial products create the kinds of opening for disruptive democratizing organization that Marx identified in relation to coal-based industrialization. The demand for higher wages and better working conditions was the specific form of class struggle under the particular technosocial conditions of late nineteenth-century industrialization. Marx was writing *Capital* during the period when the British Empire was trying to impose the gold standard on the system of world trade. When a central bank is disciplined by convertibility under the gold standard, this means that the supply of money cannot be manipulated to inject liquidity into a credit market without simply producing inflation, which is seen from a balance of payments perspective as a devaluation of the currency due to oversupply. The coal-based British Empire was financed for fifty years based on this conception of the relation of states to their internal and external markets. By contrast the petroleum-based American Empire has been financed for the past fifty years based on the ability of global investors to price currency options in relation to other financial spreads, such as volatility in the price of oil itself and the changing risks of credit instruments denominated different currencies.

Can we put Marx's account of the financial vulnerabilities of nineteenth-century commodity production in the same conceptual register as the techniques of asset valuation based on BSM? By doing so, could we come up with a credible activist political agenda that links direct action—such as strikes and uprisings—with a political program that aims at redistributing accumulated wealth?[5] Isn't the political *in*security of capitalist accumulation what Marxian analysis has always been about?

To approach these questions we must consider the embryonic role of finance in Marx's account of capitalist commodity production.

Capitalism begins, at least in theory, with the figure Smith and Ricardo called the "farmer." He is decidedly not Thomas Jefferson's "yeoman farmer" who owns the land he works, plants the seed he grows, and then sells the portion of the crop he doesn't eat on an open market, sharing the proceeds with no one. In classical political economy the farmer, rather, operates in the interstices of a feudal class society. He can in theory rent his land, buy his seed, hire landless laborers to grow his crop, and then sell it subject to whatever obligations he has incurred to finance his investment. For this minimal prototype of capitalist agriculture to get underway there must of course be some sort of market in the product and in the various inputs required to produce it. The farmer can enter this market because he is presumed to own his future crop, something that does not yet exist but that can be used to secure a loan from someone else who happens to have a preexisting supply of something that counts as money in the sense that it can also be used to purchase the future product and the various inputs required to produce it.

So, even before it can be traded as a commodity, the crop must already be available to be pledged as collateral for debt. The consequence of borrowing against the crop is that the creditor has a right to purchase it for the value of the note plus interest—he has acquired an option to put back his note at that price, exercisable on its due date. Having given up this put option in return for receiving a secured loan, the farmer is left with a contingent claim on the remaining value of the crop to the extent that it exceeds what was previously owed. This call option (or a share of it) is potentially something he can sell. The farmer thus has a second way to finance production: he can issue what we now call equity in addition to assuming debt. (And he may be required to raise some capital in this way in order to qualify for a loan that is secured by his future crop.)

Before actually producing his crop, the protocapitalist farmer must thus have the sociolegal capacity to throw off two financial byproducts, debt and equity. In classical political economy, however, there is no secondary market in these byproducts—they can't be recycled because they can't be easily priced. This is why Marx thought Smith and Ricardo lacked a good account of how capital itself accumulates in the process of commodity production.

In some moods Marx sometimes makes much of the fact that Smith's farmer, like any capitalist, gets his ability to manufacture these financial products out of thin air—we would now say that his right to do so derives from the culture rather than any specific market transaction and we would not assume such right is unjustly acquired for that reason alone. A superficial form of Marx's presumed-injustice complaint about surplus extraction is that the capitalist did not pay anyone a "premium" for his call on the residual value that enables him to buy a secured loan (which requires him to sell a put) and also to sell shares in the call he already owns. But from whom would he have bought such a contingent claim and at what price? Sometimes Marx implies that the capitalist should have paid an equity premium to the worker, who might in a Lockean state of nature have taken possession of the entire product.

But elsewhere Marx attacks Ricardian socialists who take such a view as "vulgar" rather than "scientific." The "scientific" view (which Marx rightly credits to Smith and Ricardo) isn't that the capitalist succeeds to ownership of the means of production from a feudal lord but that, *even if he rents* the means of production (perhaps from a feudal lord), he nevertheless has the ability to manufacture financial products in addition to ordinary commodities. It is thus essential to a protocapitalist mode of production that someone other than a feudal lord, who at the outset still owned the means of production, have a prior right to appropriate the surplus that was not directly purchased on the market itself (Ayres 2005).

In his "scientific" moods Marx seems to grasp that, at the innermost kernel of the mode of production defined by Smith and Ricardo, there is an outside to the market for commodities as such that is also more inside the market than the market itself (Ayres 2005). This inside/outside is the very thing the capitalist always already possesses—the ability to manufacture a *financial* asset (derivative) based on the present value of something that does not yet exist. I believe that Marx understood this—which is why he called his book *Capital* even though it is most directly about commodities.

His choice of title stresses the insight that commodity production has to be financed and that the emergent logic of finance will eventually dominate the production process.[6] But to reframe his argument in this way we still need to understand what Marx himself made of finance, given the state of capitalist development occurring before his eyes.

Approaching the question of how capitalist finance affects production requires us to confront a paradoxical fact about the structure of Marx's argument in *Capital* itself as both a critique of classical political economy on its own terms and as a first-order account of what it missed. The problem Marx saw is that Smith and Ricardo forced their argument about market-based production in order to show that the distinctive features of protocapitalist agriculture begin to pay off, not when landless peasants are hired by the farmer to do the unspecialized work of feudal serfs but when they are employed in workshops that replace the guild system and allow them to develop greater skills through specialization (see *Capital* volume 1, chapter 29). But if the classical political economists forced their argument, it can equally be said that Marx forced his own account of how a division of labor in manufacture creates surplus value by showing that the real payoff occurs when this system is replaced by "machinofacture," the large-scale industrial factory in which commodified labor becomes increasingly deskilled and homogeneous and which results in the unemployment of large numbers of workers who have been brought into the labor force through the process of dispossession that Marx's translators call "primitive accumulation" and that might be better called "original accumulation" (or "absolute rent" to distinguish it from the forms of accumulation based on harvesting the relative rents created by technology, as we shall see below (Mezzadra 2011)).

As a careful reader of Smith and Ricardo, Marx saw that the capitalist tendency toward industrialization could lie in the assumed desire of the capitalist for a larger aggregate surplus value. If this were the driving force, why would he not just hire more workers for as long as they are available, instead of investing in expensive machinery that would eventually drive down his selling price per unit? Smith and Ricardo thought that the capitalist would be biased in favor of higher employment for this very reason—a strategy that Marx called the production of "absolute surplus value," which, as he pointed out, could also be increased by lengthening the working day of existing workers. Marx went on, however, to distinguish the "absolute surplus value" that characterized the mode of production described by Smith and Ricardo from the capitalist's production of what he called "relative surplus value." It is the pursuit of relative surplus value that explains capitalism's bias in favor of productive technologies that reduce rather than increase employment, and thus its ability to transform the world through the rapid adoption of industrial technology.

Relative surplus value does this by implicitly introducing the logic of finance into the market mode of production described by Smith and Ricardo and then by asking what effect finance has on the *re*production of the social relation between labor and capital that they described. The reason that producer goods, which are means of production, can *also* function as vehicles of capital accumulation is based on the financial principle that each identical unit of output must be sold at the same price regardless of its actual production cost.[7] This principle (now called "the law of one price") favors those who can produce more units in the same amount of labor time and thus compels investment in productive technologies that throw people out of work while increasing material output.

From the standpoint of today's financial theory, the capitalist's investment in labor-saving technology is simply an example of how to create an arbitrage opportunity by widening the spread of returns on the investment in a (constant) quantity of raw materials that are used to create products that will sell at the same per unit price regardless of what Marx calls the "variable" quantity of labor employed in their production.

Marx's account of relative surplus value is thus the paradigm case of how technology can be used to both create and measure a spread that can be arbitraged by investing in an asset that serves as a vehicle to preserve, and hence accumulates, value. In this case the vehicle for financializing the spread is simply to increase investment in raw materials and other producer goods. Here (and this for Marx is the genius of capitalism) producer goods do double duty as both means of production and as financial assets—that is, as vehicles for capital accumulation. In this respect technologies of productivity function to create and measure a gradient of returns on one's investment in raw materials in much the way that, for Ricardo, there would be a wider gradient of returns on the fertility of soil (the rent on the land used for capitalist agriculture) as population grows and techniques of cultivation improve.[8]

The development of relative surplus value to produce a spread in expected returns is thus an early example of what some recent Italian Marxists call "the becoming-rent of profit." One thing this means is that profits, like Ricardian rents on land and today's rents on intellectual property, are based on variable spreads over and above a zero-rent alternative, which is for Ricardo cultivating the least productive land and in the realm of high tech using freeware.[9] In Marx's distinction between absolute and relative surplus value we see the contrast between the capitalist as a financier who can increase his return on constant capital through technological innovation and the capitalist as employer who operates in the manner described in earlier accounts of the market mode of production, such as those of Smith and Ricardo.

In summary, relative surplus value explains the effect of capitalism on technological change; absolute surplus value, the exploitation of wage labor, explains the effect of capitalism on population growth. By creating both forms of surplus value the whole of capitalism here acts to produce the mechanical result (in Marx an "absolute general law of capitalist accumulation") that in successive rounds of production the relative amounts of capital that is reinvested in hiring workers must diminish so that the surplus value that was created in previous rounds can be accumulated in the form of producer goods and money. Marx's "general law" brings these two logics of surplus value *together* for the first time in *Capital*, volume 1, by showing (in a way that we should find exemplary) the *impact of finance on production*. It describes the destabilizing financial logic of creating cost/price spreads through the use of labor-saving technologies, thus allowing real accumulation of capital to occur through growth in the total volume of producer goods and not in other ways. When Marx wrote, however, there were no technologies for valuing financial assets except producer goods (which were already priced as commodities) and, of course, money itself. Marx thus observed that emerging financial assets that were neither producer goods nor money were "fictitious" in the sense that they were not a form in which real, as opposed to merely speculative, accumulation had thus far taken place.

But Marx did not need to exclude all financial products other than money itself from "real" accumulation in order to attack speculative bubbles. His "General Formula for Capital," M-C-M′, describes in the abstract what financial economists call an arbitrage opportunity in which an identical commodity has two different prices. This violates, as we've seen, the "law of one price" if the two different prices are both simultaneous and certain because there would then be the possibility for limitless profit. If capitalism were based on perpetuating (rather than eliminating) arbitrage, the formula for capital expansion would simply be M-M′ and you (or anyone else) could borrow all the money in the world with no risk of default. In that case you wouldn't need collateral, or indeed any capital at all, to have capitalism, which is the very thing capitalism is supposed to make impossible. (Any worker could be a capitalist if the extraction of surplus value could be financed as an arbitrage opportunity that is always already fully collateralized.)

Marx famously resolves this apparent violation of the law of one price —making money from money—by focusing on the special characteristics of a specific commodity, labor power, which requires preexisting for its employment. Capital invests in labor power because there is a spread between what Duncan Foley (1986, chaps. 2–3) usefully calls the labor value of money (labor's contribution to GDP) and the money value of labor (the purchasing power of the wage). Foley's formulation suggests that in his theory of absolute surplus value Marx in effect discovers what I earlier described as a call option on that spread.

But for this very reason, what Marx described as capitalism was an abstract version of wage labor in which workers were both debt free and uncreditworthy (Graeber 2011, chap. 11). He assumed (contrary to fact) that there was enough physical currency in circulation to pay this labor in advance, but not at a high enough wage level to give workers the option not to spend their entire paycheck on consumer goods but, rather, to invest or borrow against their wage. The key to Marx's theory of surplus value is that wages are never spent on goods that preserve rather than lose their value in use—and thus what he calls "variable capital" (the labor-cost portion of total investment) is not, by definition, available for recirculation and accumulation and cannot generally be pledged as collateral. This is what we might call the capitalism-as-production side of Marx's picture, which effectively keeps the wage goods workers buy from becoming investments and thus preserving their value as capital.

But there is also, at least in embryo, a capitalism-as-finance side of Marx's account M-C-M′. Here we might imagine the middle term, C, not as a simple commodity but as a hedged *portfolio* that can itself be priced as capital. Producer goods, what Smith and Ricardo call "stock" (which, if jointly owned, is now called "equity"), can be parts of a portfolio and thus provide the vehicles of accumulation that Marx saw constant capital to be. And debt instruments (bonds) can be another part of an investment portfolio. Marx recognized in *Capital* volume 3 that the capitalist may need to borrow against his raw material and machinery to fund expanded production and that "overproduction" (the inability to sell the output at a markup over costs) puts these loans at risk of being called at a time when their collateral (at least the raw materials) may be nearly worthless. What Marx calls the "realization problem"—a phrase that appears throughout *Capital* as a kind of nervous tic—is the exposure of a capitalist investing in raw materials to the risk that they will lose value in the process of production (that he will experience what financial economists call a "negative carry") if the price of the finished product falls below the historical average on which he based his initial investment.

Marx's "realization problem" in the later volumes of *Capital* is almost always about overinvestment in producer goods because he usually assumed (unlike Keynes) that workers spend their entire wage and cannot save. The capitalist here has a portfolio consisting of debt and equity (his net investment in constant capital), but this portfolio does not include a hedge against the loss of value in his investment in the producer goods that he must "carry" until the point of sale. Without the possibility of hedging his investment in producer goods the capitalist engaged in the expanded production is exposed in the way that Marx describes, and the credit markets that finance him are likely to collapse periodically as his investments in constant capital cease to be considered sound collateral as the market for his finished product declines. From this perspective, the point of modern financial theory is that Marx's version of the realization problem can be hedged if the generic capitalist portfolio includes not merely debt and equity, but also puts and calls—and that without a financially correct pricing of puts and calls there can be no robust recycling (pricing) of the two financial byproducts, debt and equity, thrown off in the system of capitalist production that Marx describes in his critique of the failure by Smith and Ricardo to explain surplus value.

What are puts and calls when seen from the perspective of Marx's overall analysis of capitalism? A call is simply a right to appropriate a potentially unlimited gain (surplus value) without further exchange and a put is a vehicle for limiting or shedding exposure to a loss. By defining puts and calls in this way we are already talking about the accumulation and preservation of an always-preexisting social surplus in terms of managing the upside and downside potentials associated with employing labor in the manner Marx describes. But this is a matter of definition rather than technology—it is the technology for manufacturing and pricing puts and calls that allows one to decide *whether or not* investment in expanded production is the optimal route to preserving and expanding the store of capital that already exists. Here producer goods (the enterprise's "capital stock") are merely one possible store of capital that may or may not provide a safer form of collateral than investment in other vehicles of capital preservation such as pure financial assets constructed out of puts and calls.

Once we can separate out the market in vehicles of capital accumulation, we can also see that what Marx described as "relative surplus value" (the driver of expanded production) is merely one possible play on the observed volatilities (historical price spreads) in one particular market and that the general problem is whether one can buy protection for a time against the possibility that future price spreads (the volatility "implied" by the price one will actually get for one's product) will replicate past price spreads (the "historical volatility" that has been reflected in the market to date). Without being able to set a price on puts and calls, and thus to recycle them in a secondary (derivative) market, it is not possible to construct a fully hedged portfolio consisting of debt and equity that can in principle be made fully liquid at all times. And it will not be possible to set up a fully functioning money market that sets the rates at

which funding can be exchanged for safe collateral in the form of tradable government debt and its equivalent as defined by BSM when read as
a left-handed formula, as described by LiPuma in this volume.

The BSM options pricing formula, which framed the financial sector's
solution to the liquidity problem posed by oil, allows one to price (and
thus manufacture) puts and calls by replicating (or fully hedging) them by
using the put-call parity formula, which is the most basic interpretation of
the "law of one price." This means, as we have seen, that Marx's M-C-M'
formula for the self-expansion of capital (surplus value) has two sides.

On the production side Marx's argument draws on the special properties of wage labor that allow the "stock" of capital to grow by exploit-
ing the fact that a surplus in the wage goods sector provides the revenue
for increased investment in the producer goods sector. This assumes that
wage goods, relying on Marx's definition of consumption, do not hold
their value in use. Because consumer goods are defined as the only expenditures that are not also investment—we don't, for example, accumulate surplus wealth by overconsuming—the effect on capital of expansion in the wage goods sector puts pressure for increased investment in
the stock of producer goods necessary to expand growth in output. For
Marx producer goods and money are the only nonfictitious stores of the
surplus value created through the expanded sale of goods that can be
purchased with wages.

The accumulation of wealth in the form of producer goods (and base
money) generates the finance, rather than the production, side of Marx's
M-C-M' formula. But in the absence of puts and calls the basic ability of
the capitalist to preserve wealth by, for example, hedging his investment
in expanded production is simply not expressed as a conceptual corol-
lary of the theory of surplus value itself.

Put most generally the M-C-M' formula for the self-expansion of capital simply states that the capitalist invests in a portfolio (C) in which,
again by definition (and using identical underliers, maturities, and so
forth):

$$\text{Stock} + \text{Put} = \text{Call} + \text{Debt}$$

This formula is a simple identity. Intuitively, it says that, if you own a
stock plus a put giving you downside protection, you can replicate an investment return equivalent to owning a call giving you upside participation on the stock plus the present value of a loan that has a principal

value equivalent to the current stock price. The put-call parity formula also tells you how to solve for the price of a put or a call, which can be replicated by shorting stock (subtracting it from both sides) or taking on debt (subtracting it from both sides) at the prices that would balance the formula if you used it to fully hedge.

Most importantly, the formula says that if you solve for debt, you *can* use puts and calls to have a completely hedged stock portfolio that will earn a return equivalent to the risk-free rate of interest. This means lending to the US government and thus puts the dollar-denominated price of oil back into the picture. Debt denominated in a currency that the obligor can print is the new "gold standard," the definition of "safe collateral," which is now defined as US Treasury obligations. This allows the returns on all other financial instruments to be understood, measured, and expressed as economic spreads (Ricardian rents) based on the premium they pay over the least remunerative asset that can be used for capital preservation, even when real interest rates are nearly zero, or even negative, as in some places they are today.

To summarize where we have come thus far, Marx's M-C-M′ formula describes the purchase of a capital asset in three ways: (1) as an arbitrage opportunity; (2) as a play on the spread between two ways of valuing labor under the assumption that the wage can be neither invested nor collateralized; and (3) as a fully hedged portfolio based on the formula for put-call parity. It turns out, however, that the baseline for hedging is a debt instrument, the return on which is tied to the value of money and thus, ultimately, to the purchasing power of wages denominated in that money. If the return on debt instruments (bonds) is now the paradigm for the portfolio side of M-C-M′ of investments in wages on the production side, then the effect of finance on production is more varied and complex than Marx described.

A striking conclusion is that the expanded manufacture of debt/credit instruments does the kind of double duty in our account of financial asset production that the expanded manufacture of producer goods (constant capital) does in Marx's account of commodity production. In BSM debt-based financial instruments are produced means of asset production that also serve directly as vehicles of capital accumulation to the extent that they serve as collateral. The ability to manufacture puts and calls out of debt and equity is thus the ability to produce liquidity by setting the dynamically changing price at which nonmonetary assets can be converted into money at any time.

An implication for politics is that credit is no less important as a source of revenue than wages and that debt service, based on the collateralization of wages, is no less important as a vehicle for capital accumulation. An indebted student's after-debt ability to pay taxes should be discussed in the same political register as his/her after-tax ability to pay debt (Meister 2011).

Put a little differently, our capacity to assume debt, and the anxieties and uncertainties that lead us to assume it, are becoming almost as important as our labor in creating vehicles of capital accumulation. And secured debt is not merely contractual (Coppola 2013a; Hyman 2011; Levy 2012); it requires the ability to repossess—to seize—the collateral that would have to be liquidated (monetized) in the event of default. This is important for political purposes because those who are indentured are also hands-on occupants of that collateral, which is nothing more or less than the accumulated social wealth that has been alienated from them in the form of debt.

So Marx's concept of the debt-free but uncreditworthy laborer—always an abstract construct—may be obsolete in economies where finance extracts surplus from providing credit to a labor force that far exceeds the numbers employed to produce goods and services sold at a profit. Credit, alongside wages, must here be seen as another way of providing money (cash flow) that is increasingly used to pay for debt service and insurance products along with taxes. Both debt service and insurance must now be lumped together as nonwage vehicles of surplus extraction. This is obvious once we grasp the extent to which the taxpayer is backstopping the provision of expanded private credit facilities to individuals whose debts are incurred to provide housing, healthcare, education, and other basic needs.

To the extent that individuals spend their available cash on debt service, the payment of which increases the credit available to them, we have, I think, a becoming-rent of consumer spending that now goes increasingly to the financial sector that intermediates access to the means of subsistence. This credit system is feasible only because individuals spending time online, whether they are working or not, are constantly producing surplus information that can be used to construct the data spreads out of which financial products, such as credit scores, professional credentials, subprime loans, and other statistical spreads, are constructed (Poon 2009; Callon and Muniesa 2005).

The fact that this data is constantly being harvested, whether people are "at work" or not, means that an increasing amount that people spend "@work" in countries with high GDP per capita can be considered a renting back by capital of some portion of the time they spend online providing the unpaid data inputs out of which financially valuable spreads can be manufactured. What is now variable for many individuals is the spread between paid and unpaid time online, which determines on a netting basis the credit they run up and the credit they pay off in a context that is already controlled by the financial institutions that run the internet-based economy in conjunction with the tax state that allows it to be "free." What has become clear in this becoming-rent-of-wages characteristic of the online service economy is that the extension of credit and the making of payments has become part of a single (and increasingly global) netting system that is ultimately dependent on two industries that occupy its chokepoints: the global *securities* industry that produces collateral (stored value) out of information and the global *security* industry that controls and protects collateral through surveillance and violence.

The umbilicus connecting the securities and security industry in the age of oil has been, as indicated above, the US government bond. To understand the connection between finance and state violence, however, we must grasp the analytical role that risk-free government bonds play in the derivation of the BSM pricing formula from the concept of full hedging and in the technologies for manufacturing fully hedged derivatives that are based upon it.

Compare the world of finance described by BSM to that of Smith's capitalist farmer described above. The hypothetical case in the original paper published by Black and Scholes is that of a holding company, such as a hedge fund, that owns stock in other companies as its only assets. This company, they suppose, buys these stocks using borrowed money and equity that comes from issuing its own stock, based on the present value of its future earnings (which can be reduced by up to 100 percent, depending on what percentage of the total equity is sold). Once this highly financed company is a going concern it may want to generate cash by selling calls on its own shares (and, once it develops the formula for doing this, on any company's shares regardless of its exposure to them). What is the price at which it can manufacture and sell a call option in whatever quantities are demanded without making an uncovered bet on whether the underlying stock price will rise or fall?

In the original Black-Scholes paper, the solution was based on diluting the option with risk-free treasury obligations so that it had the same underlying risk as long-short position in the stock (Black and Scholes 1973). This approach could, as Derman and Taleb point out, have been derived from the definition of put-call parity described above. Here we have version of Marx's general formula for self-expanding capital based entirely on the impossibility of arbitrage between the option price and its hedge in the form of a short position on the stock price collateralized by a risk-free bond (Derman and Taleb 2005).

The solution devised by Merton was to write a formula for manufacturing a dynamically hedged portfolio of securities with known present values that would have the same return as the call option in every possible future state of the world, and could thus be used to construct a perfect hedge. Risk-free bonds are an important element in this dynamically hedged portfolio (Merton 1973). In Merton's derivation, the actual market price—what people are presently willing to pay for an option—is thus indistinguishable from the process of laying out all possible scenarios and then assigning probabilities to the spreads between them in comparison to the risk-neutral baseline.[10] Both derivations of the expected return on risk-free bonds are an important analytical element for pricing puts and calls and, thus, for hedging (preserving the value of) one's accumulated capital position. To price an option under BSM there is no reliance on psychological factors such as expected value or on transactional factors such as supply and demand. What is *absolute* for the purpose of options pricing is not any single price point but rather a historical *spread* of price points relative to the risk-free rate.[11]

But BSM is not merely a technique for pricing calls; it is also a technology for manufacturing calls in fully scalable quantities that are limited only by the supply of safe collateral needed in order to hedge the default risk of all the other credit instruments needed to satisfy the ever-growing demand of capital markets for stores of value (MacKenzie 2006). Indeed, one could reasonably say that the BSM formula for setting the price requires that this price be identical with the cost of manufacturing a perfect hedge—this is its originality. Before BSM, call options were available on boutique markets, but, because the counterparties were making bets with prohibitively high odds, these options contracts were sold in limited quantities at a very high price that discouraged demand. BSM allowed options contracts to be produced in large quantities at a competitive price without any added risk exposure provided that the manufacturer of the option who doesn't want to make a bet on the underlier completely hedges his position and thus charges only for the service performed. In this sense, the risk of manufacturing calls is no more of a gamble than that of manufacturing any other product—one can make as much as one can sell. So the hypothetical company BSM describes could simply be in a high-volume business of manufacturing financial products, such as calls, for entities that wish to hold these derivative products as vehicles for preserving or increasing stored value, depending on whether the protection they provide is being bought or sold.

The only safe collateral that does not have to be fully hedged in BSM is, as we have seen, the US government bond: it is repayable in US dollars that effectively substitute for the hedge (because the Fed can create them) and that earn the rate of return that a risk-neutral portfolio would replicate.[12] So, an increasing supply of these safe vehicles for capital preservation is necessary as the financial equivalent of a raw material for manufacturing all the other financial derivatives, based on puts and calls, that provide liquidity in capital markets and thus reduce the need for increasing the supply of base money that would be demanded for the liquidation of collateral in the event of a crash.

In this sense, the US Treasury, backed by its own banking agent, the Fed, must create enough debt to satisfy the demand of global financial markets for safe assets, while controlling inflation through limits on public spending. Not all countries can do this. But, because the US has its own central bank that has been free since the 1980s to monetize government debt without significant inflation, the US Treasury has in effect become the largest supplier of AAA-rated ("safe") collateral that allows the shadow banking system and vast global repo market to net out its accounts at the end of each trading day without any direct government guarantee. The indirect guarantee, of course, is that US government-backed assets "cannot ever become unsafe" as a result of inflationary spending policies, including economic stimulus (Gourinchas and Jeanne 2012; Gorton and Metrick 2010b; Garcia 2011; Coppola 2013b; Kaminska 2011a). The bond markets thus decree that we must, paradoxically, cut our deficits so we can be allowed to increase our total debt at lower cost.

This means, quite simply, that expanding the dollar value of the capital asset market requires, as a raw material for making hedges, an ever-expanding supply of credit that satisfies an expanding demand for debt.

This total credit market debt must be *both* public and private—both components are necessary for the equations to work so that puts and calls can be privately manufactured at a price necessary to meet the demand for both currency stabilization and capital accumulation, which requires preserving the global liquidity of financial asset markets.

This argument suggests that, just as the expansion of commodity production once required the global growth of labor force participation, so the expansion of financial asset production now requires the global growth of forms of indebtedness (or indenture) that are the social conditions of capital accumulation as we know it—along with the banks of information necessary to quantify and hedge the risks associated with such lending. The Tunisian fruit vender who started Arab Spring by immolating himself is possibly an example of an underemployed debtor who owed more money than he could repay. But I assume this possibility, not on the basis of specific knowledge but because I have read books describing how conditionalities on the refinancing of public debt by the world bank and Gulf States (where the Arab Spring was not allowed to blossom) actually require the production and measurement of relational values—social capital seen as data "spreads"—that could be used as a basis for expanding private credit, often in the form of microcredit while hedging the resulting credit risk.[13]

Timothy Mitchell has convincingly described in detail the "economization," or social production of a credit-based "economy," as a form of "biopolitics" (producing manageable subjectivities) that is essential to the program of international organizations and NGOs operating in the Middle East (Mitchell 2002; Goldman 2005; Elyachar 2005; Dalyan 2009). Our view of the same phenomenon is that greater *knowledge* of the "risks" people face in an increasingly "uncertain" world aims to develop their capacity to "make better choices"—essentially a form of hedging behavior that makes them potential customers for financial products, such as microcredit and also educational certificates from for-profit global institutions that advertise themselves as selling options to work for multinational corporations, NGOs—and even, possibly, to immigrate to a place where those credentials are transferable for academic credit (Meister 2013). The more people know about the risks they face, the more anxious they are expected to be—and the more need they are likely to feel for interactive financial products that teach them to be "better choosers" under conditions of uncertainty.[14] Eventually, they may come to see even their ethnic differences and disparate cultural heritages—often a source of cyclical violence—as "spreads" on lifestyle options that can attract global capital-seeking investment opportunities in the tourist and recreation industries (Comaroff and Comaroff 2009).

In such a global context the role of the US state in advancing financial capitalism is not primarily, as David Graeber says, to enforce the repayment of debts owed by its own citizens (which originates in the pledge of bodily indenture) but rather to provide the safe collateral that allows debt-based instruments to remain liquid rather than be liquidated.[15] This requires the repression—or silencing—of political demands in the United States that would subvert the system of extensive cross-collateralization out of which the liquidity of the global financial system is produced. But it also, and no less fundamentally, requires the funding and maintenance of a global security industry that protects the very fragile system of information and collateralization on which securitization rests from being compromised. We have thus seen, particularly since 2007, a militarization of finance on the model of the "war on terror" along with a corresponding financialization of the military as corporate providers of "security services" become the fastest-growing sector of the global defense industry—providing coverage domestically, internationally, and across cyberspace.

The political question in this paper concerns the relation of security to securitization. Can the technologies used to perform and enforce liquidity be subverted to become forms of resistance that leverage the potential for illiquidity? Did the leaders on Wall Street (picture them for a moment as saboteurs or suicide bombers attacking the general economy) show the Occupy movement the way to do this by threatening to blow up the financial system and themselves along with it when they said that *none* of their collateral could be valued unless essentially all of it was guaranteed by the government at a hundred cents on the dollar?[16]

Because all this collateral—the sum of accumulated capital wealth—is already in "our" collective hands we have (in at least a notional sense) the collective power to threaten the kind of global liquidity crisis that the suicide bombers on Wall Street threatened to bring down upon themselves. In this respect the nodes of liquidity in today's financial system are, at least arguably, parallel to the points of passage and potential worker power in industrial wealth production in the age of coal. These nodes of liquidity make the system vulnerable and open to democratic pressures that could consist of the popular seizure or repossession of what financial markets value as collateral. Threatening liquidity in this way can be seen as a complement, or even an alternative, to reoccupying semipublic spaces, like Tahrir Square and Zucotti Park, that are merely jumping-off points for a hoped-for future democratization of the accumulated wealth that now lies in private hands. Bringing on a liquidity crisis is, of course, a threat to destroy that accumulated wealth, assuming "we" as activists have the nerve to act on the vulnerabilities in the financial system revealed in 2008. Posing threats is what saboteurs and strikers know how to do; such tactics can produce a higher wage, more progressive income taxes, and some redistributive social programs in return for leaving largely intact the distribution of accumulated wealth.

But the ultimate subversion of these technologies would be to use them against themselves to appropriate and redistribute the accumulated social wealth that has been collectively produced. To do this we need to grasp where the gears of accumulation and production mesh. Marx's genius was to do this with the concepts of constant capital and technologies for creating spreads in relative surplus value in order to explain and subvert the process of industrialization. The question is whether we (whoever "we" may be) can do something similar with technologies for creating financial spreads and then for privatizing the information used to exploit them. [17] We could then potentially build upon the ways in which the financial system creates the demand for global debt necessary to absorb the ever-expanding supply by teaching an increasingly linked-in population about the multiple dangers existing in an increasingly linked-in world that they can hedge by purchasing both securities and the security systems needed to protect them (including increased state and private surveillance). In the literature on "agent-centered development" this informational process that sells "resilience" products to alleviate anxiety is known as "capacity-building" (Chandler 2013).

But for our purposes the wide use of these technologies is also a revelation of the role of subjectivity production in the technologies that produce a glut of information to the public in ways that simultaneously generate user data out of which financial spreads and the products to hedge them can be constructed.[18] The problem, perhaps obvious, about constructing knowledge as "information" is that it often tells us what we did not know about our past risks in a way that tends to heighten our present uncertainty about the future. The more we know that we did not know, the greater need we feel for more such information in order to become better choosers. And the more receptive we will be to financial and other products that will hedge our uncertainty about whether our future will be more like the past than we could have known the present to be in advance. The result is a form of data-driven ignorance about when or if one can ever know what to do next (Mirowski 2013).

We are actually part of a supply chain of data—produced through our simultaneous participation in the financial system, the security system, and the open internet itself—that is mined to produce financial wealth in the form of both securities and security. (Climate insecurity may even contribute to this wealth production dynamic.) How are we to think logistically and operationally about ways in which the capacity of this system to extract and expand information (along with everything else on the supply chain) can be used to reconfigure the power actually held by those of us who occupy choke-points in the system? Why have seizing these forms of collective power become *almost* unthinkable to us as debtors for whom every shock produces a tightening of credit conditions (Mezzadra and Neilson 2013)? The parallelism I see between the role of debt and information in financialized capitalism and Marx's account of producer goods in industrialized capitalism may help to bring back the kinds of practical questions about democracy familiar to us from the age of coal. We may then need to think of our notional collective power over the financial system as simultaneously a kind of logistical/operational power that some of "us" may have much more of than others.

What do I mean by this? I have been talking about a becoming-rent of profit based on the use of informational technologies to create what Marx called relative surplus value out of data spreads. This parallels the way that early convergences of rent and profit were created out of productivity spreads in manufacturing and fertility spreads in agriculture under conditions of industrialization. Such openings are, as they were for Marx, technological because the role of technology in capitalism is to produce spreads that can be arbitraged to create economic rents that can be accumulated in the form of assets that yield those expected returns. It should be apparent from the foregoing argument that cognitive capital, including finance, is a technology for producing spreads that are valued because the *same* system creates (and more importantly transmits) doubts about how long the present can last. These doubts are based on our ever-growing knowledge of the risks that we have born in the past. This dynamic is clear enough from the way energy crises and shocks increase the financial value of oil in the ground. It is also clear from the ways in which the revealed fragility of our financial system—the constant threat of illiquidity—has increased the financial value of securities designed to prolong the present financial system's survival, beginning with the expansion and hoarding of "safe credit."

There are, I have suggested, at least two connected points of vulnerability in this becoming-rent of profit that are subject to coordinated collective action to disrupt financialization's supply chain. The first is the liquidity of collateral. The second is the private enclosure (Marx's original form of accumulation) of the informational commons used to manufacture spreads. The simultaneous public expansion and private appropriation of these two forms of material abundance are what we might call, in Marx's spirit (and following Negri), "absolute rent" rather than "relative rent." I use this term because both making collateral liquid and enclosing the informational commons are instrumentalized forms of violence derived from a fundamental insecurity at the heart of securitization itself. This could conceivably be opposed by disruptive and subversive uses of the same technologies that are already being used to appropriate the surplus that is already present (Negri 2010). There is really plenty to go around when we are talking about wealth in the form of liquid collateral and the information on which it is based.

But today Big Data and the techniques used to aggregate and mine it are defined as either proprietary (the trade secrets of corporations) or military (the intelligence secrets of the state). Often these converge, as when the state secures, and thus conducts surveillance, on the trade secrets of corporations. We now know that the state also surveils directly in real time the trading on financial markets, ostensibly to protect them from disruptions due to hacking and subversion (as distinct from the "normal" effects of self-interest and greed). No less pervasive is the practice of private informatics companies making their intelligence gathering available to states on an exclusive or nonexclusive basis. This occurs both through consulting contracts with the state or as a result of direct seizure. One response that echoes the nineteenth-century demand for "nationalization" would be a call to socialize Big Data that, in its present form, was never owned by anyone before it was produced. The idea would be to make what is now proprietary a subject of public scrutiny upon which democratic demands could be made. This would be in contradistinction to "nationalization" of Big Data as a code word for militarization now dressed up as a populist rejoinder to the globalization and financialization of all information and communication.

ROBERT MEISTER   171

If "nationalization" won't work as our slogan, an alternative available response to "globalization" and "financialization" is to use "our" various oppositional grids and networks to consider the possibility of a new "international" movement. Such a movement would operate at a nodal site to create distributed disruptions that threaten the logic of privatized accumulation of collateral and information. Possible slogans to oppose this privatization or enclosure could be "socialize collateral" and "socialize data." Today, invoking "the social" in this way is but a gesture against the encroachment of proprietary and national access to information that we once considered "personal" and even "private." If asserting the "social" against both the private and the public can still be used to reclaim collective nonpublic information about society that is selectively hidden from its object by corporations and states, then there is still a specter of communism underlying the current movements to democratize finance. This specter is importantly not adequately captured by the idea of debt forgiveness. It is much better expressed by some idea of occupying an informational "commons" that now has been secured and securitized, but that will never have been a commons until we actually make it so. One problem with taking such an approach is the relation of the sort of democratizing movement I describe to both anarchism and terrorism. The same level of disruptions to our networks and grids can be caused by ten million individuals acting in concert (to crash, for example, a payments system or database) and by a single "malicious user" generating ten million copies of the same message or algorithm.

The fact that collateral and data notionally belongs to "us" (and may already lie in our hands) should not be a distraction from the fact that only *some* of us (perhaps very few) are needed to seize logistical power over the financial supply chain. Once we ourselves recognize how little it would take—how few of "us"—to crash our system, we must immediately acknowledge that this is already known by everyone else. This is why the general public so easily acquiesces in the use of the full state security apparatus to crack down on breaches and leaks by security workers like Chelsea Manning and even the most benign-seeming "hackers" like Aaron Swartz.

The fewer of us it would take to make the financial system illiquid, the harder it becomes to assert this as a possible form of democratic mass action. The more fragile the technologies of a financialized administrative order, the easier it is for those who claim private ownership of collateral to say that they will do this to themselves if we do anything to upset their "confidence" in the system's basic security. In speaking of inves-tor "confidence" we are talking the subjectivity of finance—what Keynes called "animal spirits." This is also a factor that left-Keynesians recog-nized from the start as a political (security) limit on the project of expert management of liquidity for democratic ends (Kalecki 1943; Akerlof and Shiller 2009). Coal miners addressed this issue by forming labor unions that entered electoral politics in order to produce the breadth of support necessary to legitimate a general strike.

Our problem is to imagine a popular movement broad enough to le-gitimate the acts of sabotage that are possible in "our" name. Do num-bers matter? Do intentions? Are McKenzie Wark's "hacktivists" the coalminers of today? Are "we" the equivalent of a union organizing to raise democratic demands (Wark 2004)? And, if we fear such possibil-ities, must we try to incrementally reverse the becoming-rent of profit with a service-based economy in which people are paid for more of the time they presently spend online providing information for free? If busi-nesses were created to organize these services, would we call the result a "becoming-profit of rent"? Such questions bring us to the role of popular democracy in alliance with a potentially disruptive movement that could engage in acts of sabotage or direct action.

One way of describing the present situation is this: People produce information and need money, but they are subject to surveillance and precarity that make them the easy prey of financial and governmental institutions. These claim to offer people better choices in a dangerous world. Our problem is to find a popular (indeed universal) truth of this situation that is inexpressible within our present situation. The expres-sion adequate to our condition would require real change rather than a mere unfolding of present tendencies.[19]

Is "making money" the idea that is supposed to drive the system met-aphorically because the system does not allow people to do it literally? Marx's argument is quite simply that workers do not make money except in a metaphorical sense that requires them to go through a ritual of sim-ple reproduction based on existential uncertainty about where they will get their next meal. He thus saw democratic potential in the demand to make money in a nonmetaphorical (that is, metonymic) sense that would unite those with power to shut production down to what he called "the reserve army of the unemployed" whose fundamental insecurity under-pinned the system of wage labor. By assuming, ahistorically, that the gold standard operated as a permanent, rather than transitional, con-straint on the British state's response to wage demands, Marx did not see the threat of illiquidity (the demand for cash because credit instruments can't be priced) as the general form of instability that drove industrial capitalism, even as he described it.

He thus failed to understand how the nonmetaphorical—literal—power to "make money" can be expressed formally as the power to incur debt that is fully redeemable in a currency that you can produce as needed for this purpose. This *exceptional* relation between credit and its repayment is, like legitimate violence, the monopoly of states—and, in a global system based on financialization and humanitarian intervention, of a very few states. Since around 1973 this global system has been excluding the state power to make money from democratic control.[20] In today's capitalism states make money literally in order to create the liquidity of investment vehicles that allows wealth to be accumulated in metaphoric (monetary) form without actually being money. If individuals could make money in a literal sense, their product would be a direct claim, or credit, against the borrowing power of the state. This is the very thing that capitalism today makes impossible. Marx tried to capture this in his inaccurate description of the worker as inherently debt free and uncreditworthy. Correctly understood, this is merely an inability to make money by earning a wage, while still being subject to the discipline of paying cash for the means of subsistence.

Put very crudely, it seems to me that the collective demand for money—neither wages nor credit, but simply money as a redistribution of wealth—could be disruptive of the financial system in the sense of making a common claim on the publicly created and guaranteed collateral that is used to secure accumulated wealth that remains in private hands. As a democratic program, what could be simpler than that? Perhaps we only now—and at long last—have what can be usefully attacked as capitalism because the financial sector (and not heavy industry or mining) is the emergent site of democratic demands that have the potential for shutting down the system as a whole if they are not addressed. But equally we must read much of what government and the financial sector do in response as a deliberate way to evade or repress such demands.

CHAPTER FIVE

From the Critique of Political Economy to the Critique of Finance

Randy Martin, New York University

W ere Marx to write *Capital* today, or if the writing of capital were to pick up now where he left off then, the critique of political economy would necessarily morph into the domain of finance. His project was to enter into the internal logic of capital's apparent self-expansion in order to discern how value is crafted. Finance is now the means by which value is adduced as once political economy had been. Before finance came to predominate what Marx termed "the wealth of society," and for nearly a century after his death, a distinct domain of the economy emerged that was meant to integrate a national population and partition the political action of the state from self-regulating markets. So our critical attentions must focus on this now predominant way of pricing what had been unpriced and aligning populations with a particular scheme of a value.

Finance operates less on the great beyond than through the spaces between, the spreads between prices where risk is hedged through arbitrage, which is the discovery and disclosure through investment of a difference in price in different circumstances that then resets what will momentarily stand as the appropriate price. Arbitrage is the means through which a volatile field of trading in assets is kept liquid. While finance is a crucial condition for industrial capitalism, its operations and logics now serve to orient the means and ends of amassing wealth, of capturing profitability, the way in which commodity production once did. But this is not a brave new world, a risk society that has moved beyond capitalism. Rather, the account that unfolds across the three volumes of *Capital* positions finance as the movement from production into circulation and the need to anticipate the risks involved in failing to realize potential profits, as a development already immanent in Marx's critique. It is therefore possible to return to his critique of political economy and read it in reverse as yielding the critique of finance if only we can derive the terms of movement that are implied yet unnamed there in what capital needed to be and what it will become.

Capital opens with a declaration of where an immanent critique of the prevalent value form must begin. "The wealth of those societies in which the capitalist mode of production prevails, presents itself as 'an immense accumulation of commodities,' its unit being a single commodity. Our investigation must therefore begin with the analysis of a commodity" (Marx 1967a). Wealth here is a matter of self-presentation, of a part, a unit, the commodity, that stands in for the whole of society. The whole is not static but compelled by ongoing self-expansion, an immense accumulation that is its ambition and its measure of success. Wealth, for Marx, has a double valence. It is at once quantitative, a seemingly self-expanding magnitude of money, and qualitative, a deepening interdependence among those whose collective efforts make society possible. The social principle named in this relation between part and whole is one of an expansive mutual indebtedness. Not simply a sum of parts that could be allocated for better or ill in some formula of distributive justice, Marx is concerned with understanding the collective social capacity evident in mutual indebtedness that makes it possible to posit what society could be. Mutual indebtedness and associated labor are more socially potent concepts than those of interconnectedness and shared foundations that inform more conventional ideas about how people and things, parts and wholes, bonds and ties comprise a given understanding of social life.[1] Taking wealth as the subject and object of the social amounts to a claim that the parts rendered whole, associated labor, can make the whole represented by means of its discretely circulating parts, that is, through money. The immense accumulation, the drive that capital expands or dies, prevails over other extant possibilities by which wealth could be generated and valued. Wealth in this regard is but a metaphor for the self-expansion of capital.

This initial sentence in volume 1 regarding wealth and the commodity amounts to a pairing of metaphor (wealth looks like a commodity) and metonym (commodities stand in for wealth as such). Linking metonym and metaphor in this way draws a proxy for the whole inside of a relation of equivalence, a coupling that gives us nothing less than the formula for capital itself, M-C-M'. The force of Marx's subsequent analysis is to demonstrate that what allows money to be made from money is the capacity to extract more value from a particular commodity, labor power, than is paid to laborers for their time in the form of hourly wages. Labor, the metonymic commodity of the formula, becomes the metaphoric equivalence of difference from capital that is turned into something just like capital, the ability to get more of it by accelerating what it gets from labor. Labor is that commodity whose ratio of return changes with the efficiency of production, a quality Marx terms variable capital. The generalization of this condition is wrought through relations of force by which labor is freed from its conditions of self-subsistence. As a consequence, labor possesses nothing but time given over to a space of production in which, lacking direct access to means of subsistence and therefore compelled to work for others, it possesses no ownership. The human capacity to make a society according to its wants is translated into that immense accumulation of things. At the same time, abstracting and generalizing labor engenders the very associations and interdependence of productive activity by which a world of things is made possible.

This labor theory of value, centered on the commodity, is purportedly what the advent of economy, as a model of price making based on information equilibrium in the neoclassical reckoning, puts to an end. Finance, as we know, posits equilibrium as its physical condition expressed in the "law of one price" but traffics in volatility. Price making is derived not simply from commodity production or information flows but from risk. Derivatives are in this regard now the unit of wealth in complex and multiple ways associated with the universal equivalent of money (as token, measure, and store) for finance in the way that commodities served for political economy. While the analysis of capital has long since commenced, it must proceed from primitive to contemporary mysteries of the form of wealth and the orientation of value—requiring a shift in terms from M-C-M' to M-D-M'. Like the commodity, the derivative is the instrument of the contemporary value form and also what drives the self-expansion of value whereby money seemingly turns itself into more money. But derivatives, even if they are called upon to craft the architecture of equivalence that had been associated with money as such, are themselves parts and not whole commodities.

Derivatives are contracts that price the variable attributes of underlying commodities such as interest, exchange rates, or swings in stock price that pose prospects of future gain or loss. Derivatives are priced through an ongoing recalibration between the relation of a specific risk exposure on a position to buy or sell at a given time and the movement of the market as a whole. While derivatives align part and whole through a calculation of shared exposure to risk, at the same time they complicate that very relationship of part to whole. They connect what is internal to production and what external to it. They also relate what lies within the self-expansion of capital and what beyond it. Marx's analysis rested upon a series of clearly delineated relations of space and time both in terms of distinct spheres of production and circulation and also of a Newtonian physics of rate (or velocity) and mass. Yet Marx can also be read as seeing the fissures in these boundary conditions by which capital is accumulated that could point beyond that particular self-rationalizing logic of social wealth.

The critique of finance, it follows, is an inquiry into the wealth of society where risk is central to the value form, its measure, medium, and store most legible in the derivative. Had Marx stopped his analysis of capital with volume 1 (a place where much Marxism also rests), there might be little reason to turn to his work to transpose the commodity into the derivative. But once he has shown that capitalist production relies upon a socialization of labor that it ultimately cannot abide, he moves on to two additional volumes and analytic turns. Volume 2 is an analysis of the circulation of capital as a drive to compress as much as possible the time between investing capital and realizing its expansion (M-M'). Volume 3 is the arc of capital's grand amalgamation in pursuit of emancipation from its own predicaments of accumulation through a turn to finance (volume 3), which he calls "social capital." With economy and finance as we will come to know them in contemporary parlance still ahead of him, Marx does not have an explicit critical vocabulary of risk. Instead, his analysis of the pursuit of profit in the face of its tendency to fall or fail to realize what capital promises and demands is a statement of the problem of risk or forces of danger in the making that lie at the center of accumulation.

Through a curious dyslexia of history his formulation of a law of a tendency has frequently been inverted as the tendency of a law: profits fall and capitalism falls apart.[2] The latter leaves us waiting for Godot, or Lefty, or the apocalypse, in the form of a final crisis or crash of accumulation, a condition of utter failure that ruptures what was from what could be and ushers in a fundamentally different order that will arise in a newly wrought space and time of the change to come. The notion of the law of a tendency instead leads to something rather different, for a tendency is about the likelihood of a certain trajectory, a moment within a larger movement. Rather than a pure break between what is and what could be, the tendency provokes an incessant reading of the future into the present and with what is happening elsewhere to what can be done close to hand. The result of mixing this grammar of time and space elicits a consistent array of maneuvers or hedges against unwanted outcomes that we would now refer to as risk management. Capital accumulates on the promise of a future that always threatens not to come. Anticipating failure, and turning it into opportunity, measures must be taken, even if they are at odds with one another. In paeans to entrepreneurialism or the intrinsic dynamism of capitalism itself, risk justifies reward, but in a Marxist key it could return us to the valuation of wealth that lie at the heart of political economy.[3]

There are three chapters in volume 3 (chapters 13–15) that explicate this tendency for profit failure or what contemporary finance treats as the impetus for pricing risk. The first states the principle of failure that is a feature of the labor process in which the effort to maximize productivity undermines the basis of profitability. Chapter 14 examines the countertendencies or counteracting influences that "cross and annul the effect" presented by challenges internal to production with a series of moves both in and outside the workplace. Chapter 15 poses the internal contradictions that these colliding forces deliver to the problem of accumulation that posits the limits of capital to continue without some kind of fundamental reformulation. From there Marx proceeds to develop the various forms of banking and financial institutions as he saw them, so as to understand the fissures among various sources of profit and the efforts to render these commensurable with the idea of social capital.

Let us look at the arguments of each of the three chapters in turn with an eye toward how they might allow us to imagine where the work of the derivative emerges from the problems posed for accumulation by commodity production, again less as an invocation of historical periodization than of how to approach the immanence of finance to political economy. First, let us recall that the production of commodities in the labor process is prior to the realization of the value of those commodities in the sphere of circulation or the market, where sale of goods converts the value back into the money form by means of price so that the cycle or circuit of accumulation can begin anew. The future in this sense is ever the enemy of the present, for it bears the uncertainty as to whether or not value will be realized. Complicating this is the opacity of the relation between production and circulation (Marx's name for the labor process, good Victorian that he is, is the "hidden abode of production").[4] This invisibility is doubled for labor, whose products are alienated from them and no longer appear as their own, but also for capital, which strives to extract as much labor as possible from the time given in the working day without assurance that what gets made on the shop floor will actually be sold in the marketplace.

This separation of spaces between the realms of supply and of demand is part of the irrationality of the market that socialist planning might rectify and that finance sought to resolve by effacing that very separation in space and time. But we get ahead of ourselves, which is certainly a tendency that the derivative seeks to correct by pricing what could promote profit failure in distant time and place to a very actionable present. Meanwhile, for nineteenth-century manufacturing the dilemma remains that for a given array of people, machines, and materials, the way to extract more value in the same working day focuses on getting laborers to work harder by expending more of their laboring capacity under given conditions of time, design, and inputs, and producing a greater measure of commodities than they receive in wages. These two measures, or the ratio between the equivalence of goods they are paid for and the portion in excess of their wages that Marx termed surplus value, is the basis for the rate of exploitation. Add to this a second ratio between the variable portion of capital that is a property of living labor and measured in wages and the constant or fixed costs that that are utilized for each unit of a commodity produced, a ratio between the living and the dead that Marx termed the organic composition of capital.

And here's the rub. Labor is compelled by management under the sway of furthering accumulation to expend more effort in the same time and generate a greater amount or mass of goods. Yet by doing so its own proportion of the total costs expended on living labor is reduced. Working harder, making more under given conditions of production results in wages being a smaller proportion of the daily wealth that their labor yields. In turn, the opportunity for exploitation is diminished and the ratio of variable to constant capital is lessened, thereby lowering the rate of profit. Getting workers to work harder in a day, the aim of management, is called a speed-up, increasing productivity, or efficiency, referencing that other meaning of rate as velocity. Marx begins the discussion of the tendency for rates of profit to fall by placing velocity of profit in opposition to mass, which in Newtonian terms of inertial mass is defined as an object's resistance to acceleration. "Since the mass of the employed living labour is continually on the decline as compared to the mass of materialized labour set in motion by it, i.e., to the productively consumed means of production, it follows that the portion of living labour, unpaid and congealed in surplus-value, must also be continually on the decrease compared to the amount of value represented by the invested total capital. Since the ratio of the mass of surplus-value to the value of the invested total capital forms the rate of profit, this rate must constantly fall" (Marx 1967b, 213). So we have a physics problem, a conflict between time and space that Marx used to figure the whole of capitalist accumulation as the annihilation of space by time, a means through which the resistant mass would be overcome by the velocity of exploitation.

Notice therefore that in volume 1 there is already a problem stated with rates of profit within the production process. Squeezing more surplus value out of the time labor is expended during the course of the working day has an immediate effect of increasing the rate of profit. At the same time, increasing the rate of exploitation sets off all manner of responses from labor itself in the form of struggles over the length of the working day, factory conditions, claims on pay—all of which is happening in the context of competition among capitalists to maximize returns. Consequently, capital will be pressed to replace workers with machines where possible and therefore hasten the change in ratio between living labor, or variable capital, and fixed inputs, or constant capital. This too is an extended narrative of pushes and pulls, tendencies and countertendencies, in which Marx is unpacking a series of measures in conflicted relation. Together these various measures describe both steps taken to force labor from populations and consolidations of those actions as appreciable gains. A tension is evidenced between threats on profit's acceleration (how much more can be extracted under any given productive arrangements), compensated for by an expansion of its mass. This interplay between rate and mass is what Marx called intensive versus extensive expansions of surplus value. All this comes before Marx gets to the heart of the realization problem, which is what to do with all the value that labor has produced once commodities have been alienated from producers. These are relations (especially in Marx's day, for something like a consumer society has been implemented to expand circuits of accumulation) largely between various capitalists. Volume 2 details the drive to accelerate this process of realizing surplus value, effectively an effort to drive the overall time of circulation as close to zero as possible. Here Marx starts with the simple circuit and adds greater temporal and spatial complexity until arriving at an understanding of what he terms the aggregate social capital, but at the heart of the problem of circulation is compressing this spatial differentiation into an accelerating temporal rate. "The more the metamorphoses of circulation of a certain capital are only ideal, i.e., the more the time of circulation is equal to zero, or approaches zero, the more does capital function, the more does its productivity and the self-expansion of its value increase. For instance, if a capitalist executes an order by the terms of which he receives payment on delivery of the product, and if this payment is made in his own means of production, the time of circulation approaches zero" (Marx 1967b, 125).

Volume 3 can be read as an account of how this expansion of wealth-making capacity creates a greater scale and scope not only of the pathways of circulation but of mutually associated labor and capital that expands the interdependencies that constitute society as a whole. At the same time the expanding social integuments, and the accumulation of capital, the wealth of society, and the sociality of wealth, can become unmoored. The discussion of the tendency for profit failure is the hinge on which capital stands in a hostile relation to the very sociality it rests upon. Chapter 13 of volume 3 on the Law of the Tendency provides the bridge between the realms of production and of circulation of the separate spheres that are the basis for volumes 1 and 2 of *Capital*, where value is made and where it is priced.

There are three moments of the analysis of the tendency that move us between these two spheres of private production and market realization where the separation opens problems of coordination and articulation much as it does in the case of the Victorian separate spheres. The spatial disjunction of these spheres places them in tension with one another— the larger point of Marx's critique—which is that capitalism amasses a productive capacity for which it has no future. The first moment is the inverse relation between mass and rate of profit as described. The second is an elaboration of the implications of changes in the rate of profit for the relation between variable and constant capital (again, what he terms the organic composition) and the consequent relation between increased productivity and increased surplus population. This last is also a problem of the relation between mass and rate, for as labor is rendered more productive through the squeeze of increasing the amount of surplus it produces and replacing it with machines that accelerate use of constant capital, relatively less working time is required to produce the same amount of commodities.

Hence, while the mass of labor can continue to increase through expansion of economic activity, the ratio of the employed to those excessed as no longer required to maintain certain levels of productivity continues to throw labor out of the workforce. Marx was observing this process in the midst of colonialism, but we can certainly see it in effect today, in the industrial workforce from Europe to the United States and Japan and in the inability to absorb rural migrant populations displaced from collapsing agriculture in India and China. The third moment of this tension between rate and mass comes with the increasing acceleration of accumulation, the rapid advance of turnover times in production but also the rush toward global markets that speed the incorporation of populations into the labor process. The acceleration of the rate of accumulation meets its limitation in the decrease in the amount of labor required for the production of commodities, which leads to a fall in commodity prices, which in turn places pressure on the rate of profit. The success in the capitalist mode of production prevailing over others cheapens the very commodities by which profit would be realized.

The chapters in volume 3 that follow this presentation of the tendency make clear that Marx does not see the falling rate as capital's endgame, but as occasioning a whole range of responses among various capitals that compel them into the mutual association or intercommensurability that Dick Bryan and Michael Rafferty see as the heart of contemporary finance. "Derivatives are thereby the bearers of contestability. So they are crucial to the link between money, price and fundamental value not because they *actually* determine fundamental values (for there are no truths here) but because they are the way in which the market judges or perceives fundamental value. They turn *the contestability* of fundamental value into a tradable commodity. In so doing, they provide a market benchmark for an unknowable value" (Bryan and Rafferty 2006, 37). Chapter 14, "Counteracting Influences," lists six factors that cancel and annul the tendency: (1) the increasing intensity of exploitation, expansion of the working day, intensification of labor; (2) the depression of wages below the value of labor power; (3) cheapening the elements of constant capital; (4) relative overpopulation; (5) foreign trade that also diminishes variable capital and encourages overproduction; and (6) the increase of stock capital that begins to associate profits from interest, rent and production.

These six influences still resonate even if their reference and significance has mutated. In the aftermath of the great financial bailout of 2008, productivity has been robust, mandatory overtime common; furloughs and nonreplacement of positions have meant that relatively fewer workers are contributing more surplus value. The UAW contract that halved wages from \$28 to \$14 per hour certainly reflects a depression of wages, as does the decline in the median household income by \$4,000 between 2007 and 2013. Apple's outsized profits until their fall in 2013 were as much a story of cheapening inputs through global supply chains as a triumph of branding and design.[5] Relative overpopulation, which Marx understood to have a historical specificity, now takes a form less of a labor reservoir that depresses the price of labor power (though high unemployment certainly has that effect) but of pressing populations out of the labor market altogether. For example, in 2000, 18.5 percent of those aged 25 to 34 were considered outside the labor force. By 2011 that figure had risen to 26.6 percent for the same age group (Leonhardt 2013). What passes as urban policy—whether deliberate, such as the "reconstruction" of New Orleans or Baghdad, or through neglect as in Detroit or Buffalo—produces large-scale depopulation from what were once centers of employment and therefore a surplus population beyond the formal workforce. For the United States, precipitous drops in auto sales were one sign of the link between foreign trade and overproduction. Finally, what came to be called the housing bubble that drove the stock market expansion through 2007 was, among other things, a means of associating profits from rents, interest, and production (of new housing starts) through such instruments as mortgage-backed securities. But Marx's larger point is to understand these factors not as a laundry list but as constituting a field of various approaches to the persistent prospect of profit failure.

Another way of understanding these counteracting influences, therefore, would be as hedge strategies to "cross and annul" the pressures for profit to fail to be realized. For each challenge, there is not only an action taken in the opposite direction but a cumulative array of possible strategies that seek to close the gap between what is internal and external to production. The tendencies and counteracting influences, therefore, begin to look something like a range of spreads in a series of price-able risks, with production standing as the underlying value from which all manner of departures in various directions are imaginable.

These six influences range from what management can do at the point of production (extract more labor over longer working days and increase the scale of machinery to lower fixed costs) to external factors such as a working population increasing faster than available employment, replacing labor within a country through an international division of labor, or facilitating the passage of profit from one site or source to another through stock exchanges. But they also represent the range of possible adjustments to profit sources that follow the logic of a balanced portfolio. If profit is jeopardized through one means it can be compensated through another. The counteracting influences therefore articulate what it would mean to manage risk in relation to the market as a whole. The relation between tendencies and countertendencies addresses the general disruption between the realms of production and circulation, but also maps a series of gaps that can be filled by acting across the spread, or by means of arbitrage. Read together, the play between tendencies and countertendencies suggests a series of gaps or spreads and movements to close those differences through action on a particular point of leverage. The dialectic of mass and rate, of space and time, would name that active and ongoing process through which arbitrage becomes necessary.

Chapter 15, "The Internal Contradictions of the Law," suggests that as for history, laws generate irregularities that they cannot contain. Here too Marx articulates three moments of tension between the tendencies and countertendencies. The first pertains to the drop in the ratio of labor in proportion to employed capital, which hastens the concentration (of market share by fewer firms within a given industry) and centralization (by conglomerates across different industries or fields) of capital and the severing of the conditions of production from the producers. The second is the conflict between the expansion of production and the production of surplus value. Consequently, less labor time is required for the reproduction of labor, as less and less of the working day is required to go toward the worker's wage as the ratio of surplus value rises. At the same time, a lowered quantity of labor is needed to set capital in motion, as labor costs become less of the total costs of production.

But as capital succeeds in suppressing the proportion of labor needed for production, its relation to its workforce, especially one that is organized or has costs of social reproduction that include such things as education and health care, shifts from a needed input to an intolerable con-straint. The labor that once provided a basis for expanded accumulation becomes in its particular configuration of wages and social benefits an obstacle for securing further profit; capital flees the workforce that had been the very social basis of wealth. Finally, the excess of capital that cannot be absorbed in further production and the absence of investment opportunities that promise suitable rates of return thereby idle capital. Wealth rendered unproductive confronts the masses of population that cannot be absorbed as labor. The internal contradictions of profit do not by themselves bring profit to an end but rather bring various forms of capital and profit-making activity into closer association. This is the significance of concentration and centralization, or monopolization and conglomeration, whereby fewer entities control more of the market for a particular line of production and more kinds of production are concentrated in large corporations.

But Marx's critique is not of size but of scale, of what it means for capital to be generalized as a condition across local sites in a manner that constitutes a world market and what it means to accelerate accumulation when less labor is required to keep capital in motion. The consequent excess of capital and of population draw disinvestment from particular profit forms so as to create conditions whereby profit itself might move in a form of general or social capital. This movement through sites of production links them together while severing their distinct moments of ownership. As Marx notes in volume 3, part 5, "The Role of Credit in Capitalist Production":

Aside from the stock-company business, which represents the abolition of capitalist private industry on the basis of the capitalist system itself and destroys private industry as it expands and invades new spheres of production, credit offers to the individual capitalist, or to one who is regarded a capitalist, absolute control within certain limits over the capital and property of others, and thereby over the labour of others. The control over social capital, not the individual capital of his own, gives him control of social labour. The capital itself, which a man really owns or is supposed to own in the opinion of the public, becomes purely a basis for the superstructure of credit. This is particularly true of wholesale commerce, through which the greatest portion of the social product passes. All standards of measurement, all excuses more or less still justified under capitalist production, disappear here. What the speculating wholesale merchant risks is social property, not his own. (1967c, 438–39)

This "superstructure of credit" that results from freeing capital from individual capitalists so that it is available for further investment in productive activity yields a "speculating wholesale merchant" who engages in risk at the level of social property. The advent of the joint stock company takes individual property and renders it into a mass of social property. This agglutination makes it possible for one form of revenue to be rendered equivalent to all others and to produce an agency for wholesale risks to become a force that further binds and blends capitals together.

The discussion of commercial paper is a meditation on the socialization of capital, of how individual and unassociated productive capacities are bound together. Capital is no longer simply for itself, for specific functions and operations, but capital for others, capital in the aggregate that has been freed to find the most propitious rate of return. The move from mass to rate, which signals the last step in the advent of finance as we will come to know it, is signaled in Marx's analysis of what he calls fictitious capital, which he discusses a few chapters later in volume 3, part 5, chapter 29, "Component Parts of Bank Capital":

> With the development of interest-bearing capital and the credit system, all capital seems to double itself, and sometimes treble itself, by the various modes in which the same capital, or perhaps even the same claim on a debt, appears in different forms in different hands. The greater portion of this "money-capital" is purely fictitious. All the deposits, with the exception of the reserve fund, are merely claims on the banker, which, however, never exist as deposits. To the extent that they serve in clearing-house transactions, they perform the function of capital for the bankers—after the latter have loaned them out. They pay one another their mutual drafts upon the nonexisting deposits by balancing their mutual accounts. (1967c, 470)

What is being described here, namely that the same underlying capital can generate a multiplicity of claims on debt that proliferates the amount and form of that capital, would today be referred to as derivatives. The notional or face value of derivatives as multiples of productive capital permits bankers to undertake "balancing their mutual accounts." Derivatives render debt mutual and make it possible to reconcile capital as a whole with its constituent exposures through an accelerating process of multiplying the face value or aggregate exposure (now the measures of volatility) to any particular claim that is being made. The issuing of commercial paper would perhaps remain "fictitious" until a mechanism was devised to price each transaction of risk in relation to risk as a whole. This fiction, that capitals could contract their interdependence in a competitive environment, still served to bond them together in what would become very material terms with actual social effects.

But here too Marx is posing the problem of capital's need for mutuality of debt that can be rendered fully liquid that will only be solved a century later. With commodity production, mass and rate remain at odds, opening gaps that need to be filled through disinvestment and investment. Once risk itself can be priced, production and circulation can be combined in a momentary conjuncture of time and space that closes the gap between a present and future, or here and there into which profit might be lost. For this to happen the notion of rate as velocity, as the ratio between two measures, would need a nonanalogic means of relating difference and of connecting parts and whole. Rates would need to be subject to a rate function, a means to quantify probability of some rare event subject to exponential decay at the tail (an asymptotic distribution).

The probabilistic or stochastic turn would make rates relate not two different measures of central tendency but an outlier that would accelerate the movement of an entire distribution. The shift in orientation from central tendency to outlier is a way of thinking of the press of volatility as a whole on the concrete particular event that is priced. The drift of Marx's account in volume 3 is to demonstrate how the effort to hedge specific risks, to arbitrage the gaps opened between tendencies and countertendencies, yields an excess—of capital, labor, and population— that cannot be readily absorbed through the profit-making process. Capital's socialization as finance surpasses concrete limits but poses a limitation to its own absorption that it cannot surpass. This is the point at which the socialization of labor described in volume 1 and the socialization of capital articulated in volume3 shift the locus of what wealth is for. No longer is accumulation just for itself; now the means and ends of wealth and indebtedness will be aligned through what Marx, at the end of his discussion of the internal contradictions of the tendency of profit failure (in chapter 15), calls "the society of the producers":

> The real barrier of capitalist production is capital itself. It is that capital and its self-expansion appear as the starting and the closing point, the motive and the purpose of production; that production is only production for capital and not vice versa, the means of production are not mere means for a constant expansion of the living process of the society of producers. The

limits within which the preservation and self-expansion of the value of capital resting on the expropriation and pauperisation of the great mass of producers can alone move—these limits come continually into conflict with the
methods of production employed by capital for its purposes, which drive towards unlimited extension of production, towards production as an end in itself, towards unconditional development of the social productivity of labour.
The means—unconditional development of the productive forces of society—
comes continually into conflict with the limited purpose, the self-expansion
of the existing capital. The capitalist mode of production is, for this reason,
a historical means of developing the material forces of production and creating an appropriate world-market and is, at the same time, a continual conflict
between this its historical task and its own corresponding relations of social
production (Marx 1967c, 250).

This contradiction between what capital can direct of wealth-making toward its self expansion in the form of profit and what it cannot absorb as
an excess of the social as such is what Michael E. Brown in his reading of
the three volumes calls "the production of society":

> It is of course true that capital created its *labor force* by bringing people to-
> gether in massive territories of work. But the essential sociality of that force,
> the conditions of interaction and mutual support, the practices by which peo-
> ple come to know themselves as members of a community of workers and a
> society of producers cannot be, nor have been provided by, any deliberately
> rational act of capital, since the cost of that sociality necessarily detracts from
> the free circulation of goods upon which the profits of capital depend. There-
> fore, *the society of producers*, society as such, the society for which wealth is
> an historical problem, must have been created by and be maintained in the
> acts of the producing population itself. This is the history of labor as a class
> against the history of its class antagonist capital. And, as will be shown, this
> antagonism, so apparent in the overall movements of the political economy,
> derives from the fundamental and interior division of production into the mu-
> tually necessary yet incompatible operations of labor and capital. (Brown
> 1986, 54)

This is a shift that moves beyond the equilibrium of pricing that the
closed system of the economy had imagined to imbrications of production in circulation that at once made each moment commensurable with

each other, but also open to an excess of wealth that would await a means to deliver it from the future. As Brown, following Marx in volume 3, recognizes, the antagonism between wealth for society and the avoidance of the risk that profit would not be realized "derives" from the mutually implicated but persistently disruptive "operations" of labor and capital that are always on the precipice of reverting to population beyond the workforce and wealth that cannot be aligned with the purposes of capital. Labor and capital set in motion a whole series of unfinished business from which compensatory and counteracting forces are derived and which now have a language in the form of the derivative that can articulate what is entailed in that abiding and irresolvable contradiction.

A Politics for Derivatives

Marx's work has inspired many a political project and taken on myriad expressive forms. In the broadest terms, three political trajectories from his work can be described. One engages the question of emancipation or freedom. Labor is in chains, the commons is enclosed; national populations are subordinated through histories of colonialism. Capitalism is the totality that must be removed and replaced for history to move forward. Typically, such aspirations are cast in terms of revolutionary movements. A second trajectory is toward the elimination of inequality.[6] The appropriation of surplus value by private owners of the means of production leaves wealth concentrated in the hands of a few. Reconfiguring the way in which wealth is held transfers private property to public needs in a wholesale redistribution. While such radical redistribution of wealth might indeed require revolutionary action to dislodge property relations, labor and other social movements can act as proxies for this future in the present and effect reforms that achieve greater equality.

While these trajectories are well represented in various Marxisms over the past hundred years, from political economy to philosophy and postcolonial and cultural studies, the assertion that Marx himself had a distinctive theoretical contribution to make toward ideals of emancipation or equality is more tenuous to maintain. Certainly he aligned himself with these values and they are consonant with his work, but it is unclear what he added conceptually. Rather, my own view is that Marx's more unique political perspective can be gleaned by following his argument regarding socialization (Martin 2001). The generalization of commodity production comes about through a universalization of mutually associated, interchangeable, and interdependent labor.

The immanent critique of capital, which begins with the commodity at the opening of volume 1 and extends to the "society of the producers" as extending beyond capital's own limit and the question of class at the end of volume 3, treats capital as self-rationalizing. Its achievement, accumulated wealth, is wrought through an expansion of mutual indebtedness, a thickening of the weave among associated producers. Insofar as production and circulation were separate from one another, socialism would consist of seizing the means of production by the direct producers, understood as some kind of workers' self-management, and aligning production and consumption, ability and want, according to a rational plan. What lies beyond the politics of redistribution, which Marx imagines as the basis for communism, is predicated on a condition where "all the springs of common wealth flow more abundantly" (Marx 1969, 87). With the intercalation of production and circulation that finance has wrought, the mutual indebtedness of labor suffuses the debt-generating relations of capital.

The derivative now bears a claim on future wealth in the present that once labor itself had to await in the form of wages. For the past century, various instruments of credit have been extended to populations in ways that most commonly disavowed the socialization of debt. Debt was a burden to be borne alone, in shameful silence or, at best, personalized conspicuous consumption, rather than treated as a collective accomplishment, a claim on what future wealth might be that could be fashioned not simply by a rational plan, but by means of gathering, assembly, and active association. Such would be the political promise of a politics for derivatives, namely that it treated the immanent mutual indebtedness of populations as a means for them to gather and enact what the social could mean and embody. Creating the world in the image of commodities made it possible to imagine what it would mean to take collective possession of the means of production. Recognizing the world crafted through the operations of derivatives leads toward the entangled constitution of mutual indebtedness, of the ways that we are social together, even if we never fuse as one.

Reading *Capital* as an argument regarding social debt where the risk of a failure to accumulate generates a spread of preemptive interventions that socialize capital brings us to the precipice of a politics based in finance without providing the vocabulary for what that might be. Such a politics remains speculative, but it is still immanent in much of what capital can now claim for itself as its own conditions of social reproduction. Rather than a society of producers, we can derive the basis for a society of mutual indebtedness, one where forms of credit, currency, and sociality itself open to become objects of historical transformation. Recall that Marx derived finance from the prevailing forms of accumulation: rent on land, profit from production, and interest from lending. Moving through these forms and rendering surplus interchangeable aggregated capital from particular sources into a general condition. What Marx called social capital, the transmutation from one stream of accumulation to another, is today the basis of finance. This account is itself indebted to Robert Meister's development of an options-based model for reparations in considerations of social justice. Meister wants to solve both the technical question of how revenue streams might be created from the unearned advantages of the perpetrators of injustice and also how we might cathect past, present, and future so as to engender a sense of collectivity that continues to pursue elimination of injustice rather than declaring that pursuit cancelled or closed. The capacity to make this common claim itself suggests a different way of constituting social indebtedness than a model that seeks to settle the claim and exonerate itself from the debts of history. Hence, "unexpired options, like running debt instruments, can be continuously valued, but their value fluctuates with the utility of an underlier rather than increasing exponentially over time as unpaid compound interest on debt would. This is highly relevant to the questions of inter-temporal justice because it directs attention to moments when historical claims might be liquidated through bargaining and when their settlement can be legitimately *enforced* at a price that has not been directly bargained."[7] Operationalizing such politics would require state-society relations where enforcement and liquidation were effected not to bail out capital but to relaminate wealth and population. This is where Meister sees derivatives as socializing property in the way that Marx grasped the commodity form in the nineteenth century. "The techniques for creating financial derivatives—new property rights—could be used to describe the redirection of social revenue flows as contingent claims to be triggered by future events. The actual use of such financial instruments has already resulted in massive, previously inconceivable transfers of wealth with no pretense of justice, backward looking or otherwise. Why shouldn't greater justice be an option too?" (Meister 2012, 259)

Marx's account of fictitious capital, the contracts that different firms and capitals enter into with one another to place credit and debt into circulation, is the basis of disintermediation, one of the cardinal effects of the derivative. By facilitating the mitigation of various risk exposures that would threaten a failure of profit, derivatives also render accumulation from seemingly disparate sources of accumulation interchangeable, concentrating these into blended flows of capital. The accumulation derived by agriculture, industry, and banking in the form of rent, production and interest shadows the three basic forms that derivative trades take: futures, options, and swaps. A future is an obligation to buy or sell a particular holding on a given date, such as a crop of corn once it has been harvested or the belly of a pig upon slaughter. This future exchange is made in the present, affecting a kind of temporal analogy between what conditions of exchange will be and what they currently are. Hence futures operate metaphorically, by treating the present in respect to a particular price as if it were just like the future. An option provides the opportunity but does not mandate a future exchange. As Marx showed in volume 3 of *Capital*, industrial production presents a spread of various strategies for hedging against a failure to make a profit, which options now perform across a whole range of holdings in a portfolio. More specifically, the right to sell an option is termed a put and the right to buy is known as a call. Puts and calls would be used to achieve parity or equilibrium in a portfolio. Thinking about the relation between a given risk exposure and the whole market, options seek to affect a kind of integration between part and whole, a trope termed synecdoche.[8]

Finally, a swap is an exchange of two different revenue streams in order to balance contrary risk exposures. Swaps were used by central banks starting in the fifties to trade their quotas of currency exchange mandated by the Bretton Woods agreements (Mehrling 2010). They are now used by banks and firms to trade off exposures to regulation, like minimal reserve holdings. Swaps have also been used to offset some perceived negative effect like carbon emissions, creating exchanges in rights to pollute known as cap and trade. Whether by getting around regulations or reducing negative externalities such as pollution, swaps operate according to the trope of irony, where the part stands in a negative or contrary relation to the whole. In practical terms these basic forms of derivatives are themselves combined and parsed into all manner of specialized financial instruments, such as swaptions, which further tie particular risk exposures to the movement of the market as a whole. Observing this tendency for derivative forms to further socialization of capital, we can note that the passage from metaphor to synecdoche to irony (the tropes expressed in futures, options, and swaps) operates as its own cycle of accumulation. Markets are initially made through analogy in which the unpriced becomes priced. They are integrated or rationalized when the attribute of a part can be said to circulate throughout the whole. They are transformed as a given regulatory framework is treated ironically, in a form of financial innovation.

Typically, derivatives are either focused on in strictly technical terms as mathematical models for hedging risk or, in moralistic terms, as purely speculative processes unmoored from the real economy. Both of these approaches overlook the profound dimensions of socialization—for capital, labor, and populations—that is the hallmark of Marx's work. Each of the three derivative forms makes different kinds of claims on accumulated wealth, assembles a distinctive relation of part to whole, and assembles a particular expression of a social agency. The financial bailout that followed the explosive rise of derivative trading used public funds as collateral for private debts but wound up cementing a politics of deficit by which present expenditures on social needs have to be sacrificed to future deficit reduction. Just as commodity production can be read immanently as disclosing the social foundations upon which it rests, derivatives suggest a politics of mutual indebtedness that is contrary to the conventional segregation of wealth and austerity by which we now live. Following the analytic procedure in *Capital* to begin with the simplest unit of wealth and see how it becomes socialized, we can track a parallel course for the various forms of the derivative.

One place to locate a derivatives futures market is in the current proclivity toward tax exemption as a means of recognizing what should count as and rewarding public goods. Tax exemption is in effect a government forbearance of future revenue, a fiscal means by which the state shorts its own capacities to fund socially necessary activities. The transfer of these future public funds into current private hands assumes that private individuals will treat that sovereign obligation to dispense of the public good and their orientation toward the present. Philanthropy becomes, from this perspective, an investment in a future public good, but one that takes a purely individuated market form even as those individuals are supposed to be making investment decisions from the perspective of a future government action. At issue is less whether such persons are capable of making these judgments but just the opposite: how those decisions might appear as measures taken toward a collective need. Currently, tax exemption operates in the name of the public good to preserve private wealth. Roughly 1 trillion dollars are ceded as tax exemptions (the largest share of this through mortgage deductions that benefit the most affluent), and only about one-third this amount is returned through charitable contributions (Mettler 2011). If these same trillion dollars were thought as wealth that could be aggregated and delivered collectively in the present, then the process of decision making, investing, and taking on a voice associated with the deliberation over the public good would itself be socialized. Metaphorizing the future, treating it as if it is like the present, summons an intervention into what might come to be. The idea that the present could be like the future could become the basis to convene a critical reflection on what could be made together with social wealth gathered for that purpose. In such a scenario, government could no longer be an enemy of the people, a drag on our common capacities for collaboration and deliberation. Rather, a form of governance would need to be summoned that made a claim on the aggregation of surplus that taxation once represented but that has now been disavowed.

Trading options is meant to be integrative. A balanced portfolio hedges expected gains against loses, protects against risk exposures in any direction, and also makes it possible to create revenue streams from expected returns. Conventionally, there is no place for labor in such calculations. But if we are referring to some kind of rise in values in an underlying commodity or market, labor will have a place. There has, for example, been much talk about creative classes sparking urban redevelopment. Artists, creatives, makers congregate in a neglected area, render that place more desirable, make rents go up, and then are pushed out, having forfeited their sweat equity. That art is purportedly done for love has meant that it is often not treated as labor, making it all the more difficult to take the measure of such contributions to enhancing the real estate value.[9] If equity were to be measured by appreciation to the market as a whole, bonds might be issued that returned some of those gains to the very creative endeavors that made them possible.

One of the key tenets of Meister's argument is that an options-based approach to distributive justice alters the intertemporal grammar by which accounts might otherwise be settled and forgotten. Hence, in addition to providing a means of revenue sharing, options sustain a means of re-membering, of reconnecting those to whom present wealth is indebted to the sources of that wealth. Here, too, options would be pricing what had been unpriced, socializing the risks of expanding the value of inhabitability, elaborating the kinds of knowledge that could be valued, posing the question of who has access to the city and what urban space might be for. The example of artists here is not meant to be metaphorical, a relatively weak or strong resemblance, such as the claim that we are all artists now. Rather, artists should be thought of as a synecdoche, as providing a means to recalibrate what kinds of form we might value so that we could say of the city, or of society, it's all art, or it's all justice, or it's all optional. This perpetual option, directing revenue streams through the anticipated enhancements of what we make together, transposes the account of commodity production in which labor disappears, to a continual repricing where credit for what could be created is extended over and over again.

As of this writing, the cap and trade market for carbon emissions lies dying, gasping for breath. By issuing credits to pollute a certain amount that could then be exchanged by those who polluted more, the expectation was that a net reduction in the amount of carbon emissions would be created, a positive incentive for industries to clean up their acts. Swaps are conventionally designed to reduce exposures to unavoidable risks. They are motivated by an effort to negate what the market might otherwise bear if a part had not been taken out against the weight of the whole. In this sense, swaps are ironic, as indeed we might say is the mature state of any regime of accumulation where risk factors have made their presence known.

Irony is itself disruptive, and swaps themselves suggest the modes of risk management that enhance the volatility that would seek to profit from. As Arjun Appadurai has noted, rituals, which are sure signs that people have tread particular tracks before, not only manage the uncertainties of existential failure (like planetary demise) but generate their share of uncertainty as well.[10] The trick might be to be able to sort out what kinds of uncertainty we would want to minimize and what we would want more of. Swaps have been oriented toward risk reduction while they have been pinned with the elaboration of risk. Perhaps we might start by asking what risk or uncertainty we want to enhance, what volatility would allow us to thrive, what excesses would expand our horizons of imagining ourselves together.

Ben Lee and Ed LiPuma (2014) have reminded us that the market works its magic in reverse, that the activity of pricing what had not been priced convenes us and orients us toward a kind of collective action. This also seems to be the trick of the derivative, to assemble something excessive and self-expansive from very divergent sources and sites that are placed in circulation together. In this the derivative may not simply socialize disparate forms of accumulation, as Marx saw for finance, but may enable us to value social wealth together as at once a surplus product, a creative potential, and populations in circulation. The derivative affords a speculative regard toward the social, not simply a return to what the people once possessed and now have lost in the form of the common, but of what a population and a society might be if people had the active means to make contingent claims on one another that would render their mutual indebtedness the object of a politics that enhanced the ways in which they could value how they make their worlds. That would be asking a great deal from the derivative—but no less than it currently asks.

PART III

CHAPTER SIX

Remarks on Financial Models

Emanuel Derman, Columbia University

Making Finance Simple

I once initiated a competition through my blog. I wrote that I had heard that the physicist Richard Feynman was asked for one sentence to leave to posterity from which our knowledge of physics could be reconstructed if all other knowledge of it were lost. His answer was "Everything is made out of atoms." (I have since heard that there is an equivalent sentence for medicine: "Disease is caused by germs.") I asked readers to send me the one sentence about finance they would similarly propose to leave behind to instruct the future. A man from Brazil, Marcos Carreira, sent in the best answer: "Time and the right to choose to have value."

I never formally studied finance or the Black-Scholes options pricing model. I was thrown into it feet first when I came to work at Goldman Sachs in 1985, the days of amateur heaven in finance, before financial theory grew so faux rigorous that many academics began to embrace it as a branch of pure mathematics. I taught myself option theory over a couple of weeks because I had to work with it. But though I more or less understood options theory at that point, I never really understood the capital asset pricing model (CAPM)—the supposed relationship between risk and expected return on an investment—for many, many years. All the proofs of CAPM that I came across relied on optimization, and to this day I pride myself on never having used an optimization model in my work. Most optimization in finance, perhaps all, is optimization over predicted future scenarios that will not occur. As a result I was always uncomfortable teaching CAPM.

Then one day, about ten years ago, I tried to understand CAPM from a purely rational point of view, from the vantage point of how little we know rather than how much we know, imagining we can optimize over it. My remarks here grow out of that decision and that effort. I want to derive everything in financial theory from one principle. That principle is the principle of replication, or what I like to call the principle of analogy.

Doing this allows me to formulate modern portfolio theory *and* options pricing on a common basis in a way that makes me comfortable. I'm going to apply the principle to stocks and end up with CAPM. Then I'm going to apply it to options and derive Black-Scholes. And finally, I'm going to talk about how people actually use Black-Scholes—not just the equation but the methodology—to trade volatility.

Theories and Models

I like to begin by emphasizing the importance of understanding the distinction between *theories* and *models* when doing financial modeling. My book, *Models.Behaving.Badly*, tries to show in detail why this is important. A short summary goes like this: Theories describe, or attempt to describe, some feature of the inanimate or the animate world on its own terms, in an absolute way. I say "attempt" because theories can be wrong and can still be, from an epistemological point of view, theories. You can have a wrong theory or a partially right theory, but by my definition, and I believe by that of most working physicists, it can still have the quality of a theory. So, for example, Newton's laws are a theory because they attempt to describe the laws of motion intrinsically, from scratch. They don't use analogies or extrinsic comparisons. They don't say "An atom is like a miniature solar system," or "The brain is like a computer," or "A computer is like a brain." Instead, they describe. $F=Ma$, or force equals mass times acceleration, is Newton's description of dynamics, and $F=GMm/r^2$ is his account of the law of gravitation. Special and general relativity approach the same topics—dynamics and gravitation—in a different way, and end up being more accurate, but that doesn't make Newton's original formulation any less a theory. Both formulations are theories, because each stands on its own legs, not on someone else's. One isn't an approximation of the other. Here's an analogy: You can't call typing an approximation to cursive handwriting or cursive handwriting an approximation to typing. They are both legitimate, independent forms of conveying information.

Models, on the other hand, are metaphors or analogies that try to compare something we don't understand very well to something we do. In physics, we have both theories and models. Newton's law, general relativity, and special relativity are theories. Then there is the liquid drop model of the nucleus. The uranium nucleus with 238 protons and neutrons behaves *like* a ball of liquid in that it rotates and vibrates in a variety of modes. That's *not* a theory. It's clearly not true that a molecule of uranium is a ball of liquid. That's an analogy that breaks down at some point, and physicists know when. Maxwell's equations, or Newton's laws, or general relativity, in contrast, don't analogize. They proclaim, "This is how the world works." It's important to be aware of this distinction in finance because many of the errors naïve as well as oversophisticated people make about financial theory revolve around mistaking financial models, which are (mostly poor but useful) analogies, for theories. They make these mistakes because both theories and models employ the syntax of mathematics, but their semantics is very different. Don't mistake advertising or propaganda for literature just because both of them employ the alphabet.

In models the overlap between something you want to understand (such as a nucleus) and something you think you already understand (the hydrodynamics of a liquid drop) is partial. A theory, in contrast, isn't concerned with overlap; it is an attempted description, attempted because it could be wrong. In brief, theories try to tell you what something is; models try to tell you what something is like.

The Use of Models in Finance

In finance there are very, very few—perhaps no—theories. I used to think that Black-Scholes was a theory. Now I would argue otherwise.

I want to highlight a few points about models based on my experience using them. In my professional life on Wall Street, I have almost always worked with a derivatives desk—with people who are trying to sell something complicated to their clients, hedge it, and not lose money. If you, as a client, want to buy a call option on the S&P 500 or on Apple from a derivatives desk because you think the market's going up, the desk doesn't want to lose money if you make money on your bet. So they sell you the option and in addition try to replicate that option out of something else and keep the replica for themselves. They are trying to sell you something complicated that you can't get somewhere else *and want to manufacture it out of simpler stuff* so that if you win, they win by owning the replica too, and therefore have the money to pay your winnings. If they are fair, they charge you for the cost of manufacturing the replica. In my working experience, models are therefore not really used to predict the future. They are best used to tell you how to value something in the present by manufacturing it out of simpler things whose prices you already know.

Models are used to interpolate from liquid ingredient prices to the price of less liquid securities that can be manufactured from them. Let me give a more accessible example. If you want to buy a ten-bedroom apartment on Park Avenue on the East Side of Manhattan, let's suppose that there hasn't been much activity in such large apartments because of the financial crisis. In the absence of recent market prices, how do you value it? Here's a sensible strategy: you can say, "Okay, there are a lot of liquid studio apartments in Battery Park City where everybody is being fired and hired all the time during the crisis. I can approximately replicate the Park Avenue apartment out of eight and a half Battery Park City apartments. My initial model is to make the price of a square foot the same across apartments of different sizes. Eight and a half Battery Park City studio apartments make one big Park Avenue penthouse." This is a replication argument that relies on going from liquid apartments to illiquid apartments through some model.

Let me insert a caveat about the model. It's not the real price per square foot we're talking about. It's the *implied* price per square foot because there are actually many things in the apartment that have value that are not related to the square footage, such as the appliances, the location, the school district, the number of doormen, the views, and so on. But if you quote the cost as price per square foot, you are pretending all that matters is price per square foot to start off with. So it is not the actual price per square foot for constructing the Park Avenue apartment; rather, it is the implied price per square foot if you insist on quoting the price as just a function of the square footage. It's an implied variable, one backed out of a market price filtered through a model.

Models are used by practitioners in ways that academics often don't apprehend. Here are some things models are good for:

One, the interpolation from liquid to illiquid prices, as I have already mentioned.

Two, models are good tools with which to tinker. They allow you to take something like price per square foot, or yield to maturity for a bond, or volatility of an option, or probability of default under certain economic circumstances—each a quantity you can picture intuitively—and use it to get to an informed opinion. You can hypothesize: "I think defaults will be 1 percent per year; total return on a particular bond will likely be 8 percent," and so on and so forth. Then, having linearly thought about the parameters (default probability or yield to maturity or price per square foot), you can translate your intuition about the values of these parameters in the future into the nonlinear current dollar value of the security whose price is determined from the parameters via a model.

Three, models give you a way to rank-order different securities by your model's idea of value. If you look at a variety of corporate bonds, for example, with different coupons and maturities and issuers, then knowing that one bond trades for $103 and another one for $99 doesn't really tell you which is a better buy. A model allows you to take the market price of a security, figure out what value of the model parameter—such as implied yield to maturity, or implied default rate—fits the market price, and hence compare the values of the same parameter for different bonds, value being different from price. You can, for example, conclude, "This bond has a higher implied yield to maturity than that one and is therefore likely to be a better purchase."

In that sense, models are immensely powerful sales tools. Everyone wants to know value as well as price, especially for complicated products. Models are, for better or worse, a way to try to peddle wares to people in a confusing world. You can say, "On this one-dimensional scale of implied default rate (or, in a different example, implied volatility), these securities are more valuable than those, at least according to my model."

Risk and Uncertainty

In physics, uncertainty enters very late into the discipline. Statistical mechanics and quantum mechanics developed at the very end of the nineteenth century and the beginning of the twentieth. In finance, uncertainty is there right at the start. You don't know what is going to happen. The big problem is how to value promises of future payment under uncertainty.

It's important to not be fooled into imagining that all uncertainty is describable in rigorous probabilistic terms. David Freedman, a mathematical statistician at Berkeley, took the statement "What is the chance of an earthquake of magnitude 6.7 occurring before 2030 in the Bay area?" and showed that this is not a statistical question at all. The answer involves models of plate tectonics and all sorts of assumptions about the way physical things behave. The occurrence of the earthquake is not itself a frequentist probability question that has any meaning. I think this is true in the financial world too.

Yet everything in finance—all its models—assumes that probabilities of the market doing something are frequentist probabilities. But mostly they are not. History matters. People learn from experience, or learn to avoid old mistakes and make new ones. The fact that something happened before affects the probability that it will happen again. Probability as measureable frequency of a foreseeable event is a giant unjustified assumption.

Replication

I have said that the one principle I will be using to derive CAPM and Black-Scholes is the principle of replication. A more precise way of formulating the principle of replication is the law of one price: if you want to know the value of a security whose price the market doesn't tell you, your best bet is to use the price of another security or set of securities that are as similar to it as possible.

More formally, this is the principle of no riskless arbitrage that claims that any two portfolios of securities with identical future payoffs in the future—*no matter how the future turns out*—should have identical current prices today. If they don't, the argument goes, people will buy the cheaper one and sell the richer one and eventually bring them into equilibrium.

If you are interested in the value of a target security that is relatively illiquid, you try to build a replicating portfolio—a collection of more liquid securities that, collectively, have the same future payoffs as the target under *every scenario you can think of* in the future. Of course the trouble is that you can't think of everything that is going to happen. So there are two parts to using this law.

The first can be thought of as the science part of finance: defining all the possible futures, or trying to define them. You have to define what you mean by "the future." This is where stochastic calculus and Monte Carlo analysis come in. You want to describe all the possible scenarios under which stock prices, interest rates, default probabilities, and so on can affect your security.

In actuality this is impossible to do correctly because things always happen that you didn't expect. So that part—trying to control for actual future events—cannot be a correct theory. It will be a wrong theory or a model with only a partial overlap with the actual phenomena. This is totally unlike physics where, for some reason, you can write a one-inch equation (the Dirac equation) that describes the way the electron behaves. The equation and the electron are, one and the other, the mental and physical sides of the same thing. You cannot write an equation like that in finance. That seems to be a fact.

The second, less difficult part is the engineering. Once you have specified whatever you think all the future scenarios are, the question becomes: How do I make a collection of stocks and bonds that replicate, say, an option, in the sense that the replicating portfolio and the target option produce equal payoffs under all scenarios? The task is to replicate a complex security whose value you don't know with a bunch of other things whose prices you do know.

People break down replication into two types: static and dynamic. Static means static, that is, unchanging. You want to replicate this complicated thing. You buy a bunch of other things and then you just hold onto them. You don't trade out of them. You just wait until expiration. On expiration, the payoff of this bunch of things is constructed to be exactly the same as the payoff from the option that you are trying to replicate, under all scenarios. With perfect static replication, there is no model involved. For the prices to be different is an absolute arbitrage. The only assumption that you are making is about credit—that everyone is still going to be around to give you the payoff on all the securities you have bought or sold when expiration comes.

Dynamic replication is the great Black-Scholes-Merton contribution to the theory of options valuation. Their paper was published in 1973, and the breakthrough achievement it represents has dominated finance over the past forty years. Dynamic replication is much riskier because you have to be trading all the time to do the replication. A host of assumptions are being made: that people will be around to pay you (a question of credit); that you can trade whatever you need to trade—stocks and bonds—over and over again, continuously, many, many times; that you can bear the transaction costs that you have to pay every time you do a trade; that there will be liquidity in the market when you want to adjust your position as dynamic replication demands; that you have access to the vast amounts of price and position information you need through connections to computer programs, user interfaces, model hedge ratios, and the security exchanges to do all the necessary computation; and, finally, that your exposure to volatility in the models will be accurate and realistic. In dynamic replication you take on a lot of model risk. This kind of replication is both much iffier and yet very beautiful in its own way. This is the engineering part of finance.

The Science Part of Finance: Modeling Risk

Now I want to talk about neoclassical finance's attempt at science and show how the assumptions involved in this attempt lead to CAPM and to Black-Scholes. Let me explain one thing, though, to address a common misconception. People in finance—quants and traders—aren't stupid. They know that Brownian motion and diffusion, which I'm about to discuss, aren't correct theories by which to understand price variations and movements. Nevertheless all the models commonly used are based on the mathematics associated with Brownian motion, as invented by Louis Bachelier in the early 1900s and then independently formulated for the random bumps experienced by dust particles in the air by Einstein in 1905.

The underlying assumption is that *the return* you can earn on a stock (not the stock price, but the return earned on the price), instant to instant, is distributed normally with a mean value for the return and a *volatility* that is the standard deviation of returns. Brownian motion is an actual theory (in the technical sense that I've defined theories) for dust particles bumped by atoms in the air. It really describes their movements based on reality. But it is only a metaphor—or a model—for stocks. Stocks do not really behave like dust particles and nor do their returns. It would be a much more mathematically tractable world if they did. This model does capture something plausible and significant about the uncertainty of stock prices that is very relevant to finance. But stocks, though their returns are uncertain, do not experience exactly that kind of uncertainty. The analogy with Brownian motion, physically inspired, is limited. Physics is about what is really going to happen in the future. Finance is about what people expect to happen in the future. And, once people have watched the movement of stock prices, they know that they should expect wilder motions, at least some of the time, than Brownian motion allows.

Nevertheless, let's proceed to use Brownian motion as a *model* for stocks. Then the stock's motion is completely specified by its expected return and the volatility or standard deviation of returns. You can build a binomial simulation and you can implement it on a computer.

Figure 1 is a diagram that models a stock's return. There is a 50 percent probability of the motion associated with the up arrow, with a positive return corresponding to the stock price moving up. (Note that the use of the word "up" for the larger return, conflating "higher" and "larger," is a gravitational metaphor, linked to our having lived on earth rather than in empty space.) There is similarly a 50 percent probability of it moving down. The mean return in the middle is μ (Mu) per unit time. Over time, Δt, meaning a short time, the return is μ Δt on average. On the upside, it is $\mu \Delta t + \sigma \sqrt{\Delta t}$, where σ (sigma) is the volatility. On the downside, it is $\mu \Delta t - \sigma \sqrt{\Delta t}$. That the fluctuations are of order $\sqrt{\Delta t}$, whereas the drift is of order Δt as a function of the time interval Δt, is what characterizes Brownian motion: for small Δt, if you remember your math, the fluctuations are larger than the drift. If, for example,

The evolution of a stock's return

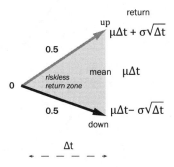

FIGURE 1. The evolution of a stock's return

$\Delta t = 1/100$ of a second, the square root of one hundredth of a second is one tenth of a second and one tenth is much larger than one hundredth. So, the fluctuations are much bigger than the return. That is the characteristic of Brownian motion.

If you repeat this over and over again and you assume that stock prices move only when fresh news arrives, and that stock prices fluctuate either up or down depending on whether the news is good or bad, and if you assume (unrealistically) that the volatility is always the same, then you can model the evolution of the stock price through time, as shown in figure 2.

Figure 2 shows a possible path for the stock price that goes initially up once (to the left), then down three times, then up twice, and then down once more. At the end of it all, although you've taken seven steps, you don't really move seven units because some are up and some are down. On average, you might only move two or three. You can show rigorously, from the mathematics of Brownian motion, that after N steps, the *average* distance the stock price moves up or down, to the left or to the right, is actually the square root of N. This is sometimes called a drunken man's walk. After time T, on average, a drunken disoriented man has moved away from his starting position only a distance proportional to the square root of T.

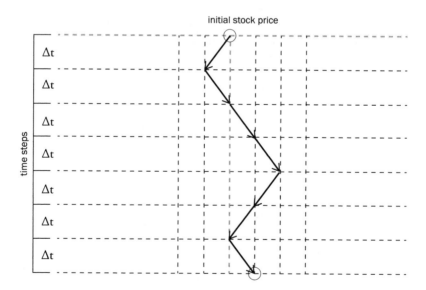

FIGURE 2. A stock's path through several time steps

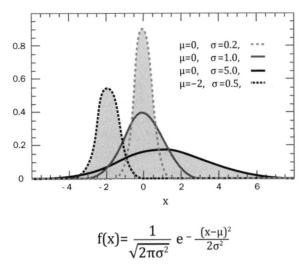

$$f(x)= \frac{1}{\sqrt{2\pi\sigma^2}} \ e^{-\frac{(x-\mu)^2}{2\sigma^2}}$$

FIGURE 3. Several normal distributions of returns with different mean returns and volatilities

This type of evolution does have the qualities of a risky investment. It may not be realistic, but it does have essential uncertainty in there. If you repeat these Brownian steps over and over again millions of times as you let the distance between the steps in time and price go to zero, you get a normal distribution for returns that looks just like the bell curve, as shown in figure 3. Figure 3 shows three different normal distributions. The center on the x-axis of each distribution corresponds to the drift μ. The width of the distribution corresponds to each distribution's volatility σ.

All of this assumes that there are only two unknowns that affect the future movement of a stock, the mean return and the volatility of returns. If you really believe this model of risk, or pretend to believe it, you believe that every possible future of every stock is characterized by only two numbers. You don't care whether it's Apple or Walmart or the S&P. According to Markowitz portfolio theory, all that matters is μ and σ, the expected return and its volatility in the future. If you believe all this, you shouldn't care about what the stock is. You should only care about what its expected return and its standard deviation/volatility are.

How realistic is this? Not very, because although Brownian motion specifies a kind of uncertainty, it's still much too mild a kind of uncertainty for the real world.

The sample paths for a stock shown in figure 4 are generated from a Monte Carlo simulation of a normal distribution with a fixed 20 percent volatility. You can see the fluctuations, but the stock does not fluctuate very wildly. The actual historical path below for J. Crew's stock price during the great financial crisis from 2007 to 2009 is shown in figure 5.

The moves in figure 5 are much more dramatic than those of figure 4 and don't fit the normal distribution. It is a mistake to characterize it in terms of by how many standard deviations it disagrees with the normal distribution. The real world is much rougher than Brownian models presuppose. And there are much more dramatic examples than this one, where entire markets drop 20 percent in a day, or currencies drop 20 percent in a literal instant.

But I'm going to stick to this model anyway, to see where it leads. There is a line from William Blake: If a fool would persist in his folly he would become wise. I think that's the right way to behave with financial

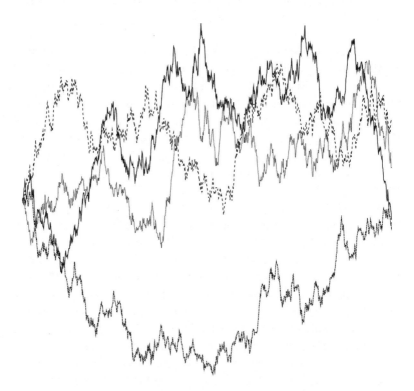

FIGURE 4. Plot of stock prices executing a random walk: Four possible paths

FIGURE 5. Actual paths of the stock price of J. Crew during the great financial crisis

models. Indulge yourself by assuming something incorrect and persist in pushing it. See how far you can go. You may learn something interesting and become wise. But at the end, remember that it is based on folly.

The Relation between Risk and Return

We have defined a model for stock price evolution, that is, for the risk of stocks. Now assume that risk is defined by μ and σ, no matter what company the stock represents, and assume that you know the values of μ and σ.

The major question of finance is: Given a certain amount of risk, what return should you expect to earn? The variables μ and σ have so far been independent, with risk and return unrelated to each other, but now we want to know what μ you should rationally expect for a certain σ. I will derive an answer using the law of one price, or the principle of replication.

The law of one price states: Two portfolios with exactly the same future payoffs must have exactly the same price today. In the model I described above, future payoffs are defined by the standard deviation or risk σ. I will now coarsen the law of one price to state that portfolios that have identical expected risks must have identical expected returns. If all that characterizes securities is their risk, then securities with the same risk had better have the same return. There would be a statistical arbitrage if that weren't true. Thus portfolios with the same σ had better have the same μ.

However, if I assume that everybody is behaving rationally, then some risks can be avoided. You don't have to take every risk that is out there. Therefore I will modify the law of one price once more time to state that identical *unavoidable* expected risks must have identical expected returns, arguing that if you can get rid of some risk, nobody's going to pay you for taking it. I am not saying that this is the way the world really behaves, but simply assuming that in order to proceed. So identical unavoidable risks have identical expected returns. Now I have to think about how I can avoid some risks.

There are three ways you can reduce the risk of a given security or set of securities. The first is: if you have a risky security, you can dilute it. If there is a riskless security somewhere, say a Treasury bill that lets you lend money to the US Treasury, you can add that T-bill to your security to dilute its risk. The US Treasury is pretty likely going to pay you the interest they promise you, at least in the near future, although even this isn't an absolutely sure thing. The second way of reducing risk is diversification. If you take a whole bunch of risky securities together, the fact that you put them together usually diminishes the risk, because much of the time some of them will go up in price while others do nothing or go down. The third way to reduce risk is by hedging. If two securities are correlated with each other, if you buy one and short the other, you can reduce the risk.

Now I want to show how that principle of identical *unavoidable* risks having equal returns, combined with these ways of avoiding risk, leads to the result that risk and return are proportional. More risk, more return. Let me pause and be really careful. In finance we are always talking about what is going to happen: More *expected* risk, more *expected* return.

Making Use of Dilution

Figure 6 shows the evolution of a riskless bond and a stock over a short time Δt. The light grey trajectory represents the stock going up, the darker grey, the stock going down. For a riskless bond, it doesn't really matter which way the stock price goes. The riskless bond pays you a return $r\Delta t$, the riskless rate r times Δt over some infinitesimal period Δt. In the same time period, for a stock that's risky, it's return will be either $(\mu \Delta t + \sigma \sqrt{\Delta t})$ or $(\mu \Delta t - \sigma \sqrt{\Delta t})$. If I combine w dollars invested in the stock with $(1 - w)$ dollars invested in the riskless bond, where w is a fraction between 0 and 1, I have a portfolio worth $1 that has the w-weighted average of the returns and the w-weighted average of the risk of the two securities (where all the risk actually comes just from the stock because the bond has no risk).

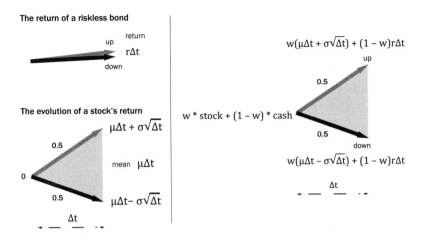

FIGURE 6. Combining a stock and riskless bond

The expected return for the mixture is then the $w-$weighted average of the up and down returns of the portfolio in the figure above, namely

$$w\mu\Delta t + (1 - w)r\Delta t = r\Delta t + w(\mu - r)\Delta t$$

Similarly, the w-weighted average of the risk of the mixture is

$$w\sigma$$

The return per unit time of the mixture is therefore $\mu' = r + w(\mu-r)$, and the risk of the mixture is $\sigma' = w\sigma$. If w is less than 1, you get a smaller risk and a different return somewhere between r and μ.

The mixture I've created from a high-volatility stock with volatility σ and a riskless bond with return has a volatility $w\sigma$ that is lower than the volatility of the stock alone. I have replicated a low-risk security from a high-risk security by diluting it. And by the law of one price, all securities with this volatility $\sigma' = w\sigma$ must have the same return $\mu' = r + w(\mu-r)$.

When $w = 0$ then $\mu' = r$. When w is greater than zero, you expose yourself to additional risk above that of the riskless bond, and you get to expect an additional excess return $w(\mu-r)$. This is the excess return over the riskless rate that accompanies an extra risk $w\sigma$. The ratio of the excess return to the additional risk is

$$\frac{w(\mu - r)}{w\sigma} = \frac{(\mu - r)}{\sigma} \equiv \lambda$$

This ratio λ has to be the same for all securities no matter what the value of w, because w cancels in the ratio. This ratio λ is called the Sharpe ratio and describes the excess return you can expect for exposing your portfolio to additional risk.

In deriving this relation I've assumed (1) that equal risk earns equal return and (2) that risk is completely defined by the risk of a normal distribution. I like the principle that equal risk expects equal return. It would be hard to argue otherwise. I think the real flaw in this derivation is in part (2), the assumption that risk is just the value of σ. Risk is more complicated than σ. But if you believe it is just σ, then the Sharpe ratio has to be the same for all stocks, if they are uncorrelated with each other.

Rewriting the above equation, we obtain

$$\mu - r = \lambda\sigma$$

This says that the excess return over the riskless rate is proportional to volatility. But we don't know the value of the proportionality constant, λ, the Sharpe ratio.

Making Use of Dilution and then Diversification

Now I want to figure out the value of λ by using the law of one price together with another method of avoiding risk. Suppose that I live in a world where there aren't just a few stocks, but there are thousands of stocks. They are all—this is not yet realistic—they are all uncorrelated with each other. I can take a giant portfolio of a thousand stocks and put them together. Again, since they are uncorrelated with each other, I can show, just from Markowitz's theory, that if you put a lot of uncorrelated stocks together, the risk asymptotically goes to zero as the number of stocks becomes infinite. The portfolio of stocks becomes riskless.

But a riskless bond also has zero risk. Therefore, I can replicate a riskless bond asymptotically by putting a million stocks together. But the previous formula, $\mu - r = \lambda\sigma$, must apply to all securities and portfolios of securities. If I take the portfolio that consists of all the stocks in the world, its risk σ becomes zero, so its expected return μ had better be the riskless rate r.

We can now prove that λ is zero, by a reductio ad absurdum. I can also regard μ for the portfolio as the sum of all its component μ's. Now suppose that λ is not zero. Then each of the individual stocks in the portfolio has its own particular risk σ and its own expected return μ, which, if λ is not zero, is greater than the riskless rate. Since the average of these individual expected returns is greater than the riskless rate, the entire portfolio's expected return must be greater than the riskless rate, and yet its risk is zero, inconsistent with the relation $\mu - r = \lambda\sigma$.

The only way the whole portfolio—the sum of all these individual stocks—can have zero excess return is if λ is actually zero. The only way a portfolio's excess return can be zero when its risk is zero, and yet be made out of many risky stocks with nonzero expected excess returns, is if the Sharpe ratio of each of the stocks is zero. But if the Sharpe ratio is identically zero, then $\mu - r = 0$ for all stocks. So, if you can diversify, all stocks should be expected to earn the riskless return $\mu = r$.

We don't expect this to be true in practice because, in fact, stocks tend to be correlated with the market. We will now examine how this relation $\mu = r$ changes when all stocks are correlated.

Making Use of Hedging, Diversification, and Dilution

I want to go one step closer to the real world. You can't always diversify to eliminate all risk by creating a large portfolio of stocks, as I assumed above, because stocks actually move together. If the whole market goes up on average, all stocks are more or less correlated with the market, with some assumed correlation, different for different stocks. If the whole market goes down, they all go down together. Sharpe and Lintner and Treynor assumed that there's a correlation between stocks and the market as a whole.

Now in order to be less technical, I'm just going to say this in words: Assume that every stock has its own particular correlation with the market that doesn't change with time. It could be different for different stocks, but let's assume it's constant through time. Then for each stock, if I know its correlation with the market, I can go long the stock and short some fraction of a share of the market to exactly cancel out the market risk of the stock. For example, I can buy a particular stock and short one-eighth of a share of the S&P that exactly cancels out its market risk in theory. The fraction that is one-eighth in this particular case depends on the volatility of the stock, the volatility of the market, and their correlation. That miniportfolio consisting of a long position in one share of the stock itself and a short position in the entire market just enough to cancel its market risk is what I call *the market-neutral version of a stock*, meaning it has no sensitivity to the market. Then I can take all the stocks in the universe of thousands of stocks and, in theory, hedge out the market risk of every single stock and make a market-neutral version of each stock. Then all of those market-neutral stocks are uncorrelated with each other because all they have left is their residual risk, which isn't market risk. Let's suppose that these residual risks are all uncorrelated. Now, if I put all of the market-neutral versions of each stock together in a giant portfolio, I have a giant portfolio of thousands of uncorrelated (market-neutral) stocks. To this I can apply the two previous arguments involving dilution and diversification: by dilution, all market-neutral stocks must have the same Sharpe ratio, and by diversification, that Sharpe ratio has to be zero.

The expression for the Sharpe ratio of a market-neutral stock, being the Sharpe ratio of a portfolio that is long the stock and short the market in some particular ratio, is a little different from the Sharpe ratio of a single stock. By working out the algebra and setting the Sharpe ratio of all market-neutral stocks to be zero, one obtains the formula

$$(\mu - r) = \beta(\mu_M - r).$$

This is simply the capital asset pricing model (CAPM), which expresses that the expected excess return (μ-r) of a stock is related to the excess return (μ_M-r) of the market via the proportionality constant $\beta = \rho\sigma/\sigma_M$, the usual beta of CAPM. In this equation σ_M is the volatility of the market and ρ is the correlation between the stock and the market.

From my point of view, CAPM is really just a statement that portfolios with equal unavoidable risks, after dodging all avoidable risks, should expect, on average, to earn equal returns. You avoid the market risk of individual stocks by hedging, and you avoid the residual non-market risks of individual stocks by diversifying. The result is that the only risk you can expect to get paid more than the riskless rate for is the part of the market risk that is intrinsic to each stock, which is determined by β. The expected return of every stock is therefore related to its β times the expected return on the market. That's CAPM.

This is not usually the way people derive CAPM, but I like it because this allows it to be seen as coming from one basic principle, the principle of no riskless arbitrage. Instead of employing optimization, my derivation says that if you regard risk as being simply volatility, and if things with the same risk have to have the same return, then CAPM follows. CAPM is an equilibrium statement saying that portfolios with the same risk, after removing all avoidable risks, must have the same Sharpe ratios. If they didn't, the assumption is that people would come into the market and buy the lower Sharpe ratios and sell higher Sharpe ratios, and eventually the prices would equilibrate.

The Black-Scholes Equation

The original derivation of Black-Scholes involved the insight that if you have a stock, say, Apple, and you have a call option on Apple, then both the stock and the call really give you access to the risk of the underlying stock. When you buy Apple stock, you're getting access to the risk of Apple stock. When you buy a call on Apple, you're also getting access to the risk of Apple stock. Black's original argument is that over a short instant of time, over one millisecond say, both of them give you access to the risk and expected return. To be consistent with all that we've derived, they had better have the same Sharpe ratio. One of them can't have a higher Sharpe ratio than the other—they're one hundred percent correlated because the β is one—because there is nothing (in theory at least) in the Apple option that there isn't in the Apple stock if you consider that all that matters is volatility over the next instant of time.

So, to repeat myself, the Black-Scholes model and equation are both really statements that the Sharpe ratio of the stock is the same as the Sharpe ratio of the option. The only technical difficulty is that you have to figure out mathematically how to calculate both the volatility of the call and its expected return—i.e., the Sharpe ratio of the call—from the fact that it is a derivative of the stock's. Ito's lemma, the mathematics behind this, is the calculus of stochastic processes that tells you how to do that when the stock undergoes Brownian motion. If you do that, you get the Black-Scholes equation. Black-Scholes is really just a statement that the Sharpe ratios of stock and call are the same, expressed in stochastic calculus.

Because Black-Scholes relates the stock to the call, it also indicates that you can replicate an option (that is, to be precise, get the return of an option under any future scenario for the stock) by borrowing money and buying the appropriate amount of stock to get you the right Sharpe ratio, *assuming*, as I keep stressing, that all that matters risk-wise from your point of view is the volatility of the stock and that you know that volatility.

Options theory, which I learned before I ever learned CAPM, but which is based on CAPM, is much better, that is, more reliable, than CAPM. CAPM says roughly that two stocks with the same risk have the same return. But stocks have all sorts of risk beyond their volatility alone, the volatility that CAPM assumes is the only constituent of risk. That's too limited. There are many worse things that can happen to a stock than Brownian motion, and CAPM is deeply flawed because it neglects all those other things—sudden jumps, sudden changes in volatility, all sorts of violent occurrences.

Options theory is flawed too, but less so than CAPM because it only demands that the risk of an option be related to the risk of the stock beneath it—and they are related, even when more violent things happen than Brownian motion can imagine. The risk of an option on a stock has more in common with the risk of that stock than the risk of two different stocks have with each other.

What is revolutionary about Black-Scholes is that it says that, independent of your opinion about the future profitability of the stock, independent of your views about the economy, politics, business, and so on, you can still estimate the appropriate value for the option (assuming all the things I've indicated about risk being fully described by volatility, as I've reiterated). The option pricing formula is rationally derived from those assumptions. The reason everybody embraced Black-Scholes when it arrived was that, before then, everybody thought that option pricing depended on your opinions about the future direction of a stock price and about how much you liked or abhorred risk. Everybody had a different risk preference, and therefore everyone got a different value for the option. Black and Scholes showed that, because of hedging, all options could be derisked, and so everybody could agree on the same price, provided you knew the future volatility of the stock. This is why the op-

tions market has become so liquid—because people can use the formula
to approximately get rid of some of the risk of options.

The Merton Method

I want to look at Black-Scholes also from another point of view, from the
way that Robert Merton derived it. It is actually presented in the Black-
Scholes paper itself—it appears as the first of the two proofs they give. It
has to do with convexity.

Figure 7 contains a graph of the profit or loss (P&L) that you get
from owning a stock if you bought it at the price indicated by the dotted
line's intercept on the x-axis. If the stock goes up from there, the P&L
increases linearly. You make more money. If the stock goes down, the
P&L decreases linearly. You lose money. But if you look at a call option,
it has a payoff like the one shown in figure 8, with the kink occurring at
the strike price.

If the stock price is below the strike price at expiration, the owner of
the call gets paid nothing. If it's above the strike price, he gets a dollar
for every dollar increase in the stock price. This asymmetry between a
move down and move up is the characteristic called convexity of the payoff. And this particular curvature is called positive convexity.

The big question of option pricing before Black-Scholes was: What
price should you pay for a call given that it has this convex nonlinear
shape? The Merton strategy for valuing an option is that you put the option in a portfolio with the stock so that, together, they replicate a riskless bond. Since you know the price of a riskless bond and the price of

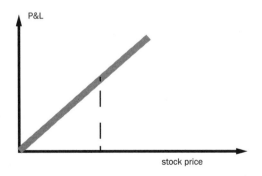

FIGURE 7. The P&L of a long stock position

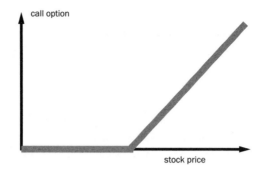

FIGURE 8. The payoff of a call option at expiration

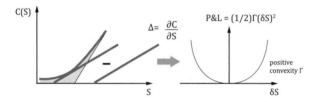

FIGURE 9. Hedging an option
Buy a call option C and short Δ shares of stock against it to create portfolio Π = C − ΔS.
On the left side: Long a call and short Δ shares of stock produces a parabolic positive pay-
off for all changes ΔS in the stock price.

stock, you can back out the value of the option. It's as though you know
the price of a fruit salad comprised of apples, pears, and pineapples, and
you know the price of apples and pears, and can hence back out the price
of pineapples. You use the law of one price to determine it, but you apply it at each instant, dynamically. You do it for one millisecond, and
then the stock price changes and time passes and you have to do it again,
slightly differently.

On the left of figure 9 is the convex payoff of a call at expiration. The
thicker curved line is the supposed value of the call at an earlier time.
The diagram plots the value given by the Black-Scholes equation that
we haven't found yet. Assume you own the call shown. If you look at the
tangent (the straight line) to the thick line, it tells you how much, for an
instant, the call's value will go up or down as the stock price moves. The
value of the tangent is called *delta*, and defines the number of shares you
need to own to match the behavior of the call value in the next instant of
time. So now you can short that number delta of shares against the call

and thereby remove the linear risk of the call. For one instant, then, you have eliminated all the up-down risk of the call by shorting one fraction delta of a share of stock against it. The riskiness that is left is the difference between owning delta shares of stock and owning the actual option, that is, the difference between the linear line denoted by Δ and the curved option value denoted by above $C(S)$. It is the difference between the thick curve and a tangent line that runs through it at a given stock price.

The right part of figure 9 shows the difference between the call option price and a tangent to it that is produced by shorting delta shares of stock. The difference in value $\Pi = C - \Delta S$ for a range of S values is the parabola shown on the right. The difference is zero at the actual stock price that prevailed when the delta shares of stock were shorted. If the stock then goes up a small amount δS from there in the next instant over time, the profit of the call option increases compared to the profit of owning the stock. And if the stock goes down δS, the loss in value of the call option is less than the loss of just owning the stock, so again the portfolio makes money. You are left with a parabola, and the parabola has a curvature whose value is conventionally denoted by the Greek letter Γ (gamma).

If the parabola is described by the formula $\Gamma(\delta S)^2$, where (δS) denotes the small move in the stock price away from its initial value, then the payoff of owning the call and shorting the stock, as the stock moves through (δS), is $\frac{1}{2}\Gamma(\delta S)^2$, that is, one-half gamma times the move in the stock price squared. This payoff is parabolic and depends only on the *square* of the move δS in the stock price and is therefore the same whether the stock price moves up or down a given amount. Thus, the payoff is riskless, in the sense that you get a positive payoff from the hedged portfolio $\Pi = C - \Delta S$ whether the stock moves up or down, unlike owning the stock itself. If you go long the call and short just the right number (Δ) shares of stock, you have a riskless payoff for Π. It doesn't lose money on the way down. It doesn't lose money on the way up. If you knew how large δS was going to be in the next instant, you would know exactly how much money you would make. The future size of δS, positive or negative, is determined by the future volatility of the stock, assuming Brownian motion.

The portfolio Π that consists of the option and the appropriate short position in the stock is riskless and therefore behaves like a riskless bond, at least for a short instant. It gives you the same payoff no matter whether the stock goes up or down. By the law of one price, that parabolic payoff, that was gotten by buying the option and hedging it with stock, which for a short instant replicates a riskless bond, must therefore earn the return of a riskless bond.

Let me assume for pedagogical purposes that the riskless rate is zero, as it almost is today. The return of a riskless bond is therefore zero. Thus the return over the next instant of the hedged portfolio Π must be zero. How can that happen?

There are two things that can happen over the next instant of time δt. First, the stock price itself can move up or down by an amount δS. If you know how much, you know the *volatility* of the stock. Second, the call option can change in value too. But the combination of both these effects on the hedged portfolio Π must make it be equivalent to a riskless bond whose return is zero. That is, the price changes of the hedged portfolio Π must cancel. One of those changes is the parabola we plotted above, whose profit arises from curvature as the stock price moves an amount δS during the instant of time δt. That profit must be exactly cancelled by the decrease in the value of the call option during that next instant δt. The change in value of the option is called "time decay." The gain from convexity and the time decay have to exactly cancel. This is an instantiation of the principle that there is no free lunch. If you want to be able to make money in the hedged portfolio from the stock moving, from convexity, then you have got to lose money when the stock doesn't move as time passes. That statement, when expressed in mathematics, is the Black-Scholes equation.

Trading Options

Now I want to explain how people actually use options to trade volatility, assuming one believes all the results derived above from the assumption above. Suppose I'm a trader. In that case, all I have to do to value the option is to solve the Black-Scholes equation. I usually know the stock price, and I know the level of interest rates. All I need for the Black-Scholes model is the expected future volatility of the stock, which I don't really know. So, I'll look at the past or I'll take a guess at the volatility, using the value Σ (the capital Greek letter sigma) to represent the volatility I expect. (In real life, because I know the model isn't right, I might inflate the number for volatility to put in extra cushioning.)

But let's say for now I just fill in what I think the volatility is going to be. Then I hedge according to Black-Scholes. I go long the call and short the stock. The hedge ratio I choose is the solution to the Black-Scholes model with this guessed-at future Σ. That determines the price of the option and so is also the option's *implied volatility*. Inserted into the Black-Scholes formula, it tells me how many shares of stock to short. Then I wait an instant Δt. And, horror of horrors, the stock price doesn't move with the volatility Σ that I expected but with a different volatility, the *realized* volatility, σ (the lowercase Greek letter sigma). So the move in the stock price isn't $\Sigma S \sqrt{\Delta t}$ that I forecast but $\sigma S \sqrt{\Delta t}$, because the world doesn't behave exactly the way I expected.

Figure 10 describes what happens when you trade options using the Black-Scholes view that I describe below. The profit I actually make from the curvature when an amount of time Δt passes is $\frac{1}{2}\Gamma\sigma^2 S^2(\Delta t)$, which depends on the square of σ, the volatility that describes the stock's actual movement. Here Γ is the curvature of the option value calculated from Black-Scholes. The money that I actually make from owning the option and shorting stock is related to the difference between

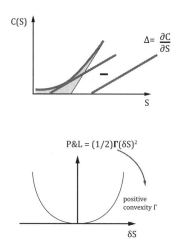

FIGURE 10. Trading volatility: Hedging an option is a bet on volatility
(1) Buy the call at implied volatility Σ; (2) hedge away the stock risk by shorting $\Delta = \frac{\partial C}{\partial S}$ shares calculated at the current implied volatility Σ; (3) (long call − short stock) has a parabolic payoff over next instant that profits whether the stock moves up or down, as in figure 9; (4) when the stock moves $\delta S = \sigma S\sqrt{\Delta t}$ with actual volatility σ the gain from curvature is $\frac{1}{2}\Gamma\sigma^2 S^2\Delta t$; (5) the net P&L during time Δt is $\left[\frac{1}{2}\Gamma(\sigma^2 - \Sigma^2)S^2\Delta t\right]$.

1. what I thought was going to happen, i.e., volatility Σ with an expected gain $\frac{1}{2}\Gamma\Sigma^2 S^2(\Delta t)$; and

2. what really happened, i.e., volatility σ with an actual gain $\frac{1}{2}\Gamma\sigma^2 S^2(\Delta t)$.

The net profit that I make over time Δt is therefore $\frac{1}{2}\Gamma(\sigma^2 - \Sigma^2)S^2(\Delta t)$, that is, one-half the curvature, times the difference between the real volatility squared and the implied volatility squared, times the stock price squared times Δt. This is positive if σ is greater than Σ and negative if the reverse holds. Option trading, at least from this point of view, is therefore a bet on whether real volatility is greater or less than implied volatility.

Black-Scholes is the most important formula in options theory, but the second most important, if you are a trader, is the one above that says that if Black-Scholes is right, then the profit and loss from trading an option at every instant is proportional to one half the curvature of the option times the stock price squared times the difference between real volatility and implied volatility squared. If you buy an option and hedge it, you are hoping that in the next instant actual volatility will be greater than the implied volatility that you bought it at. If you sell the option and hedge it, you are hoping that actual volatility will be smaller. Summing over all the instants of time between when you buy (or sell) the option and when it expires, you obtain the formula in figure 11.

The thick gray curving line in figure 11 shows the Black-Scholes value of a call option at different stock prices. When the stock price is far above the strike, deep in the money, you have very little curvature or convexity. Everything is linear. Deep out of the money at low stock

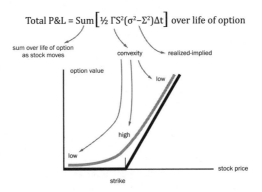

FIGURE 11. The second most important formula for options
Having convexity means uncertainty in the stock price is good for you.

prices, there is also very little convexity. When the stock price is in the vicinity of the strike, when the likelihood of the option moving into the money or out of the money is most unclear, you have the highest convexity—the most curvature of the line representing the value of the option. Having convexity means you have large exposure to uncertainty in the next move of the stock price, and this is good for you as a trader if you own an option. If you have convexity, it means you want the stock to move, up or down, because you'll make money from moves either way.

People who trade options often talk about being "long volatility" or "long convexity." Nassim Taleb's book about antifragility is in essence about the advantages of being long volatility or long convexity, metaphorically, in everyday life, meaning you are antifragile if you are happy when things change because change is going to be good for you, as is the case if you own options.

The biggest problem with the description above is that risk is much more complicated than the risk embodied in normal distributions. In a real market crash, stock prices jump. Furthermore, volatility itself is stochastic. Stock returns, according to Benoit Mandelbrot, may actually have infinite volatility, which would make the Black-Scholes theory even more vulnerable.

Difficulties Using the Model

Let me show you what happens if you're a person who buys or sells options for a living. If you buy one call option, by definition you bought it at the option price's implied volatility, say $\Sigma = 20$ percent, and let's assume for example that the realized volatility turns out to be $\sigma = 40$ percent, then you are going to make the money shown in the diagram below over the life of the option as you keep rehedging the option at every instant to get zero exposure to the stock.

The diagram in figure 12 shows the range of different profits you might make depending on the different paths the stock price might take to expiration of the option. They are all calculated by summing up $\frac{1}{2}\Gamma(\sigma^2 - \Sigma^2)S^2(\Delta t)$, over all the instants of time along the particular stock path that takes you from the moment you purchases the option to its value at expiration. The curvature Γ itself is a function obtainable from the Black-Scholes formula and depends on the prevailing value at every instant of the stock price, time to expiration, strike, and volatility.

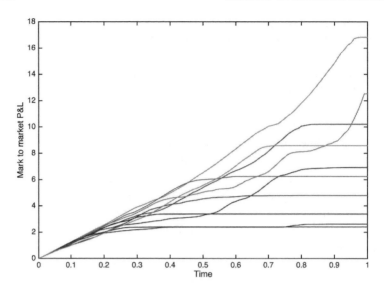

FIGURE 12. The P&L from hedging an option illustrated for several different stock paths
You profit more if (1) realized volatility is greater than implied and (2) the stock price
moves through a region where Γ is large, i.e., close to at-the-money. So, hedging an option
is not a clean bet on volatility. It depends on the path the stock price takes to expiration. If
it stays near the at-the-money region, where Γ is large, you get the largest effect.

Owning and hedging the call option is not a pure bet on volatility because the P&L is modulated by the curvature or convexity Γ of the option. If the stock stays close to at the money all the way to expiration,
you have a lot of convexity all the way and you keep making money all
the time, assuming, as we have, that realized volatility is 40 percent and
you bought the option at an implied volatility 20 percent. But if the stock
price goes very high or very low and then stays in that vicinity, far in or
out of the money, as shown in the diagram above, the convexity becomes
negligible and no more profit is captured from hedging.

That diagram shows a simulation of some of the paths that the stock
price might take, assuming you know its volatility (which, of course, you
really cannot know in advance, and so even this calculation is a bit Pla-
tonic). You would make a lot of money if you guessed right about volatility, meaning you bought the option at a cheap implied volatility and the
stock had a much greater volatility afterwards, and if, in addition, the
stock price as it fluctuates stays near the point where it has maximum
convexity, that is, at the money. But if the stock price drifts up or drifts
down, the cumulative P&L in the diagram stops growing and stays flat

because there is no remaining convexity. You would be perfectly hedged for small movements of the stock when there is no remaining convexity, and so you would not need to rehedge at all, and it is the rehedging that produces the value associated with manufacturing or replicating the option.

So this is one difficulty—that your P&L on an options position depends upon (1) guessing correctly the direction of volatility (rather than the direction of the stock price) and (2) having the stock price stay in a region of high convexity.

Another problem is that you are required to keep rehedging continuously. Black-Scholes *assumes* you can hedge instantaneously at every instant. Every time a second passes, you are supposed to look at where the stock price went. You look at how much time changed. You calculate the Black-Scholes formula for the new delta, and you are supposed to dynamically rehedge and adjust the number of shares you short according to what the formula tells you. In real life, you can't do that. It takes too much effort, and it costs you too much money in transaction costs to hedge so frequently. You are stuck with having to choose a middle road between hedging very often, where you may be perfectly hedged but it will cost you a vast amount of transaction costs, and hedging very seldom, where the hedge keeps deviating from the "perfect" Black-Scholes value because you adjust so seldom but then you pay little in transaction costs. You have to do something in between. The diagram in figure 13 illustrates the difficulty.

This plot on the left of figure 13 illustrates the range of profits made, relative to what you should make if you could hedge perfectly, for a one-month option, assuming that you know exactly what future volatility will be. If you hedge according to your assumed perfect knowledge of future volatility, even then you still will sometimes make money and sometimes lose money because you are only hedging once a day, every twenty-one business days until expiration, instead of hedging continuously. Your hedge is imperfect during the day until you rehedge, and this causes random fluctuations in the replication and in the money you make from rehedging.

Even if you know the future volatility, you will still make mistakes because you cannot hedge continuously. If you hedge twenty-one times a day, you get a one-standard deviation error of about two dollars in the example above. If you hedge eighty-four times, which is four times as much, you get half the error. As you increase the frequency of hedging, your er-

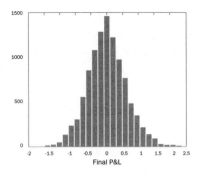 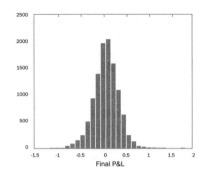

FIGURE 13. The hedging errors that arise in trading volatility
In order to trade volatility, you must hedge an option at every instant, so that you always eliminate the stock risk. But one cannot actually hedge continuously. If you hedge n times over life of option, the error in your future P&L is proportional to $\frac{1}{\sqrt{n}}$. Note: If there are transaction costs for each hedge, these increase with n. If you hedge more often, there are fewer errors in hedge, but you pay more in transactions costs.

ror goes down by something like the square root of the number of rehedgings. But then there is still the problem that with more rehedgings you pay proportionately more transaction costs. You are always caught between two imperfect alternatives. As one gets better, the other gets worse.

And this is all still assuming that you *know* what volatility will be. In real life, to avoid some of these difficulties, market makers try to diminish their need to rehedge. They try to buy as big a portfolio of options as possible, long and short, and try to hedge out as much of the risk as possible by buying and selling options against each other and only hedging the residual risks. They do not generally buy one option and hedge it. The errors are too large. Instead, ideally, they buy and sell thousands of options and hope most of them cancel out. They use the Black-Scholes formula just to hedge the convexity that is left over. If you are a market maker, you want to buy something cheap from somebody and sell it to somebody else and have no risk at all for yourself. You try to get as close to that as possible.

The Volatility Smile

Now I want to talk about the so-called volatility smile: Something is wrong with Black-Scholes.

Black-Scholes assumes that the stock has a definite volatility. All the options on Apple, for example, are "looking" at the same stock. There are options with a variety of expirations and strikes. If the model is right, the stock has a unique volatility, and that everyone should agree on. A stock that satisfies Brownian motion cannot have two different volatilities. I like thinking of options as being a bit like a CAT scan of assumed future volatilities, in the sense that an option photographs the underlying stock and tells you how people think the volatility of the stock will behave over the lifetime of the option. People using options with different strikes but the same expiration are looking at the stock from different angles. If they don't agree on the underlying volatility of the stock, there is something wrong with the camera, not with the stock. It is as if you took three pictures of your house with three different cameras from three different angles and your house had a different size in each. But your house has a definite size.

Figure 14 displays implied volatilities as a function of strike levels and expirations, first as expected according to Black-Scholes and then according to the S&P options market itself. If the model is right, you can only have one future expected volatility. In that case, the diagram of volatility should look flat as in the plot on the upper right of Figure 14. In fact, it looks more like the diagram on the lower left, which is a graph of S&P implied volatilities in 1995. It has a term structure that varies over time, and implied volatilities vary very sharply from low strike to high strike. It displays a massive variation with strike level, from implied volatilities of 24 percent down to 18 percent. This is a significant violation of the Black-Scholes model. People call it the "smile" because originally it looked like one in currency markets—a very slight smile. Now it's much more dramatic in equity index markets and resembles a lopsided smirk.

In fact, the smile or smirk now exists in all markets, in each in slightly different form. Figure 15 compares the graph of implied volatility for three-month Nikkei options as a function of strike divided by index level before 1987 with what it looked like after 1987. After the 1987 crash, lower strikes acquired a relatively higher implied volatility. This reflects the fact that people witnessed a crash and from then on, having seen it happen once, feared a subsequent one. They were willing to pay more for a put with a low strike than the Black-Scholes model with a constant fixed volatility would have led you to expect.

When you force market prices to fit the Black-Scholes model, Black-Scholes low-strike options have a higher implied volatility. This makes no strict sense in the framework of Black-Scholes because Black-Scholes

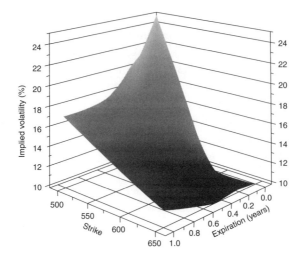

14A. The volatility surface according to S&P options markets

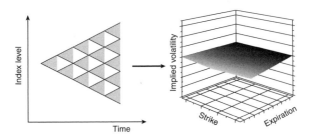

14B. The volatility surface according to Black-Scholes

FIGURE 14. According to classic theory, the Black-Scholes implied volatility of an option should be independent of its strike and expiration.
Plotted as a surface, it should be flat, as shown at right. Prior to the stock market crash of October 1987, the volatility surface of index options was indeed fairly flat. Since the crash, the volatility surface of index options has become skewed. Referred to as the volatility smile, the surface changes over time. Its level at any instant is a varying function of strike and expiration, as shown at left.

says all strikes should have one and the same volatility. But they don't. And so people now use Black-Scholes to describe what's wrong with Black-Scholes. What's most characteristic is that low strikes have high implied volatilities. The diagram in figure 16 summarizes the characteristics of the smile for equity index options.

For equity index options, low strikes have higher implied volatility. For gold options, it tends to be the other way around. In the late 1990s,

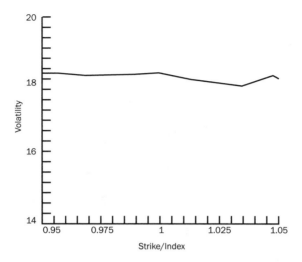

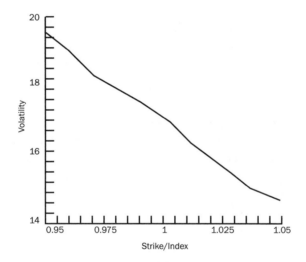

FIGURE 15. Above: Representative S&P 500 three-month implied volatilities prior to 1987. Below: Representative S&P 500 three-month implied volatilities after 1987.

the gold smile was almost nonexistent. Then, when the central banks announced that they might stop selling gold, gold developed a skew that was upward sloping, meaning *high* strikes had higher implied volatilities. The high implied volatilities tend to gravitate to the region of fear. The pattern of movement of S&P markets is to drift up slowly in small increments and crash down fast in large ones. So, with the S&P, the fear is at

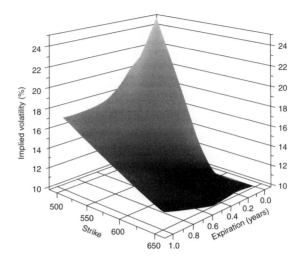

FIGURE 16. Characteristics of the equity index smile
(1) Volatilities as a function of strike are steepest for small expirations; (2) low-strike volatilities are usually higher than high-strike volatilities, but high strike volatilities can also
rise above at-the-money levels; (3) the term structure is usually increasing but can change
depending on views of the future; (4) implied volatility tends to rise rapidly and decline
slowly, going back to a long-term mean; (5) shocks across the surface are highly correlated
and there are a small number of principal components or driving factors; (6) implied volatility is usually greater than recent historical volatility.

low stock prices. A market drop will hurt the entire investment world,
so there is a higher premium for low-strike options. Gold tends to drift
down and then crash up when people get scared. The volatility smile for
gold therefore tends to rise at high gold prices. You pay a lot more for
protection against moves that will hurt you. Whether these fear-driven
premiums are actuarially fair, "fair" meaning that the options prices are
the appropriate insurance for the actuarial risk of the crash, is an interesting and relevant question, and I don't know the correct answer to this.

So, people in markets still use Black-Scholes. When they calculate implied volatility from the Black-Scholes model, this wrong model is forced
to match the market and give you the right (i.e., market) option price by
calibration. People half-jokingly say that they are using the wrong model
with the wrong volatility to get the right price but the wrong hedge ratio.
In fact, one can estimate that the hedge ratio for a standard index at-the-
money option might be off by as much as ten percentage points. When it
comes to exotic options, Black-Scholes is again the wrong model and will
produce not only the wrong hedge ratio but the wrong price too.

An Overview of Smile Models: Beyond Black-Scholes

Figure 17 illustrates the binomial view of stock evolution. The binomial tree shows heuristically what the possible future moves, up or down, of the stock price look like when volatility is constant in the future. Each of the little triangles represents volatility. Black-Scholes assumes that whether the market goes up or down, the volatility is always the same in the future. It calibrates this volatility to the observed market prices. But different options have different volatilities. To fit options with different volatilities, the binomial tree must be wider for low-strike options and narrower for high-strike options. Yet, the tree is supposed to describe the same underlying stock. How can the same stock have a different tree of imagined future movements for different options? There is only a single stock.

There are three classes of models that most people use to move beyond Black-Scholes and to accommodate the smile.

Local Volatility Models

Figure 18 shows schematically what the volatility surface really looks like. The surface has a shape. It's not flat. Local volatility models claim that the implied volatility surface is implicitly telling you that, for index options, when the market moves up, the instantaneous actual volatility

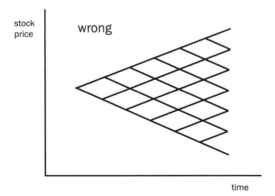

FIGURE 17. The discontents of Black-Scholes
Black-Scholes assumes geometric Brownian motion with a fixed volatility. We need to develop a different model for the evolution of the stock price.

of the S&P has to decline, and when the market goes down, volatility has to increase. It implies a directional element to volatility. Thus, local volatility models lead to a binomial tree of future possible stock price moves that looks schematically like the one in Figure 19.

This tree in figure 19 represents the notion that future index levels, when they go down, will decrease with an increasing instantaneous volatility (called the *local* volatility) and vice versa: when index levels go up, local volatility declines. The size of the triangles at each node in the tree schematically represents the magnitude of the local volatility.

These local volatilities can be calibrated to the smile, that is, determined by them. The procedure resembles the one used to determine forward rates from the yield curve in fixed-income markets. If you know the

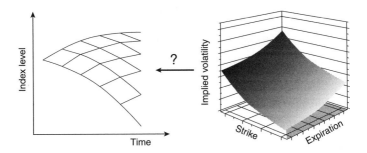

FIGURE 18. A schematic view of the volatility surface

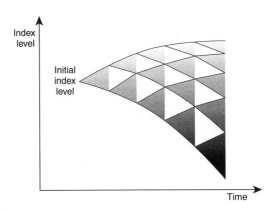

FIGURE 19. The local volatilities in a local volatility model that accommodates the volatility smile
Note the contrast with figure 17.

yield curve, you can back out what forward rates are. So in the same way, in these local volatility models, you can show that if you know three option prices with three different adjacent strikes, you can use them to figure out what the future local volatility has to be at a particular future time and future index level, as shown in figure 20.

You can build a tree as in the diagram above, which in practice requires mathematics and computer programming. There are appreciable

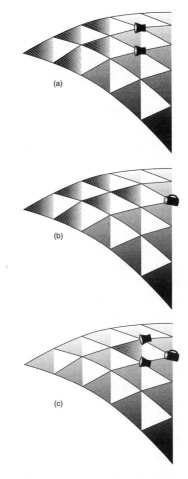

FIGURE 20. How the prices of three options can illuminate the volatility in one node
(a) Two options with adjacent strikes illuminate the triangles to their left. (b) A single option expiring one period later illuminates all the previous triangles plus one more. (c) Subtracting the earlier expirations from the later leaves just one internal node illuminated.

technical difficulties. One of them is that you need a continuum of option prices at all strikes and expirations to determine the local volatility, and there are only discrete strikes and discrete expirations traded. But one can persevere and handle these difficulties, and then local volatility models produce a formula for how volatility must vary with future stock price and time. In local volatility models, the local volatility is a deterministic function of the stock price, determined by the implied volatility surface.

Stochastic Volatility Models

In actual markets, the instantaneous volatility of an index isn't exactly determined by the index level, though it may be correlated. There is a correlation between volatility moves and index level moves, but the relation is statistical. Stochastic volatility models assume that even volatility is volatile. As shown in figure 21, instead of drawing a binomial stock (or index) tree to represent possible future stock price moves, one draws a double binomial tree in which the stock can go up or down along one dimension the instantaneous stock volatility can go up or down along another dimension.

If you want to think about this in a Black-Scholes framework, crudely and approximately, then, at any instant, the volatility of the stock can go up and you're effectively on a high-volatility Black-Scholes tree, or, at any instant, volatility can go down and you're on a low-volatility Black-Scholes tree, as sketched in figure 22.

The average option price that results from the possibility of being on a low-volatility tree or a high-volatility tree is *not* the price of being on an average-volatility Black-Scholes tree. You *shouldn't* use the average volatility. You should use the average of the Black-Scholes prices, *the price average, not the volatility average.*

As is always the case with models, you have to calibrate the stochastic volatility model to the market prices of liquid options. That means that you have to say to the market: "Tell me the volatility of the stock, tell me the volatility of volatility, tell me the correlation between the volatility of volatility and the volatility of stocks, and then I'll tell you the option price." Those kinds of details mean asking a lot of the market and the people that comprise it. No one knows those numbers reliably. So, in some sense, you can easily have garbage in and garbage out. It's difficult

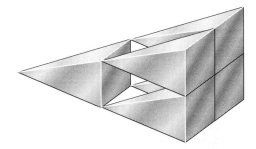

FIGURE 21. A quadrinomial tree that allows for a stochastic stock price and stochastic volatility

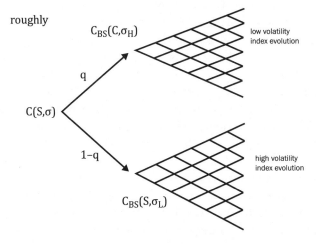

FIGURE 22. A schematic view of stochastic volatility
At any instant the stock may move between two regimes, a low-volatility future regime or a high-volatility future regime.

to calibrate these models to the market in a convincing way. Nevertheless, there is something realistic about them.

Jump-Diffusion Models

The third class of models are jump-diffusion models.

These models, though they were developed before the 1987 stock market crash, recognize that the crash of 1987 was a jump and that the experience of this jump and the fear of it occurring again cause a substantial part of the skew, especially for short expirations. If, for example, you look at a three-day, 10 percent out-of-the-money option, you are not worried about diffusion making the stock go into the money. The market isn't going to move 10 percent to get into the money in a smooth diffusive way over three days. If that option is going to end up in the money, it is going to be because the S&P has a large 10 percent jump in a short amount of time.

Jump diffusion models allow two scenarios at any instant for the stock price: a small probability—one percent, two percent, three percent—of a large jump down in the stock or index by a percentage, J, or a much bigger probability of nothing dramatic happening and just having diffusion. Figure 23 contains a diagram representing [a small probability of a jump] and [a large probability of diffusion]. At every point in the future, this possibility repeats, though we haven't sketched that. At every instant the stock or index can either jump or diffuse. The result of this evolution is shown for the stock price distribution at expiration is shown in figure 24, assuming that the jump J is downward.

The distribution of stock prices breaks into bands that look like Black-Scholes with no jumps, or Black-Scholes with one jump, or Black-Scholes with two jumps, or Black-Scholes with three jumps, and so on. Each jump takes you down a certain amount and then has a continuous distribution of the stock price around the center of the jump. Zero jumps have less probability than one jump which has less probability than two jumps, and so forth. The distributions with higher jumps are probable but contribute a tail to the distribution that gives you something like the observed skew, especially for short expirations. To be practical, one should allow the jumps to be of a variable size.

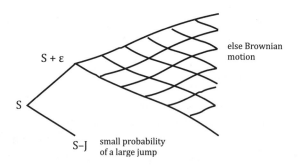

FIGURE 23. A schematic model of jump diffusion

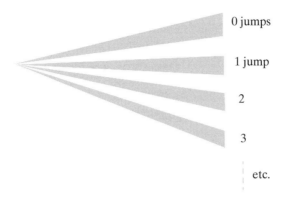

0 jumps

1 jump

2

3

etc.

FIGURE 24. The distribution of future stock prices in a jump-diffusion model

There is something realistic about this model too, but one cannot really hedge a distribution of jumps, which makes it difficult to put these models into practice.

Brief Conclusion

After the stock market crash of 1987, people imagined that we would discover one new model that would replace Black-Scholes and that would become the truth, so to speak. I don't really believe that. I don't believe that there is one better model out there that will handle all the vagaries of markets, especially since markets change their behavior as the people who participate in them learn more about their behavior. There is no easy answer or mechanical procedure to finding a better model to value options. The difficulties of quantitative finance are less mathematical in scope than conceptual.

Nevertheless, Black-Scholes, I believe, captures something significant and qualitatively real about the behavior of volatility as an asset and has opened up the way, for better or for worse, for markets to create many more derivative assets. One has to use these models in an exploratory way for a while, even pushing the envelope with them, but then one must always remember that markets are more complex than any model you write down. To assume that a model equation is actual reality is a form of idolatry—subject to all the biblical punishments idolatry incurs.

CHAPTER SEVEN

On Black-Scholes[1]

Elie Ayache, ITO 33

I'm radical. I don't believe there is value. There are only prices. I don't believe there is a statistical model that you can use to figure out, from God's point of view, what the real volatility of anything is. The major thing that the Black-Scholes-Merton model (henceforth BSM) brought into finance was the locality of the dynamic hedging strategy. After BSM you don't have to wait for the long run to break even like an insurance company with a portfolio of contingent claims. BSM has made the breakeven instantaneous by allowing you locally to hedge the derivative or contingent claim. But this is predicated on the fact that the derivative price is given by the market for you to track. It is local. Implied volatility is the only thing you have. That's why you need the market maker. I can't tell you where implied volatility comes from—how the market figures it out—and then inverts it into a value for "actual volatility."

The market is its own theory. It is a metaphysical theory in the sense that it is a theory of the event and the event is not reducible to any set of states of the world. The market *is* the model of the event so you need look no further. You have to be immersed in it. By that very immersion in the market—in the faith that no derivative should be redundant (this is my act of faith) and that every derivative has to have a price because it is eventually nonredundant with any model producing or representing it— you destroy any possibility that you could frame the market with a theory. Then you still have the market at the end of the day. The only computational theory of the market is the market itself.

The market is not the problem. It is the answer. It *is* the quantitative model of history and its numbers are what we call "prices." You will always have markets no matter what happens or how history unfolds. I know there are Marxist philosophers of the event who disagree with me. I don't think markets will ever disappear. There is no going back.

I traded derivatives for ten years, five years roughly in Paris on the MATIF from 1987 to 1991—and then in London. My first day happened to be in October 1987. I went to the floor, and the crash occurred, and I returned to the bank. It turned out the bank had lost huge amounts of money because it so happened that as market makers we were short out-of-the-money puts. Somehow the market had sensed that something was wrong and that the price of the underlying stock was abnormally high. So people were building up positions, buying out-of-the money puts. So it happened that when the crash occurred and the market jumped down by twenty percent, not only our firm but the five other market-making firms in Paris were massively short out-of-the-money puts. So we all lost money. Our firm lost ten times more money than the budget for the whole year allowed for.

That was October 19. What happened the next day was that the four other market-making shops—I'm not going to name them—closed. They did not want to make markets. As a market maker you are supposed to be committed to answer anybody who's asking you for a price. To ask you for a two-way price is not telling you I'm going to sell to you or buy from you. They're asking you for a two-way price, and then you have to be subject to whether they're going to sell or buy. So the four other shops just didn't open up for business on the day that followed the crash. We remained the only market maker.

My boss was clever enough to convince management that we should remain open. What happened the next day—this is true—is that our bank turned out to be the only market maker left in options on the ten-year French government bond futures (which were trading on the MATIF, or the market of financial futures). There had been a bid-and-ask spread from before the crash that, if I quote an option, was from, say, two twenty-five to two thirty-two, a spread of seven cents—that went to a bid-and-ask spread of something like two twenty-five to four twenty-five because we were the only market maker or provider of liquidity. Because such a huge movement took place and the underlying price had fallen by 10 percent or 20 percent, and because people who had bought the out-of-the-money puts from us during the four previous months had made so much money on the move, they wanted to sell and take their profits at any cost. They would sell us at two twenty-five. At the same time, other people were panicking and saying, well, this is only the beginning of a major collapse, so they were buying from us almost simultaneously at four twenty-five. The increased bid-and-ask spread was the only way we could face such pressure. It was the only way we could mitigate the risk of addressing such a crowd. As a result, by the beginning of the next week we had made back thirty times more than we had lost that first day.

So I was a big user and a big fan of the Black-Scholes-Merton model because BSM, as you know, was a revolution for the derivatives industry. It made the derivative valuation more or less independent of risk preference. BSM came up with a deterministic formula linking the value of the derivative with the value of the underlying. Keep in mind that the value of the underlying is stochastic as a price process.

I was a great user of BSM because it brought market makers to the floor and gave them the capacity to price derivatives continuously. BSM assumes that the value of the derivative is determined in all states of the world—that you will be able to readjust the hedge in the underlying in all states of the world. It's based on the assumption that you can represent the whole future as a number of states and you can assign them certain probabilities. But there is always something in the future as it actually unfolds that will be in excess of the representation you had of it as a mere random generator. Look at the work of philosophers of the event and you will see that the event is always radically new.

The event is something that is always beyond expectations. It is a new, emergent state that was not part of your previous stochastic model. Possibility, Bergson argues, is always fabricated *after* the real. The real happens. Nobody can predict the real because the real event is always a surprise. Bergson famously shows that it's always after the fact that you trick yourself into thinking that you could have been in a position to predict the event. The real—as opposed to possibility—always comes first. There is no way to stand in a position in which it is possible to know an event beforehand. It is only by a mental illusion that you place yourself in a position in which you could have predicted some past event as a realization among past possibilities, and it is by the same mental illusion that you think you are now in a position in which you can predict future events as realizations of future extrapolated possibilities. Time extrapolation, past and future, is actually irrelevant to the essence of the event.

This is what I want to say: if you believe in the essence of the market—that every derivative brings a radically new, nonredundant price to the table (in the sense that no derivative of greater complexity should be valued redundantly with the simpler derivatives)—then you are creating a criticism of the framework of possibility. This statement is analogous to philosophers of the event who are saying that the schema of the realization of possibilities is always weak compared to the reality of the event.

BSM assumes that you have a fix on the crucial parameter of volatility that you can put into the formula. You suppose that you can know the instantaneous volatility of the underlying price—you suppose that it exists and therefore you create a number for it. Then you may value the option. But this is only a mathematical derivation, the valuation of a mathematical function, which depends on an underlying variable and a fixed parameter, in this case volatility. This valuation is not put to practice. The practice is to hand the calculation over to the trader who will then trade the derivative in the market.

Here's the paradox. If the value of the derivative is the deterministic function of the underlying stock price and time given by the formula, why trade the derivative at all? It is mathematically valued. It's as if a computer could value it. The very fact that you are trading it means that the event of trading is going to be an event in the sense that the event exceeds any given representation in terms of fixed states of the world.

Traders don't use derivatives to trade the underlying; they use derivatives to make volatility tradable. BSM is used by traders (I was one of them) to place bets on the parameter that is supposed to be a constant. So the only meaning, according to me—the only purpose—of BSM is to hand over the calculative model of value to traders (not to social theorists or to university-based economists) so that trading can take place and acknowledge that the volatility number has to be stochastic. And if it is stochastic, it has to contradict the assumptions of BSM, according to which volatility is a constant parameter. This is not a sequential process. It is not as if volatility was constant at some point and then later became stochastic. If we recognize that the purpose of the whole BSM technology is to trade options, it is at the same time, as we hand over the BSM formula to the trader and recognize that he is a trader and not somebody who is just listening to a theoretic argument, that we recognize that the volatility number must become stochastic. In the actions of the trader there is a simultaneity in which value is modeled so that the model of value can be ruined.

The trader is a market maker. You are handing the theoretical model to the trader so he can make a market in options continuously. Although the model is continuously ruined by the market and the theoretical value that the model outputs is continuously overridden by the market price, crucially the market maker needs the model in order to compute the hedging ratio of the derivative (a.k.a. the delta). The options market requires market makers. Supply and demand don't clear themselves automatically. Because there are so many options trading, with so many different strikes and maturities, you need a specialist to quote their prices beforehand and to warrant liquidity. This specialist, or market maker, computes the hedge so he can immunize himself against the next movement of the underlying and then turn to the next option quotation and to the next trade. Even though he will not make a price outside the market and the BSM formula he is using is ultimately adjusted to fit the option market prices, the exercise is not empty and the formula is not tautological. As technology, its purpose is the option hedge. Technology is not pure theory. It is theory *plus* practice. BSM as a model of reality is wrong. As a technology, however, it allowed market makers to crowd the trading floors because it gave them a way to price options instantaneously and to hedge them. This was the way that the financial markets became more and more liquid.

The natural reaction to this by scientists and quantitative engineers over the last twenty years was for them to make the model more complex. They adopted a second generation of models with added parameters that made volatility stochastic. But the same logic applies—the logic of the event. There are no limits on the kinds of derivatives—the complexity of derivatives—that we can write because we can always write derivatives on derivatives. The reason you are writing those contingent claims and making them tradable is because they register a new price and therefore bring a dimension to your states of the world that was not in the model. Because no derivative can be redundant, the trader produces a continual criticism of any representation of the world based on the BSM model or its successive complications.

My understanding of the market is that this potentially infinite chain of derivatives has to admit of a price on the spot. By price I mean something that is not determined by underlying variables, like a function that is being valued. Price is not value. It is something new. You cannot frame the market in a probabilistic framework anymore. My conclusion—and maybe I'm too quick to draw it—is that the market is the ultimate, absolute criticism of the paradigm of possibility.

It is as if the market was telling me that I cannot frame the event of price within a totalized number of states of the world. I believe I can turn this negative definition of the market—the market as something one can never frame—into a positive statement: the market is the medium of the event or the market is itself a model of the event.

The event is unrepresentable and cannot be modeled—that is what its philosophers tell us. Now it is as if I were saying that the market is a communication channel inextricably coinciding with the unrepresentability of events. I'm not predicting the event, while being immersed in the market, because I'm not totalizing the states of the world. The present market price of the contingent claim takes place in time before the final event of the contingent payoff, yet there is no tree of possibilities that you can develop at any point in time from the present spot price to reach the actual unfolding of the event. It's as if I were getting what I wanted: I am situated in the middle of the event; I am in the real, the real that always takes place with the event; yet I manage somehow also to be standing before the event in chronological time. According to this new metaphysics, the market is the actual means that you have available to you of being chronologically standing before the event, yet of sitting logically in the middle of the event, because the market is as untotalizable in terms of states of the world as the event is.

I am saying there is no value—only prices. My problem is how to live as a market maker in a world where there is only immanence—where there is no value looking from above—and to survive. The only way that you make money in the market, according to me, is a very modest way: by being immersed in the market as a market maker trying instantaneously to buy things and sell other things with a spread, keeping in mind that, by definition, the model you are working with is going to be recalibrated. It is of the essence that the market maker determines the point at which he recalibrates his model. There is no substitute for the trader. Just as you need a subject for the event, according to the philosophers of the event, you need a market maker on the floor to produce a price. He has to be there as a performer rather than as a program. If you are standing on that floor, you are prepared to face contingency. I acknowledge that it is a somewhat mystical point of view that I am arguing for. I'm saying that every model has to fail. Otherwise there would be no market. To me the reality of the market is the positivity of this infinite sequence of failing models.

By my definition of it, the market is constituted by 99 percent non-market makers and 1 percent market makers. The non-market makers are not performing dynamic replication. They are buying financial products for ultimate reasons—they may be investing or speculating. The market is democratic in the sense that everyone is entitled to do whatever they want. However, *understanding the meaning of the market* is not democratic. There you are down to 1 percent. The ontology of the market is only perceptible through the market makers' point of view that, in derivatives, leads from dynamic replication (and the concomitant act of implying volatility from the derivatives market prices instead of reading it from God's point of view) to the whole bottomless pit where every model fails in succession.

I'm saying that to understand what price means, provided it is the price of an asset that is exchanged on a trading floor—to understand what even the next tick of price means—I need instantaneously to open this whole bottomless pit of derivatives. And what is the major trigger of my whole argument? It is that price means the result of an exchange. If you create a place of exchange and define price as the thing that will emerge from it, I am saying randomness—even of the underlying—will be of such a nature as to be irreducible to any probability representation. You need to unfold the whole story of derivatives in order to understand what a price means. You need to understand dynamic replication and what the market maker does with derivatives in order to understand what I mean when I say that the market is a bottomless pit and that there is no such thing as value, only price. This is how radical an act exchange is.

There are no such things as random generators in the market. I believe it is a mistake to see the market as a complex reality for which we do not yet have adequate tools of complete description. A quant's orientation leads many to adopt this point of view. Though present models are only approximations of reality, these people hold onto the hope that eventually their models will converge to coincide with reality. I don't believe this. I hold the opposite: Every model has to fail—otherwise there can be no market. There is no final, stable truth about the market. In a way, it is a terrible situation to be in.

It's not by accident that I'm tackling this angle of the market through derivatives. Derivatives are quantitative. Because they are formulas that are written down on a piece of paper and that prescribe what to pay off in what condition, they have given rise to the whole quantitative approach to their pricing problem. I know as a mathematical fact what a derivative is worth at the moment it expires, so it is very tempting to introduce mathematics the minute before it expires. However, despite the mathematical valuation model, the whole bottomless abyss of the market opens up in that one minute, because even a minute before expiration you are going to depend upon some parameter whose value you assume—some probability, some volatility—and this parameter is going to be put into trading in turn by the corresponding derivative. Despite the quantitative temptation inherent in derivatives and expressed in the models we use to value them, derivatives, as they are traded by a market maker, undo all calculations of probability and possibility.

Yet we cannot dispense with the quantitative tools or the mathematical models. We need them for market making. But the paradox is that by using them, we are at the same time criticizing the whole framework of possibility and probability. It is as if I had news to break—not to the financial community, because every trader is more or less aware of the limitation of the model, but to the philosophers of the event. It is as if I were telling them that I have a quantitative illustration of their philosophy and of their criticism of possibility—an illustration that materially exists because the market of derivatives materially exists.

In my narrative of derivatives, what I mean by value is what comes out of the theoretical valuation models. (I do not mean the value that actors in the market attach or deny to the derivative for whatever subjective, ethical, or political reason.) Now, against value as given by the valuation models, I argue for the immanence of the market and, consequently, that price is all there is. For instance, the fundamental parameter in the BSM valuation model is instantaneous volatility. This is a formal theoretical concept. However, given that there are only prices and no transcendent view of volatility, the only working concept in BSM is implied volatility. My whole investigation starts by trying to make sense of implied volatility. It consists in pushing things to their ultimate conclusion—as is appropriate in speculative metaphysics. If implying volatility means trying to figure out that number that is the fundamental parameter in this valuation problem from the only thing I have (prices of derivatives trading in the market, assuming liquidity), I thereby inherit a technology problem that to me is more materially pressing than any ultimate concern with value. It is a technology problem that justifies my metaphysical reformulation of the market.

Here is my problem: How do I devise and sell a technology to traders—based on definitive valuation models such as BSM and all the generation of models that come afterward—knowing that at every stage of

calibration of the given model to the market, the inferred parameters become stochastic? Because they are stochastic, they call for a higher-order
model whose own parameters will only be determined by calibration to
the market price, either actual or virtual, of a derivative of higher-order
complexity. How do I proceed to make the case for this activity without
a terminus?

If the market is the absolute matter, then every stochastic model of
the market that assumes an identifiable set of states of the world is like
a temporary section taken in that compact matter. However, it is only
through calibration to the traded prices that the model ultimately establishes contact with matter. The materiality of price is so significant
against the transcendent immateriality of value that even when basic
constituents of the underlying stock are concerned—such as the dividends it will pay out (as opposed to an abstract number such as volatility)—it is from the traded price of dividend swaps, or from the traded
price of futures contracts, or from put-call parity relations obtaining between options prices that they will be inferred rather than from some
forecast given by a financial analyst. The market trades dividend swaps
because there is no reliable forecast of dividends. Therefore it is once
again a matter only of price.

Every time something is not intrinsically subject to arbitrage with
something else, it requires a relative valuation model, or a temporary
section taken into the absolute matter of the market. Intrinsic arbitrage means that some derivative can be replicated, therefore valued, using other stuff without depending on any model. No particular assumption of states of the worlds and no particular probabilistic dynamics are
needed in that case. This is also called static arbitrage, or static hedging. But as soon as you have a derivative that is not replicable in a model-
independent way by another derivative, you will have to adopt a relative
valuation and a dynamic model. You will have to depend on the parameters of a model, keeping in mind that those parameters are going to become stochastic at the next stage because some higher-order derivative is
going to make them tradable.

Only when a given model prescribes the possible states of the world
can it price anything relative to everything else. However the market is
always destroying any model's ability to represent the total of possible
states of the world. If we push things to the limit and define the market
as the complete chain of failures of all (relative) models of states of the

world, we end up saying that there is a unique tool that prices everything in a model-independent way and that tool is the market. This is a tautology but it is also saying that the only (absolute) way of pricing anything is the market. It is absolute, yet it is changing all the time.

This is a different way of saying that the market prices of derivatives verify a kind of intrinsic arbitrage relation except that it is dynamic and not static. This ends in a paradox: Even though intrinsic arbitrage is supposed to take place only when there are no dynamics left (typically at maturity of the derivatives), now, with this ultimate form of intrinsic arbitrage known as the market, it is as if the market were not taking place before the expiration of the contingent claim and before the contingent event of its payoff but in the middle of that event. It is as if chronology no longer mattered and we were only accidentally standing before the event in time, yet as if we were nevertheless in essential communication with the event itself.

A young French philosopher, Quentin Meillassoux, has been key to all my reframing of the market in metaphysical terms. In his book *After Finitude: An Essay on the Necessity of Contingency*, he argues that the only thing that we can necessarily think, or the only absolute that philosophical speculation can purchase, is the necessity of contingency. Everything is contingent. Before we say that anything is, we need to say that the thing may be this or may be different, or may not be at all. It's as if he were saying that the basic matter in the world is no longer matter in the way physicists know it, but that the basic matter is now contingency.

Let's then assume that contingency is matter and that it is the absolute. It is absolute because you cannot frame it in any relative frame of reference and reduce it to a list of identifiable possibilities. What is the invariant lying behind this relativity, or the intrinsic difference lying behind all the probabilistic sections of the contingent event? What is the geometry that relates to absolute contingency in the same way that the geometry of the universe relates to the matter it contains, in Einstein's general theory of relativity? My answer is that it is the market.

The market is when the future is of concern—when the future becomes the issue and the only thing that matters. To me the market is the material process that puts you in contact with future contingency. It is the technology of the future. Price is only meaningful insomuch as it means price volatility. The dynamics of the future are embedded in it. I am not referring here to Brownian volatility in the sense of BSM.

Brownian volatility and BSM are only the first step in my reasoning, the first instance of the chain of calibration and recalibration leading to the bottomless pit and to the radical contingency that it reflects.

Price is linked to the fact that something is exchanged. As soon as you put traders together in a pit and tell them to exchange things—even basic stuff such as commodities—you virtually have derivatives. Nothing stops a trader from writing futures and other derivative instruments on top of the exchange of a potato or anything else. It is as if when you were throwing the dice you were also throwing the probability distribution of its outcomes and the probability distribution of the probability distribution, volatility, and the volatility of volatility, all in the same throw. And it is as if the throw never actually lands—this is radical contingency.

I need market makers to complete my philosophy. I need them to use the software my company develops and to extend the theory into a technology. The only way for option market makers in vanilla options to be able to run hedges is to become market makers in exotic options. Recalibration of the BSM model, used to price the vanillas, leads to a stochastic volatility model, and only the prices of exotics can help calibrate the latter. There is no end to the chain. The only way to close it is to put this philosophy in the hands of the market maker who will not close the circle and frame the market. On the contrary, he will open it up because he will be standing on the market floor.

Statistics from past performance or past returns do not matter. All that matters is the present of market prices and the market maker standing on the floor prepared for any contingency. Prediction is out of the question because probability is out of the question. The market itself replaces prediction. You hedge in order to be able to close your books at the end of the day and wake up the next day to start again.

The software we develop in my company gives our clients a less naïve model than others. The crucial thing is captured in the word "recalibration." "Recalibration" means that you have to start from somewhere because we all live accidentally in time. Time is unavoidable but not essential. At any point in time a trader needs to have a way to expand the model, the randomness, or states of the world, so that he has a new context to frame new events. He needs to be able to expand the state space to accommodate the volatility that becomes stochastic the next day without throwing the model away. He wants to keep the model—or let's rather call it the tool.

We found that a regime-switching model can give him that capacity. The regime-switching model is a jump-diffusion model for the underlying whose parameters (Brownian volatility, size and intensity of the jumps) change stochastically in bundles called "regimes." Different regimes of volatility mean stochastic volatility. However, this stochastic volatility model can itself vary in regimes of regimes, and this implies a stochastic model of stochastic volatility. Since regimes of regimes translate into further regimes that are similar to the first, and since the regime is an open bundle that can virtually contain anything, a given regime-switching model is structurally similar to its stochasticization. As a result of my company's technology, the pricing tool can sustain recalibration and the market maker can keep it and not throw it away.

A virtuous circle flows from being a market maker and creating liquidity and using liquidity to recalibrate the pricing tool. I don't know where the beginning of this circle lies. The market is a continual change of contexts and cannot be reduced to a Bayesian probability updating because of the emergence of new worlds. These worlds are incompatible with the previous ones and cannot be subsumed with the previous ones under a more encompassing world or larger set of states.

The market "writes" history in its way, and history is certainly superior to a stochastic process. History is a series of history-changing events. It so happens that the market is made up of numbers (prices going up and down) and this tempts us to use probability models. The market is quantitative history. Instead of looking for probabilistic models of the market, we should understand the market as the quantitative model for history (a kind of numerically constituted soundtrack of the far richer movie of history).

The market exists. It is real, if only in the sense of the marketplace where the market maker acts. It is material, the medium through which history is transmitted. Somehow I want to turn the gap between contexts, or the void out of which the event emerges, into a positive matter. I want to define the market as the endless failure of probability models, only turned positive. Perhaps in this way a reality that is alternative to the reality of statistics and temporal processes can emerge.

CHAPTER EIGHT

Mapping the Trading Desk

Derivative Value through Market Making

Robert Wosnitzer, New York University

Mapping the trading desk is not a description of its topography, nor a catalogue of the people, machines, and models used by traders in the everyday exchange of financial instruments. It is neither abstract nor a self-evident object where economic value in the form of price is mediated. Mapping the trading desk in the context of this volume refers to the work of trading and, in what follows, the specificity of the kind of work by particular subjects that is performed in the circulation of credit instruments through the bond market.

The markets for capital—whether stock, bonds, or formal derivatives —are often imagined as sites of speculation par excellence. For neoclassical economics and financial theory, this is considered a good thing when things go according to plan, as these markets emit data in the form of prices that reveal the value of various capitals for circulation in the economy. The assumptions are well documented: information symmetry, fundamental value, actors behaving rationally, and so on. So, too, are the exceptions, made most famous by Keynes (1936), identifying those moments when "productive" speculation morphs into "animal spirits" (Akerlof and Shiller 2009). Taken up by Shiller, "animal spirits" help to explain the financial crisis of 2008, much in the same way that former Fed Chairman Alan Greenspan identified "irrational exuberance" (1996) as what explained the bubble for tech stocks at the turn of the millennium (Shiller 2000), as "fundamental value" was imagined illusory or, more accurately, as Dick Bryan (2012) has pointed out, no longer a measure for meaningful value. On the heels of the 2008 near collapse, a new form of speculation emerged as the culprit, where Paul Volcker targeted "proprietary trading" as the institutionalized form of speculation that was making the banking system unsafe for everyone.

Suspicion toward speculation, as Martijn Konings (2014) and Marieke de Goede (2005) smartly trace, has a long history, and today is no different. Following that work, and perhaps on a more granular level, I am interested in how a particular form of work—in this case, credit trading—that is geared towards the circulation of socially and technologically mediated financial instruments carries a structure of speculation that is understood as an ethos, or spirit that drives it—a speculative ethos of proprietary trading in the credit markets. To refer to a speculative ethos is not to assert the crude amplification of chance, or conceptualizing a "casino capitalism" (Strange 1986) that informs some critiques of financialization. Rather, the speculative ethos is a particular kind of work that is exemplified by its immanence in the day-to-day practices of proprietary trading as it is mediated across and through a dense network of actors, machines, and models. Its structure—the structure of speculation that follows a derivative logic, if you will—carries the imprimaturs of temporality, calculation, audit, and volatility as the labor of making liquidity for financial derivatives through the circulation of differences. These differences are economized by spreads, the quantifiable, calculable, and numerical representations that measure the spaces between differences in the valuation of financial instruments, enabling competing claims of value to emerge in the production of wealth.

One of the most fiercely debated and contested elements within the sweeping Dodd-Frank Financial Reform is the so-called Volcker rule and its attempt to limit, or ban altogether, proprietary trading (prop trading, for short). Prop trading is notoriously difficult to define with precision, and it is this lack that underwrites much of the debate as regulators attempt to construct the rules that define the practice. Simply put, prop trading is a form of exchange in financial instruments whereby a trader is authorized to buy or sell on the sole behalf of the firm, using the firm's own capital, and assuming all risk. The bank is responsible for all losses, while also entitled to all profits. This definition of prop trading is what might be called "pure" prop trading, insofar as the trader within the bank is not interacting with any of the bank's clients.

This form of "pure" prop trading stands distinct, both in practice and regulatory definitions, from what is called market making in the capital markets. Market making is the general practice whereby traders actively and consistently provide prices for counterparties to exchange financial instruments; in the parlance of the industry, this is simply providing a bid-ask spread, or the prices at which a trader is willing to buy (bid) and sell (ask) in specific quantities. As may be seen from contemporary debates—a veritable cottage industry has sprouted up around the Volcker rule—figuring out where the line between market making and prop trading is a difficult exercise, leading Jamie Dimon to claim that "if you want to be trading, you have to have a lawyer and a psychiatrist sitting next to you determining what was your intent every time you did something" (Protess 2012).

Yet, the specifics of market making are notoriously diffuse and are practiced differently in each capital market. For example, most public exchanges, like the NYSE, require market makers (known as "specialists") to always provide a bid-ask spread to all counterparties in order to maintain orderly and liquid markets; counterparties are typically other traders, acting as intermediaries for public customers. In over-the-counter markets, by contrast, market makers are expected but not required to make active bid-ask spreads, and rarely do traders transact amongst themselves—their counterparties are either clients of the bank, or another set of intermediaries, known as street brokers, that act on behalf of other traders. For OTC markets, the distinction is between "client-facing" desks, also known as "flow" desks, or the "pure" prop trading desks, where the former is authorized to speculate on the future demands of counterparties and the latter is operating much like profit-maximizing hedge funds that seek out small price anomalies in credit instruments.

The distinction is important in three dimensions. First, OTC traders can withdraw liquidity at any time, as they are not required to make bids or offers; indeed, in 2008, it was the collection of traders in the credit markets that withdrew bids, making access to capital—and thus circulation—impossible for some counterparties. Second, because any bid or offer in the OTC market is always contingent, price discovery is opaque and densely uncertain, requiring a "long chain" of mediation in the process of making a claim on the value of a financial instrument. And third, in the provision of bid-ask spreads, market makers often wind up building inventories, or portfolios, constituted by long or short positions that are a consequence of making the market—and inventories require capital.

Herein lies the rub for the definitional problem of prop trading, whereas once market makers build an inventory, they are exposed to a variety of risks financed by the firm's capital. Because they can't always know when buyers or sellers might appear, nor at what price, market making, or "flow" trading, is thoroughly speculative, and desks deploy different hedging techniques that, like Black-Scholes, attempt to price and assuage different kinds of risks in the market.

Here, too, lies the crux of my argument. In the act of making markets, credit traders are concretely performing the market and themselves as a series of unfolding events through price taking. Market makers pronounce their actions as making liquidity for the markets, but the process of liquidity making is the staging of uncertainty and the constitutive act of releasing volatility. Uncertainty is the raw material that flows through the various levels of mediation, binding and blending different future possibilities in the same logic of the derivative. Each consummated trade, or event, produces a price in time that sets the stage for the subsequent unfolding for the next price, using the produced price to calculate and measure a newly calibrated volatility. Their method is thoroughly speculative in the more complex sense of making multiple claims on multiple futures by mediating chains of value through a dense sociotechnical grid, and its form is derivative in the decomposition and recombination of social and economic attributes to make claims on the risk objects that circulate through these spaces.

As such, the form of speculation in the making of markets takes on a distinct character that renders it different from crass speculation and is productive of value. In this sense, this project shares an affinity with Max Weber's (2009) magisterial work, as Weber's "Protestant ethic" made the routinized and methodical work historically and materially distinct from other forms of labor, providing a deep structure of belief and value for the Protestant sects.

A mapping of the trading floor, then, is an attempt to construct the very specific kind of work of trading, specifically for the global credit, or bond, markets. Choosing the bond market as a site of study is not accidental, as I would argue its sheer size and depth not only make it relevant, but also so that so many forms of wealth pivot around credit today. The bond market is also a bit anachronistic, neither fully automated nor marked by a foundational calculative model, yet carries those markers within its structure. The OTC structure of the bond market renders it as a space that requires multiple forms of mediation, making it an entanglement of actors, machines, and models.[1]

The bond market does not exist in the sense that, say, the NYSE exists—there is no centrally organized exchange, nor the orderly flow of transactions through computer systems that match buyers and sellers. The bond market is constituted by trading desks residing within investment banks, dense sociotechnical assemblages. They serve as intermediaries in the circulation of surplus capital, matching buyers and sellers of capital—typically institutional investors, such as hedge funds, insurance companies, pension funds, and the like who seek returns through the ownership of a variety of risk exposures—so that corporate bonds, mortgage-backed securities, asset-backed credit card receivables, student loans all circulate through credit-trading desks in the transfer of capital.

The central site for the making of credit markets is known as the "trading turret." The turret is a technological apparatus that positions the trader with a panoptical view of the market in space and time. The central object of all contemporary turrets is the Bloomberg terminal, the software package that not only displays active prices for various markets but also connects every credit trader, salesperson, and customer in a closed network. The system runs powerful calculations of pricing models, holds descriptions of instruments, maintains the trader's book, or inventory, with real-time profit and loss calculations, and has a private, closed instant-messaging system that allow traders to communicate across multiple dimensions simultaneously.

It is from the turret that the trader makes markets both in competition and cooperation amongst other participants both internal and external to the firm. In the interest of time, I just want to decompose the act of market making into its constitutive elements, starting with the trader's run.

Flow and Proprietary Trading

Each morning one of the hallmark rituals of credit trading is enacted, known as "the morning run" (Abolafia 1996; Zaloom 2006; Miyazaki 2013; Lepinay 2014). It is a shared ritual, performed by virtually every trader on every trading desk, every morning, constituting what Anderson (2006) has called the "imaginary" social space that is bound together by a commonly shared routine or ritual. The morning run is a running ledger of financial instruments assigned to that trader, a list of all securities in which they are "axed," indicating prices at which they will buy or sell throughout the day and indicating the market for each bond. Being "axed" means that a trader has "an interest" in a particular bond. The nature of the "axe" is ambiguous, as it could mean that (1) the trader owns these bonds in inventory and is making active markets in them; (2) the trader knows of a customer—through a different salesperson— who has indicated that they are a buyer of this specific bond, or bonds in this maturity range that carry similar ratings; (3) the bank arranged the bond offering in this issue, and the trader is expected to maintain active markets in the bond (or at least appear to—being "axed" is one way to signal "interest" without being really interested); or (4) the trader has been thinking about using this particular bond as part of a "pure" prop strategy and is seeking to build a position. Some bonds will have both bids and offers, others just bids or offers only. Once this run is compiled, traders send it through the Bloomberg message system to a predefined list of institutional accounts, salespeople, street brokers, and regional dealers.[2]

However, not all runs are identical. That is, the run that a trader shows directly to the bank's institutional accounts and internal sales professionals reflects prices that are, to one degree or another, different from the prices shown street brokers and regional dealers. Because the competition for accounts is of paramount importance, the run reflects the preferential treatment afforded the institutional client. For example, if a trader on his run indicates that he would sell 5 million Apple Computer ten-year bonds at +50 directly to an institutional account, he would likely show that same amount to street brokers and regional dealers at +45. The logic is that the trader does not want their competitors to show their accounts an offering of bonds that is the same or cheaper than their own. Their competitive advantage in this example is price and their ability to control it.

The morning run exemplifies a derivative logic that blends attributes and binds time across the spatial dimensions of the market. The production of multiple runs is not merely a speculative bid in the conventional sense, where the trader is understood to be opportunistically taking a series of chances in the hopes of a particular outcome in a "hyper-rational" manner (Abolafia 1996). Rather, the multiplicity of morning runs is mediated through a ramified social and technical network, with each iteration making contingent value claims, composed in the language of spreads. The multiple spreads are "spreads of spreads," illustrating the manner by which traders attempt to produce value through the small differences between uncertainties. In a sense, the collection of agentive spreads represents and articulates the subjectivity of the trader as a dividual and the social relations emerging from a circulatory mode of production that is animated by this particular structure of speculation.

A trader on a flow desk can originate a proprietary trade without mediation from a client. Here, the trader identifies something more than a simple arbitrage opportunity. In this instance, the trader may simply go to the street market, by way of the interdealer brokers, and begin to buy positions in the credit, placing the bonds in inventory. No client of the bank was involved, and the trader's position is financed by the bank's capital.

Another version of the "pure" prop trade from the flow desk would begin similarly—a trader identifies a credit in the market that he (and likely the team of analysts) thinks to be cheap. After going to the street market to buy bonds, he may find that no offerings exist. To fulfill and execute the position, the trader will then exhort the sales force to contact their accounts and show his bid.

Here lies the central "conflict of interest" between traders and clients of the bank and a powerful source of tension between salespeople and traders. The first presumption is that the trader, as being on a flow desk, should allow the customer access to the information he and the analyst have used to make their decision. As the trader makes his intentions known to the sales force, he does not reveal that the position is proprietary; rather, he allows the impression to form that he's buying on behalf of another client of the bank. The conflict of interest presumes, of course, that the trader is right—but that can only be known in retrospect. The claim that prop trading creates such conflicts of interest is never quite clear and, like many features of prop trading, is ambiguous at all times.

Furthermore, for a "pure" prop trade on a flow desk, the trader may not fully hedge the position, in order to amplify exposure to the market and capture the gains when the corporation's credit improves. For example, if the position is a total of twenty million dollars in bonds, it would normally be paired (hedged) with a short position in an equivalent amount of correlating Treasuries. Here, though, the trader might short a fraction of the equivalent amount, leaving exposure to the credit risk more fully. If the credit does wind up improving over time, rising in price, the trader will reap profit, which will accrue to his bottom-line trading P&L statement; conversely, any loss will negatively impact his book.

Seen in this way, "the proprietary trade" complicates the claim of providing liquidity to the market and more acutely reveals the way traders' self-interest is expressed. The main point here is that any proprietary trade is deeply contextual and deeply social and cannot be reduced solely to an external logic ("shareholder value") or mathematical equation (Black-Scholes options pricing model or value-at-risk), which are often tools and rationalization schemes deployed by traders at particular junctures.

Rather than act as a "pure" prop trader, most traders will perform prop trading as it connects to the flow of client inquiry—not the flow of prices in the market. That is to say, providing liquidity to credit markets means that the trader is often put in the position of trying to anticipate buyers and sellers, using an inventory to position bonds that are likely to (re)circulate to the clients of the bank. In this sense, then, much of the work that goes into the circulation of credit instruments might best be categorized as a form of affective labor; much time, effort, strategy, and capital is expended towards maintaining and intensifying the relationships between trading desks and their institutional counterparties. Rather than seeing trading desks solely as sites of competition over prices, it may prove productive to see them as the stagings of different kinds of labor that best cohere at the moment of price taking, and where the entire social structure of trading becomes visible.

Thus, the prop trade is always more than just providing liquidity, or facilitating and arranging buyers and sellers in some objective manner. It is a total social fact within the world of credit trading and has the potential to fracture as well as bind the social totality that is always emergent. The prop trade is also a validating structure, in that its success in generating profit confirms the status of the trader—while traders rationalize prop trading as liquidity provision, this validating mechanism suggests something more is afoot.

A salesperson will communicate an inquiry from a client, say, NIMCO—who wishes to sell ten to twenty million Caterpillar Tractor due in 2038—and the salesperson knows that the trader is "axed" as the bonds appeared on the morning run.[3] The salesperson might relay the inquiry in an ambiguous manner, simply asking the trader, "How are you making CAT 8 1/4s of '38?" Phrasing it in this way opens up a series of unknowns to the trader, uncertainties that can be decomposed into different attributes that have social and economic meaning in the space of the trading desk.

Who is the account? What is the potential size of the transaction? What is the price of this particular bond? Are they circulating in the market at this moment? How many are available for purchase or for sale away from this particular customer? What is the price and liquidity level of similar bonds, for example those in a particular sector with a similar maturity? What are the potential event risks? What other customers of the bank are axed in this bond and in what direction? And what are his current credit limits?

Therefore, when receiving a customer inquiry, a good salesperson would say something like, "NIMCO is asking us to make a market on CAT 8 1/4s of '38. They're better sellers and are looking to move up to twenty million. They've been in the street already." What the salesperson has just informed the trader is that a large and relatively aggressive institutional account (NIMCO) is trying to sell, and likely offload a position in, CAT 8 1/4's of '38 and that other traders at competing trading desks have been asked to make a market for this account as well, at the same time.

Other unknowns still remain. What price have other traders quoted NIMCO? How many bonds has NIMCO already sold? How many bonds are bid or offered in the street? Are there more buyers or sellers in the street? What other accounts of the bank that we have relationships with own these bonds and would be willing to buy more? And, most importantly, why is NIMCO selling? Because NIMCO, relative to other accounts, is a large and active actor in markets, traders and salespeople want to insure that their relationship to NIMCO remains strong and that they can maintain a dialogue. In other words, because the bank is reliant upon NIMCO at any given time, they do not want to do anything that would upset NIMCO or give it reason to be suspicious.

The other important uncertainty faced by traders is the extent to which the market for any particular security is liquid internal to the bank. This is to say, the quoted market from the street broker reflects the external price at which traders can sell or buy bonds with counterparties. Traders would prefer, at all times, to transact trades internally, with their clients. That is, buying or selling bonds from inventory directly to the account through the salesperson (a prop trade that "worked") or, similarly, buying bonds from one account and immediately selling them to another—a riskless trade.

Therefore, if a trader knows that specific institutional accounts who are clients of the bank are buyers or sellers of any security, it will enable him to be more aggressive and responsive to any inquiry. However, because traders do not often talk directly to the bank's customers, it is incumbent upon the salesforce to assiduously monitor and know the activity of their customers either in real time or the future, situating the salesperson as a key mediant in the circulation of instruments, as salespeople operate with similar speculative logics but with different means and ends.

So, when NIMCO asks for the market, the trader will check then with the street brokers to see if there has been any change in the street market since the morning and, if so, how many bonds are being bid. He will then recheck his inventory to see how many bonds he would be willing to buy from NIMCO and, if necessary, update the level at which he would be willing to buy.

Here, the trader is trying to gauge the market so that (1) he can calibrate his price to be competitive and (2) if he can't find a buyer, or feels he paid too much, he can try to see if he can offload the bonds to street. That is to say, the trader wants to make a competitive bid to the account, and should he win, he also wants to have the option to sell the bonds he buys from the customer to the street. Remember, the trader would rather sell the bonds to another customer internal to the bank, and he's willing to use his balance sheet to take that risk until the buyer can be located. Yet if the street bid proves to provide a profit opportunity at any time, he is free to sell his position and capture the spread between the price paid and sold. This is, precisely, the way that flow traders trade proprietarily, using the bank's balance sheet to buy bonds from an account, taking risk in order to generate a profit.

The issue is that the street market might be an indicated market, as other traders are trying to gauge the market by showing bids and offers, but have no intention of honoring the price. Remember that traders are not required to stand up to any bid or offer unless it is expressly qualified as being "firm." Remember also that traders use different runs for different constituencies, and street brokers usually get market quotes that are bit less aggressive than what the market would be for clients internal to the bank.

Traders intuitively understand this game and always view street markets with a bit of suspicion. Acting more as a guide than actionable prices, the street market is more accurately the source of what Fischer

Black (2012) refers to as "noise" in the market—the information that constitutes price discrepancy that stands outside of any "rational" or quantitative pricing model and is the source for all arbitrage opportunities. As such, it is the site from which traders can create new spreads in between the old spreads, generating opportunity from the noise.

Traders report this ephemeral feel as that moment when they can sense the market's direction and have accounted for as many variables as possible. Of course, what they are feeling is the volatility in the market, something that they become attuned to with the pulsing of the daily activity. Ayache (chapter 7, this volume) reports a similar feeling—what he calls "riding the volatility wave"—for derivative market makers, who are forced to make bids and offers constantly. The critical insight being made (with Ayache) is that with the trading of financial instruments, there is a moment when all rational and quantitative models are exhausted, leaving only the effect of the social interactions and accumulated social knowledge with which to act in the market.

Returning to the salesperson asking the trader for a market on CAT 8 1/4s of '38, the trader (if he has or hasn't engaged in the machinations in the street market) will decide to buy the bonds at a price he's comfortable. Depending on the trader's "axe," that is if he is either an aggressive buyer or seller, he may qualify the quote to the salesperson, saying something like, "I'd make them +140–130, but I'm a better seller." By qualifying the quote in this way, the trader is signaling to the salesperson that if the account is looking to buy the security, the trader may be willing to sell at a lower price than +130. Here, the trader and NIMCO are both better sellers, and because the trader is a better seller, he may actually want to buy the bonds more aggressively.

While this appears paradoxical, the trader is trying to protect his position in the CAT 8 1/4s of '38 that he already owns. The salesperson may or may not have known this, or the trader did not reveal this position. By aggressively buying the bonds from NIMCO, the trader is assuring himself that a competitor will be prevented from offering the same bonds that he owns in the street—or to accounts that are covered by both firms—at a cheaper level than he would like to sell.

If the trader is not "axed" in the security, he will tell the salesperson to "wait a few moments" so that he can contact his street broker to find out where this particular security might be trading—here, he is speculating as the opportunity to, perhaps, be in a position to make a winning bid, but at a price that will enable him to immediately sell them to

the street market, at a profit (riskless trade). The trader will usually call
the street broker using his direct line and ask the same question asked of
him by the salesperson: "How are you making CAT 8 1/4s of '38?" The
street broker then might say, "The market is +145–140, ten million up."
While adding, "We traded thirty million at this level already this morning." Again, in layperson's terms, the street broker has just informed the
trader that the market is +145–140 where traders at other firms are willing to buy ten million bonds at +145 and simultaneously there are traders willing to sell bonds at +140. Keep in mind that these amounts and
price levels are intended only for insiders. That is, they are intended only
for traders at other firms. Institutional accounts and retail investors are
prohibited from being in contact with street brokers.

If a trader is not axed in a security and does not wish to buy it for his
inventory, he will often use the street market as a reference and "back
off" the levels he will quote to the bank's customers. This is to say, knowing that there are traders in the market at other firms who are willing to
pay +145 for ten million bonds, the trader will quote a price "in back of"
+145 (say +148). Here he is "hedging" in case the customer wants to sell
bonds to the bank. He can pay the customer +148 and then immediately
sell those bonds to the street broker at +145, making a three basis-point
profit without taking any risk.[4] Keep in mind that the street bid of +145
is only good for ten million bonds.

Should the trader decide that he wants to buy the bonds from NIMCO
for his book (a prop trade derived from customer flow), the trader will
tell the salesperson to make a +135 bid for the bonds. The conversation
would sound as follows:

TRADER: "I'll pay +135 for ten million bonds. If they want to sell all twenty million, that's fine. But I need to know if they have more they want to sell . . . I'm
long these bonds, and don't want any more coming back into the market away
from me."

SALESPERSON: "If they have more to sell, will you pay +135 for those too?"

TRADER: "Let's buy these first, and then see what happens. Just be sure to tell
them that I'm a good buyer and that I want a look at whenever they go to
sell more."

Here, the trader is "testing" his market. He's already decided that he
"likes" the credit, and that if he should wind up buying the bonds, he's
comfortable owning them in his book; in other words, he's willing to

take the risk that at the price of +135 he will be able to locate a buyer—
either internal to the bank or externally in the street market—in the
(near) future who will pay more than +135. How he comes to possess
this knowledge is not the result of "fundamental" analysis, nor an algo-
rithmic model that imputes +145 to be a price that is more likely to go
higher. It is the feel of the flow of the market that tells him not that he is
certain of generating profit but rather that it is worth the speculation. Of
course, the trader is mobilizing an experience of past events and trades
in calculating the feel, as well as the rhythms of the current market in the
present.

To maximize his speculation, before he even buys the bonds from
NIMCO—recall that he's only been asked to provide a bid, and is yet to
know if it is the "winning" bid—he may go about offering bonds in the
street at a high level, say +125, in order to see if anyone might buy them;
if someone does, then he's short and must buy the bonds from NIMCO
(or remain short). It is more likely that should someone in the street be
axed in the bond—and not being asked to bid for NIMCO's bonds—
rather than outright lifting his offering of +125, they may show him a bid
slightly cheaper, which is usually three to five basis points less than the
offering—constituting the bid-ask spread—at +128. He's not required to
sell bond to the street at +128—he can simply say, "let me think about it"
or even outright "pass," meaning he won't sell them there. In this case,
the trader likely wants to keep the bidder bound to him, so rather than
pass, he will stall for time.

This is a shrewd move by the trader, as he's been able to gauge the
market more accurately. His bid of +135 to NIMCO looks decent in light
of the +128 bid he is seeing in the street. That is to say, should he buy
the bonds from NIMCO, he can immediately hit the +128 bid in the
street and make seven basis points on the trade, without using his balance sheet. Additionally, it may just make him more comfortable owning the bonds outright in his book, and he would keep the +128 bid in his
pocket to return one day. More likely, though, is that the trader will read
the +128 bid as a sign that he is buying the bonds cheap and that there
is more opportunity in generating more spread as the future unfolds. It
also allows him to decide that should NIMCO have more bonds than the
twenty million, he could be more aggressive—and, in fact, he may use
the information to increase his bid should NIMCO not be inclined to hit
his bid of +135.

Again, contingency rules. It is also possible that by offering bonds in the street at +125, the trader receives no bid whatsoever, leaving him with less information to calibrate his future actions. Also, it is a risky move, in that by offering bonds at +125, he is revealing one side of the bid-ask spread before a bid is available. A trader at a competing firm may also be asked to bid the bonds from NIMCO and, upon checking the street, see the +125 offering, and calculate a bid of +130—five basis points higher than the trader bidding +135, which would result in NIMCO trading the bonds with the competing trading desk, which, when actually occurs, is reported as "bond traded away [from us]," leaving the trader and salesperson wondering what the price paid might have been.

While the trader begins to engage with the street market, the salesperson returns to her desk, calling (or Bloomberg messaging) the client:

SALESPERSON: "Okay. Dave [the trader] will pay +135 for your bonds, for ten million"

Notice here that the salesperson did not say that they would immediately buy all twenty million bonds. She is trying to comport with the trader's desire to start with ten million bonds. But she also didn't say that she wouldn't buy more. The exchange would ensue, and keep in mind that the salesperson knows that she is authorized to buy another ten million should the account wish.

NIMCO: "Okay. I'll be right back."

The account has not committed to anything, and it is likely that NIMCO is still waiting to receive bids from other trading desks. The wait is fraught with anxiety, for both the trader and salesperson. The trader begins to monitor the street activity more forcefully, calling his street broker and asking, again, if he is seeing anything move in the market for CAT bonds. Other traders from competing trading desks may have tried to make shrewd maneuvers similar to his own, and the bid-ask spread in the street might start to fluctuate.

Typically, this is expected, and as long as the street market does not reveal that his +135 bid is too strong or too weak, the trader will be content to let the situation play out. However, if the established limits of the bid-ask in the street begin to move—and there are suddenly more bonds being offered—the trader will begin to suspect that NIMCO has sold their bonds "away," presumably to a higher bid.

The stakes ratchet up, as in the intervening time, the trader has contacted the salesperson that covers one of the accounts on the holdings list, asking her to see if they might want to buy more CAT bonds, and tells her to offer them bonds at +130. The trader is attempting to execute a quick riskless trade and make a five basis-point profit should the account take the offer.

Assuming that this is the case—the new account, called GENCO, has said that they would buy ten million CAT 8 1/4s of '38 at +130. However, the other salesperson has yet to hear back from NIMCO, leaving the trade in a precarious state. The salesperson covering GENCO is now another interested party and is asking the trader if they are done.

The trader demurs—either by ignoring the salesperson entirely or by a wave of the hand—as he tries to check the street market again to glean what might be happening "away" from him. Seeing bonds offered in the street now at +130, the trader could try to bid those bonds to fill the order for GENCO, but there is no assurance that his bid will be hit. He might then "throw" a bid into the street at +138, accomplishing two purposes: first, if another trader is trying to price the CAT bonds to make a bid to NIMCO, he would see +138 and (perhaps) see this as the "correct" price, leaving our trader's bid of +135 to appear strong. Second, should he get hit at +138, instead of making the five basis-point profit, it would now increase to eight basis points.

As he's doing all of these things, he's likely using his second telephone handset to cajole the salesperson covering NIMCO, shouting over the hoot, "Hey, Carol [salesperson covering NIMCO], what's the fucking story with my bid on these CATs?" It is an effective tool, as the entire trading floor hears the question, prompting the salesperson to respond.

The salesperson is also anxious, as she wants to put in a good performance for both the trader and account. The stakes for her are ratcheted up even more with the fact that another fellow salesperson is now dependent upon her being able to buy bonds from NIMCO to fill the order from her account GENCO. Salespeople loathe disappointing other salespeople, more so than traders. The camaraderie and similarity of purpose binds them in ways that it can't with traders, with salespeople understanding the difficulty and impotency when dealing with both traders and accounts.

The salesperson then calls NIMCO to push the issue, and her resources are limited. She can, however, use the bid for the extra ten million as bait, as it is a form of capital that she can use to enhance her bid—
perhaps the other trading desk will only take ten million, and by being
able to buy more from NIMCO, she might be able to make this gesture
decisive.

Calling NIMCO back, though, is fraught with danger, as it is bad
form to pester accounts. They may honestly be waiting for another trading desk's bid, or they may have been pulled into a meeting or something more mundane like a trip to the coffee shop. At the same time,
these possible scenarios—the account unreachable—are fodder to feed
the anxious trader, belaying his request for information. It is also a sign
of poor "account control" to let the account disappear in the midst of a
transaction.

After calling several times, the salesperson finally gets NIMCO on
the phone.

SALESPERSON: "Gosh. I thought you took off for the day. Everything okay?"

The salesperson is effectively shaming the account for leaving at a crucial time, while showing concern at the same time. Classic passive-
aggressive tactics are often used by salespeople in deploying "account
control."

NIMCO: "Oh yeah, I just got pulled into a quick meeting."
SALESPERSON: "Okay. So Dave is all over me here—he really wants your bonds
. . . how do we look?"
NIMCO: "Ah, the bid looks good, but I'm still waiting to hear from one more per-
son [a competing trading desk]."
SALESPERSON: "What if I wanted to buy all twenty million—at the same level. If
I can get Dave to agree to the full twenty [million], can we be done?"

The salesperson is responding to the amplified anxiety, and quickly
plays her only card by offering to buy all twenty million bonds. At the
same time, she's prudently cutting off another trading desk, leaving the
impression of her own savviness and aggressiveness to do business with
NIMCO. Importantly, she's also just left NIMCO with the impression
that she has leverage with the trader, by casting doubt whether or not she

can buy all twenty million bonds, when she has already been given the go-ahead from the trader at the outset.

NIMCO: "Really? Hmm . . . okay, I will sell you the full twenty million at +135"
SALESPERSON: "Okay, give me a minute. Don't hang up."

The salesperson need not do anything for a beat, as the trade is effectively done. She sits quietly for a moment and then, with her other handset, calls the trader on the "inside line" (not over the hoot)—to get the trader's attention, she may yell his name, instructing him to pick up the line, and being attuned to her for this trade, he picks up.

SALESPERSON: "Okay. You bought twenty million CAT 8 1/4s of '38 at +135 from NIMCO."
TRADER: "Okay. Fine. That's done."
SALESPERSON (INTO OTHER HANDSET): "Okay, you're done. I buy twenty million CAT 8 1/4s of '38 from you at +135."
NIMCO: "Great. That's done."

The spoken phrase "that's done" or "you're done" is the performative utterance that makes the trade "official," binding all parties to agree to the price and specific security exchanged—which is the reason for the particulars and price to be repeated often, ensuring that all parties are in agreement.

The trader can now go tell the other salesperson that she's done on her side of the trade, selling ten million of the bonds to GENCO—rendering half the trade a riskless transaction. The remaining ten million bonds go into his trade book, where he is now "at risk"—a prop trade, yet used to facilitate customer inquiry. He will immediately sell ten million US Treasury thirty-year bonds to hedge his remaining ten million bonds, leaving him exposed to the basis risk (+135) and interest-rate risk.

The salesperson writes a "ticket," entering all the trade details on the Bloomberg screen, and sends it to her client. She checks her P&L and sees that the trader credited her account two basis points for ten million bonds: he's paid her a portion of the five basis profit from the riskless portion of the trade, while paying the salesperson covering GENCO two basis points and keeping one basis point for himself. He can justify this because he is now at risk for ten million bonds—if he had only arranged the ten million between accounts, he would have split the five basis points evenly between the salespeople.

To complete the trade, the public of the trading floor is informed, where the trade is reperformed in the dense narrative of the hoot-and-holler: "Fantastic job Carol and Susan . . . we just traded ten million CAT '38's, in-house. I'm a better seller, with ten million more to go at +130." The reception of the announcement is met with admiration and envy by both the sales and trading force: someone else has just made money, increased their "number," and the performance is expected to be duplicated, if not enhanced.

The ten million "prop" position remains and is the trader's responsibility alone. If he makes ten basis points in a future trade, he keeps the entire profit in his P&L, and if he loses ten basis points, he takes that loss as well. The singular trade alone does not have too much determinate effect on his overall P&L, but, cumulatively, all the trades such as this that are entered into his balance sheet constitute not just his P&L but his understanding of himself in relation to other traders, as well as his external lifeworld. For in the overall P&L, which is scrupulously accounted each day—literally each moment and instance of the market movement—lies the indication of whether he possesses the derivative of grace, a job well done. Nothing is more stark than the end of the trading day when, required to submit his daily P&L statement to management, the number stares back, a vivid reflection of his worth, status, and sense of well-being in this world. There is no ambiguity in the number and, oddly, this is what trader's report as what is ideal about their job. The lack of mediation necessary to interpret the meaning of the number is what matters, leaving only the self-possessive individual to claim the wealth that has been created from the speculative circulation of spreads or bear responsibility for its lack.

At the moment of consummation, traders talk about a feeling of routinization, and seem to devalue their role in the process. As one trader responded, "I honestly don't think about much, and I hope that I am right more often than I am wrong." Other traders offered variants of this sentiment, and indeed the routinization speaks strongly to the ritualized nature of flow trading. Of course, the only way that traders are able to know if they were "right or wrong" is when they either decide or are forced to liquidate the position, realizing a profit or loss.

Appadurai and LiPuma (this volume) have offered a reading of this phenomenon through the ritual performance, arguing that all rituals are performative in that, when they succeed, the sociality of the group is affirmed and the object of the ritual is produced. The culmination of the ritual, though, produces the conditions of uncertainty for which it has been constructed to address, compelling the staging of the ritual in future contexts. Crucially, both argue strongly that all rituals carry the possibility of failure, producing the social fact of uncertainty itself.

Seen this way, the trader's statement of being right more often than wrong appears as crude speculation—making as many bets as possible and merely hoping that more win than lose. Through the lens of performativity in the ritual of trading, what is being secured and produced is the market itself, its conditions of uncertainty for continued action. Along with the social totality of the market becoming constituted through the ritualized flow that carries risk in its proprietary form, the self of the trader and the salesperson is constituted as well, forming a subject through the dense mediation.

Embedded in the turret, bombarded by data, information, and narratives of value, the trader must apprehend those attributes which he can then blend together in order to make the contingent claim of value in the near or distant future. The structure of the ritual trade is arbitrage, where the trader—and salesperson—are simultaneously "going short" and "going long" through the combinations of social and economic attributes available for circulation and exchange. In this "work of arbitrage," the structure of the speculative ethos emerges, rendering the process of speculation in this particular way as the means by which the self might experience success. While it is a truism that profit in the market emerges as the modern-day equivalent of God's grace, there is more to it than just that which is meaningful. It is the trade itself, the process by which it happens that provides the trader with a sense of mastery and transcendence over the radical uncertainty that is the market.

The trader's romanticization of the P&L number occludes the density and velocity of the mediation involved and denies the forms of association and dependency upon which its generation relies. While there is some passing acknowledgement of, perhaps, the sales force, the structural conditions that enable these circulations remain distant and abstracted. Indeed, the social itself is denied in order to lay claim to that which was created, a wealth accessed through these instruments that is animated by a form of speculation that is generative, valued, and reproduced the next day in the procession of ritualized trading.

There is an odd paradox at work, in that the "pure" and flow prop trade is the most forceful and individuated means by which a trader can generate profit. At the same time, it exposes him to multiple uncertainties and threats beyond his control, forcing him to construct narratives and trading techniques that operate to allow the trade to remain open until the profit can be realized.

Again, the preceding material constitutes the trader's consciousness as he begins to engage a trade. Of course, it is not elaborated in the manner in which I have represented it, as a slow and careful unfolding like a chess game. Rather, all of what I have just described is thoroughly routinized and enacted methodically. Yet it is riddled with speculation, the possibility of many outcomes, and it is this orientation in which the trader becomes comfortable, able to feel the market in his gut.

Despite the collaborative engagements, which hold for so long as they are effective, what comes out of this description is the individuated space from which each actor operates and develops hedging strategies of their own. In this type of work, it resembles not so much the high-stakes collaboration necessary for creative cultural work, as the velocity is markedly different. Rather, it resembles athletes from extreme sports, such as big-wave surfers, who are in a collaboration with the ocean's wave but are left to their own gut as to when they make the crucial decision of "stepping into liquid," beginning to assume all risk as they hurtle down the wave's face. Their maneuvers may be sublime, in the same way that a trader's "surfing" the street market for volatilities takes on an effervescent character that only he can effect, while "the street" watches.

The prop trade, then, contains the structure of speculation, where the outcome of the sublime is rendered meaningful, productive, and even transcendent, just as Weber shows how it was not work itself for the Protestant, but the way that work was structured to attain a human, direct experience of the unknowable mystery of God's inscrutable will, that gave it its enchanted character. The essence of this cognitive experience is the knowledge of unknowability, in the same way that the knowledge experienced through speculation invites direct apprehension of the radical uncertainty of the market.

It is not just speculation in hope of an outcome, of taking a chance. Nor is it crass opportunism that requires the astute observer to act to achieve a particular outcome. Rather it is the way that the type of work rewards and valorizes a particular form of speculation. The actors in this space are speculating through the act of hedging, of using different attributes derived from their social lives and quantitative calculations in different combinations, with no particular affinity between one or the other but for that blending of attributes that produces value.

Like the derivative, the blending of these attributes is bound to different temporal horizons, different possible futures. In fact, what makes prop trading prop trading is the element of time. That is to say, the ability to bind time in the present act of trading is what makes prop trading effective, and to have a value that cannot be reduced to nominal profit. The trader's "shrewd" actions in the street whilst engaged with the salesperson and account is a series of hedges, using quantitatively calculated attributes of the instrument and the social structure present in financial culture. Similarly, the salesperson's parsing of the narratives is the selection of attributes that, connected to the instrument, create possible futures. Going short and long simultaneously, vividly captured by the trader's decision to short bonds in the street whilst being long in the future, binds action in the present. The cumulative effect of these combinations of attributes placed in circulation produces the consequence of uncertainty, from which trading can begin anew, with new attributes from the generative volatility of the trade being placed in circulation, animated by this new ethos that values speculation.

Conclusion

Arjun Appadurai's chapter from this volume radically proposes a new kind of subject that is emergent in this structure of speculation, as opposed to the solidity of the coherent individual necessary for a kind of capitalism that preceded it. In detailing the work of credit trading, I want to show how the practice of proprietary trading produces subjects that mobilize multiple attributes of themselves through space and time in order to make claims in multiple possible futures with a set of probable outcomes. These attributes are put into motion through technical prosthetics, financial models, and narratives in a manner that cannot be accounted for in advance but only renarrated through the evaluative performances of audit and reflection. The actors—bond traders and salespeople and the array of counterparties in the market—can, in some sense, be seen as operating in a regulatory enclosure that not only allows them to extract value in an often disproportionate manner but also allows them to risk together in the circulation of values. The metaphor is not so much the rational, opportunistic—and often morally flexible—homo economicus swinging through the jungle of the market that is typically inscribed upon these actors but more like players in a game that operate in different registers of competition and cooperation.

Given that last statement, let me be clear and state for the record that this is not about recuperating the figure of the bond trader, or the Wall Street financier. I'm convinced that finance cannot be recuperated from within its own logic and practice. But reducing the practice of credit trading to intentionality—we all know they are out to make money—is to lose the opportunity to identify an analytic that carries a potential for the creation of wealth—a wealth that must break out of its enclosure within finance itself and become more socially expansive. So by asserting that bond traders have figured out a way to risk together in order to create wealth, albeit for themselves, the political question of how we might open up these wealth-generating capacities is placed on the table. "Desk, firm, God, country" is a rallying cry for traders, mobilized as an orienting discipline that, intentionally or not, assumes a harmony between the actions of traders and society, echoing the Smithian (1776) relation between self-interest and the wealth of a nation. The phrase stands in as the moral weight by which traders rationalize their actions and by which Lloyd Blankfein's claim to be "doing God's work" at Goldman Sachs is sincere (Alridge 2009). Yet, the ordering of value is neither uniform nor equivocal and might speak to the plasticity of value on one level, or perhaps illustrate the deep structural connections between finance and society. What is at stake then is not so much the imperative to remove or contain speculation but rather to reverse the value of the trader's rallying cry so that the social comes first, where the structure of speculation might be mobilized toward an expansion of the social itself.

Acknowledgments

This book was the product of the Cultures of Finance Workshop sponsored by the Institute for Public Knowledge at New York University. We would like to thank the directors of IPK, Craig Calhoun and Eric Klinenberg, for their support, and Samuel Carter and Jessica Coffey for their assistance running our Summer Institute in June 2013, which provided the first public platform for our collective work. We would also like to thank Stephen Bruce and the Bruce Initiative on the Future of Capitalism at the University of California, Santa Cruz, for its sponsorship of student fellows at the Summer Institute, Peter Dimock for his editorial guidance, and Eli Nadeau for her technical assistance in producing this volume.

Notes

Chapter One

1. This essay owes a special debt to all the members of the Cultures of Finance Group at the Institute for Public Knowledge at New York University: Benjamin Lee, Edward LiPuma, Randy Martin, Robert Meister, and Robert Wosnitzer. They prodded me to flesh out my ideas about the "dividual," and their own chapters in this volume, as well as our conversations over the last three years, have contributed immeasurably to this essay.

2. For an excellent overview of this burgeoning field, see Diana Coole and Samantha Frost (2010).

3. My understanding of the story of the subprime mortgage crisis of 2007–8 is deeply indebted to Michael Lewis's riveting book *The Big Short* (2010).

4. For a superb synoptic account of the political and ethical implications of the explosion in "Big Data," see Alice Marwick (2014).

5. See Alan Schrift (1997) for a superb overview of this French genealogy.

6. My understanding of performatives, as well as of retroperformativity, owes a great deal to many years of conversations with Benjamin Lee, also a contributor to this volume, who shares my University of Chicago graduate school immersion in cultural anthropology and brings to the table a strong grasp of financial formalizations as well as linguistic forms and practices.

7. The idea of the dividual is having a welcome revival in contemporary anthropology due to a series of arguments about comparative cosmology by such thinkers as Viveiros de Castro (2012), Descola (2013), and Sahlins (2013). This development promises a dialogue with new trends in science and technology studies and the new materialisms, as I propose in Appadurai (2015).

8. Elie Ayache's *The Blank Swan* (2010) is the first serious work of social science and philosophy to examine the critical role of backward equations, backward causalities, and backward narratives as features of the logic of derivative

trading. His account, as well as his chapter in this volume, points to a major common property of ritual and financial performativities.

9. Here my argument is especially indebted to the essays of Martin, Meister, and Wosnitzer in this volume, each pointing to the complexities of liquidity, surplus value, volatility, and spreads in the categories and practices of contemporary finance and the ways in which these forms can be mined for their immanent and socially generated wealth.

Chapter Two

1. At one point in the mid-1970s economists began to scan the ethnographic literature much like an invading army learns the terrain of the region it seeks to occupy. The idea was that since all humans are innately utility maximizers, formal models should be universally applicable. They were, however, turned away by economic anthropologists, led by Marshall Sahlins, Stanley Tambiah, Terence Turner, and Clifford Geertz, who illustrated that an economistic model could not capture kin- and community-based societies whose economics centered on gift exchange and competition for social status.

2. From this perspective, the intervention of social forces to redirect and inflect the reproduction of the market does not appear social at all. They are thus characterized as "noise," "herd-like behavior," "animal spirits," "primal fear," "contagion," and the like. All of these terms reintroduce the social by way of metaphors that point away from it, thereby preserving the ideology of systemically natural reproduction through systemically natural replication.

3. Rituals such as Sunday church services foreground faith, though they are one of the most lucrative markets in the United States judging by the many billions of dollars that churchgoers contribute annually in exchange for improving their odds of salvation. In her account of the relationship between *Faith and Money* (2011), Lisa Keister shows just how inseparable religion and economy are.

4. This progressive fitting of platform and practice has been referred to as "Barnesian performativity" (MacKenzie 2006, 33) in the sense that platform and practice are self-referential because they mutually confirm and sustain one another.

5. This formulation intends no metaphysics, only that the market cannot be real the way concrete categories such as earth and water are real. Rather, the market is "real" the way the nation-state is real, brought into existence in the late eighteenth century by virtue of a particular historically specific imagination of peoplehood configured in respect to territorial sovereignty and governance. There was once a world without nation-states, and there may so be again in the future, but for us nothing is as ontologically real as the nation we live in, that collects and pools our taxes, that replaces and elevates citizenship over kinship, that

defends our borders, and that on occasion asks some of us to put our life on the line for a totality composed of persons the vast majority of whose very existence we will never know of, other than abstractly.

6. Since risk is a relation that objectifies itself in other relations, most notably the wager internal to financial derivatives, its function in defining and stimulating liquidity is inseparable from the moment of objectification. Thus the production of derivatives, by amalgamating numerous context-specific risks in order to model and price them, objectifies risk in an abstract form. Even the notion of counterparty risk is inherently plural and social, inasmuch as it may encompass an open-ended ensemble of otherwise incommensurable risks, from a run of the mill bankruptcy to a government's seizure of counterparty's assets to a terrorist attack.

7. It is worth pointing out that the efficient market theory is actually not a theory of the market. It is a theory of circulation—i.e., trades that define prices—that presupposes a process of production that it cannot account for. For example, that a market is self-correcting (whether true or not) presupposes that that market is closed and complete but cannot possibly account for the production of that closure or completeness.

8. This information is critical in that it can cut both ways: it can assure the players that the market is liquid and that they can exit their positions, but also that a large player may have so much financial ammunition that it can afford to wait, sustaining or doubling down on a position in the hope that its prospects may change. This was precisely the situation in the recent debacle at J. P. Morgan.

9. For anthropology and social theory generally, the social has a specific reference. It constitutes the unmarked term that encompasses all of the ways in which concrete human actions enacted with sociospecific practices (such as executing a derivative trade) are the product of the organization (both institutionally and through the habitus) of deeply imbricated social, economic, political, and moral/ethic dimensions of contemporary life.

10. The logic of the argument, whose use of law plays off of physics, is that if there were more than one price simultaneously for a security then the model would not work, and since we know theoretically that the model does work, then arbitrage must be impossible. We know that for those not familiar with finance economics it is hard to imagine that this is an accurate representation of its argument, what with its mind-boggling circularity and its conflation of theory and practice. But that is precisely its underlying logic once the mathematical adornments are stripped away.

11. In practice, certain arbitrage spreads, motivated by social forces, can remain open for years at a time. This is especially true in the credit markets. A salient example: in the United States, AAA-rated municipal bonds and US Treasuries have a common history in this respect, since for both instruments,

the default rate for the previous century is zero. Nonetheless, the AAA muni has paid a higher interest rate—sometimes by as much as 250 basis points—over comparable treasuries with an identical coupon and maturity date. Moreover, the AAA municipal bond is free of federal income tax. Accordingly, an extremely profitable arbitrage from 2008 to the present has been to short US Treasuries and to use the money gleaned from the sale to buy comparable municipal bonds, thus capturing the difference or spread in interest rates. One reason for the persistent arbitrage spread is that it does not pay foreign governments to hold municipal bonds as opposed to the infinitely more liquid US Treasuries, which can be sold instantaneously in the event that a nation's currency is under attack from speculators.

12. In 1933, Kolmogorov set out in remarkable fashion the set theoretic foundations of modern probability theory. Note that the Black and Scholes equation for implied volatility is really only a permutation of the *backward Kolmogorov equation,* which sets out a means for determining the transition probability density function for a stochastic process. The permutation is that Black-Scholes substitutes the discount rate r for the drift rate u. The basis for the substitution is that inasmuch as we can always perfectly hedge a portfolio we should not be rewarded for taking unnecessary risks.

13. For example, Hull and White (1987) argue that adding a stochastic volatility measure would improve the accuracy of the equation. But this improvement would require determination of two more parameters, the volatility of volatility and the correlation between the volatility and an indicator of the underlier's price, both of which are well-nigh impossible.

14. When we sat down with two active derivative traders and went through how a deterministic volatility model works, they looked at us with a mixture of bemusement, puzzlement, and a dash of incredulity that anyone would think this was an accurate reflection of the real practice of trading. Traders as a group tend to know very little, nor do they care to know anything, about finance economics.

15. A real, albeit somewhat complex, example: a trader recognizes that due to a large stake in a security held by Berkshire Hathaway (Warren Buffett), his huge cash hoard and his intention to augment that stake if the price of the security falls, and that any number of well-endowed hedge funds mimic Buffett's trades, that security will in all likelihood have a very smooth ride—mathematically appearing as a smooth curve—in the upcoming months. This price tranquility means that the manufacturing costs of a derivative through gamma rebalancing will be relatively inordinately low, producing an improved risk-reward ratio. At the time of writing, this is the case for IBM. Note socially that the foundation of the trade is the trader's understanding of Buffett and even more so of how investors' respect for him inflects their investing behavior.

Chapter Three

1. This chapter is the result of conversations of the Cultures of Finance Group at New York University's Institute for Public Knowledge. I've learned immeasurably from Randy Martin, Robert Meister, and Robert Wosnitzer. But most of all I would like to thank Arjun Appadurai and Edward LiPuma for conversations that stretch back to our graduate school days at the University of Chicago.

2. There's a famous joke that a financial economist and his friend are walking down the street and the friend says, "Look, there is a twenty dollar bill on the sidewalk!" The economist replies, "That's impossible. If there was, someone would have already picked it up."

3. Von Neumann and Morgenstern's distinction is between static and dynamic theories—"A static theory deals with equilibria. The essential characteristic of an equilibrium is that it has no tendency to change, i.e. that it is not conducive to dynamic developments. An analysis of this feature is, of course, inconceivable without the use of certain rudimentary dynamic concepts. . . . For the real dynamics which investigate precise motions, usually far away from equilibria, a much deeper knowledge of these dynamic phenomena is required" (1944, 45).

4. The information on Black comes from Perry Mehrling's excellent biography of Fischer Black, *Fischer Black and the Revolutionary Idea of Finance* (2005), which provides enough personal detail to paint a portrait of a brilliant thinker torn between his mathematical and analytic abilities and his interest in creativity and innovation.

5. It has been pointed out that there exist some exceptions to the axioms of expected utility developed by Von Neumann and Morgenstern (see Luce and Raiffa 1989 for a good overview). The continuity assumption seems to be violated when the choices involve existentially large stakes—one's life, reputation, or total wealth. For example, it doesn't seem that it would be irrational for someone to reject a lottery choice between death and a large monetary reward; nothing would be worth putting one's life on the line, no matter how small the risk and great the reward.

6. This argument of Derrida's is a reprise of his earlier critiques of Benveniste's (1973) treatment of the predicate "to be" in Indo-European languages, which appear in "Form and Meaning: A Note in the Phenomenology of Language" and "The Supplement of the Copula: Philosophy before Linguistics," published in 1972 and translated a decade later in *Margins of Philosophy*, only with the gift replacing the problem of the being of language in the earlier papers.

7. Emile Benveniste introduced the idea of performativity to French audiences after the famous 1957 conference at Royaumont between French and Anglo-American philosophers, which he and Austin both attended.

8. Marx's example of the "Indian commune" as a society of nonalienable exchange confirms Appadurai and LiPuma's insights about the dividual nature

of gift relationships; the Indian caste system was one of the sources for the development of the notion of dividualism by South Asian anthropologists such as McKim Marriott. Caste relationships governed social relations in India, and the exchange of substances such as food also entailed "codes of conduct" for the exchange partners—in a deep sense, you are what you eat. The disgust or revulsion that one felt upon ingesting food prepared by someone from an inappropriate caste was not a product of some internal decision-making process but rather an embodied response to the recognition of the infraction. The behaviors that governed caste exchanges were seen as inseparable from the objects exchanged and were embodied dividualized reactions rather than the product of individual intentionalized decision making.

9. Edward LiPuma has pointed out that the speculative moment in Catholicism concerns the existential timing of one's death. Under its doctrine, a person who has lived a mostly exemplary life will be sent to hell if, for example, after committing a rare offence, he perishes so suddenly that he had no opportunity to confess and hence confronts God in a state of sin, while a lifelong sinner (even the murderer) attains heaven if he should confess and thus die in a state of grace. The Catholic wager is that every unconfessed mortal sin could potentially result in eternal damnation. Commission of a sin is thus a bet that the moment of my next confession will precede the moment of my death—about which, of course, I am uncertain, though not radically so perhaps.

Chapter Four

1. On the relation between base money creation and government borrowing see Cook (2011) and Kaminska (2012d).

2. For the argument that "liquidity" is not a separate attribute of an asset affecting its expected return, see Black (1970).

3. The above formulation describes the project of controlling 1970s "stagflation" undertaken through "central bank autonomy" combined with "financial innovation." See, e.g., Roberts (2010) and Krippner (2011).

4. Federal Reserve Statistical Release Z.1, *Financial Accounts of the United States: Flow of Funds, Balance Sheets, and Integrated Macroeconomic Accounts*, http://www.federalreserve.gov/releases/z1/Current/z1.pdf ; cf. Amato and Fantacci (2012a) and Duncan (2012).

5. See, e.g., Bryan, Martin, and Rafferty (2009, 1–15); Bryan (2006).

6. For an accessible narrative of how this happened see, e.g., Fox (2009).

7. On this point see Ben Lee's contribution to this volume.

8. See Foster (2000).

9. See Vercellone (2011); Marazzi (2011).

10. In the baseline scenario this is the zero spread between the option price and its perfect hedge; in alternative scenarios it is the nonzero spreads that occur when different possible payouts have different probabilities, of which their actual market prices are the best prediction. See Gisiger (2010).

11. This is how the efficient market model, which applies to asset markets, presents itself as a full alternative to the forms of state planning of production decisions and investment allocation decisions that addressed the problems Marx raises in *Capital*, volumes 2 and 3. EMM looks at capitalism from the point of view of the investor, rather than the state, and conceives of it as an asset market that incidentally produces goods, services, and the current cash flows necessary to buy them.

12. Some analysts argue that base currency stands in relation to a nation's debt liability as tangible common equity stands in relation to a banks depositor liability. See, e.g., Kaminska (2012a, 2012b, 2012c, 2013).

13. See, e.g., Elyachar (2002, 2012).

14. For a prescient account see Martin (2007, chapter 1).

15. Graeber's grounding debt in slavery—as the redemption of bodily pledges —is the strongest part of his book. Here, he rightly understands the role of money in quantifying such obligations and allowing them to be partially settled and partly written off. But in his account, marriage pledges between kin groups are also bodily pledges that get redeemed. And these redemptions of debt are seen as building social bonds, and thus good forms of debt, unlike slavery and capitalism in which the settlement of debts tend to wrench people from their social context, which is for anthropologists a kind of ur-crime. In this respect, Graeber misses—as Appadurai, Lee, and LiPuma in this volume do not—the cultural specificity of capitalism and, more particularly, financial capitalism, in which the general function of debt is to serve as collateral, a store of value, out of which liquidity can be manufactured on an ever-expanding scale. On related themes, see Maurer (2013).

16. By threatening to pull that trigger, they got the US government to effectively guarantee the total global credit market, collateral valued at over ninety trillion dollars, by pledging thirteen trillion dollars, which is not its total tax revenue but its total tax base.

17. I here leave open the question of whether "we" want to be (or identify with) the people who can do these things. The answer may well depend on what actions are made available.

18. For a sketch of globalized, technology-enabled, higher education as a marketable financial product—literally a way of giving third-world students "first-world options" that are more resilient in the face of global financial change than the educations they currently receive, see Meister (2013).

19. This formulation is indebted to the distinction between "real change" and "ordinary becoming" elaborated in Badiou (2009, chapter 5).

20. The trade-off between financial repression and political repression is the underlying theme of Reinhart and Rogoff (2009). See also the account of financial globalization in James (2009).

Chapter Five

1. Interconnectedness has emerged as a central explanandum of the financial debacle but is also a key trope in communitarian-based conceptions of social life. If the insight that remains from these analyses is an appeal to the ideal that "we need one another," then the responses are more likely to be procedurally regulatory and moralistic than to explore what the politics, political economy, and wealth valuation implications of the social might be. While not commonly thought of in relation to one another, the underlying conception of financial interconnectedness is not only a standard approach to "crisis economics" but of the behavioral entailments of irrational exuberance. The communitarian approaches even when, as in the foundational work of Amatai Etizioni, they do not omit direct consideration of economic structures assert connection as the primary social good. See, for example, Roubini and Mihm (2010); Shiller (2000); Etzioni (1993).

2. See, for example, Gillman (1958); Moseley (1991); and, for a consideration of the deterministic terms of the debate itself, Cullenberg (1994).

3. Mark Blyth's *Austerity: The History of a Dangerous Idea* (2013) sketches these links across economic doctrine (Smith, Hayek, Schumpeter) and policy with elegance.

4. See Marx's *Capital*, volume 1, chapter 6, "The Buying and Selling of Labor Power."

5. In 2012 and 2013, the *New York Times* ran a series of articles describing Apple's political economy that won the Pulitzer Prize. See Duhigg and Bradsher (2012).

6. For a synthetic statement of these positions see Cohen (1995).

7. Meister (2012), 251.

8. For a discussion of literary tropes as employing sociohistorical narratives, see White (1975).

9. This instrumentalization of the arts is the basis for the arguments for gentrification assembled under the rubric of the creative class. See Florida (2012); and for more critical accounts of what he calls the cultural discount, see Ross (2000) and Pasquinelli (2009).

10. See Appadurai, chapter 1, this volume.

Chapter Seven

1. Pages 246–48 of this chapter were published in Elie Ayache, 2015, *The Medium of Contingency*, London, UK: Palgrave Macmillan. Reproduced with permission of Palgrave Macmillan.

Chapter Eight

1. With the exception of US Treasury bonds, virtually all bonds are traded over the counter—that is to say, all exchanges are conducted privately between counterparties, with no formal rules of disclosure and limited price discovery. Unlike the stock market, where one can access the price of a stock from a smart phone, prices in the bond market must be individually collected from each trading desk, and each trading desk may have different prices for the same instrument.

2. In the ecology of credit trading provided in chapter 2 of my dissertation (Wosnitzer 2014), I purposely omitted the category of "regional dealers." Regional dealers are those investment bank trading desks that are significantly smaller in size relative to "bulge-bracket" firms, both in capitalization and personnel. Because regional dealers operate with a minimal capital base, they often rely upon the inventories from their larger bulge-bracket competitors. Regional dealers will often expressly engage with "medium" to "small" institutional accounts that fall outside the purview of the bulge bracket firms, such as small insurance companies, fledgling hedge funds, city and county cash assets, and public pension funds.

3. NIMCO is an acronym for a fictional institutional fixed-income client, National Investment Management Company. The behaviors and actions of NIMCO are based on my fifteen-year career as a capital markets professional, where I traded, marketed, and placed fixed-income (credit) products with transnational institutional accounts.

4. Traders calculate profits on the capture of basis points. The value of a basis point is relative to the maturity, or term structure. For example, one basis point for a five-year security is worth $0.625 per million (face, par value), and for a thirty-year security, one basis point is worth $1.25 per million. Thus, to make five basis points on five million thirty-year bonds equates to a profit of $31,250.00. If a trader makes $31,250 every day for a month, he would generate over $600,000, or $7.2 million annually. If bonuses are calculated at 5 percent of gross profit, then the trader could reasonably expect to receive $360,000 in bonus. Generally, traders at bulge-bracket firms are expected to generate approximately $20 million in revenue each year.

References

Abolafia, Mitchel. 1996. *Making Markets: Opportunism and Restraint on Wall Street*. Cambridge: Harvard University Press.

Akerlof, George, and Robert Shiller. 2009. *Animal Spirits: How Human Psychology Drives the Economy and Why It Matters for Global Capitalism*. Princeton: Princeton University Press.

Allen, Franklin, Elena Carletti, Jan Pieter Krahnen, and Marcel Tyrell, eds. 2011. *Liquidity and Crises*. Oxford: Oxford University Press.

Allen, Franklin, and Douglas Gale. 2011. "Financial Intermediaries and Markets." In *Liquidity and Crises*, edited by Franklin Allen, Elena Carletti, Jan Pieter Krahnen, and Marcel Tyrell, 78–110. Oxford: Oxford University Press.

Alridge, John. 2009. "I'm Doing 'God's Work.' Meet Mr. Goldman Sachs." *Sunday Times of London*, Nov. 8.

Amato, Massimo, and Luca Fantacci. 2012a. *The End of Finance*. Vol. 1. Cambridge: Polity.

———. 2012b. *The End of Finance*. Vol. 2. Cambridge: Polity.

Anderson, Benedict. 2006. *Imagined Communities*. London: Verso. First published in 1982.

Appadurai, Arjun. 2001. "Deep Democracy: Urban Governmentality and the Horizon of Politics." *Environment and Urbanization* 13 (2): 23–43. doi:10.1177/095624780101300203.

———. 2013. *The Future as Cultural Fact: Essays on the Global Condition*. London: Verso.

———. 2015. "Mediants, Materiality, Normativity." *Public Culture* 27 (2): 221–37. doi:10.1215/08992363-2841832.

———. 2016. "The Sacred Market" and "Sociality, Uncertainty, and Ritual." In *Banking on Words: The Failure of Language in the Age of the Derivative*, 55–81. Chicago: University of Chicago Press.

Austin, J. L. 1962. *How to Do Things with Words: Second Edition*. Edited by J. O. Urmson and Marina Sbisà. Cambridge: Harvard University Press.

Ayache, Elie. 2005. "What is Implied by Implied Volatility?" ITO33. Accessed August 12, 2015. http://www.ito33.com/sites/default/files/articles/0601_ayache.pdf.

———. 2007. "Elie Ayache, Author of the Black Swan." ITO33. Accessed August 12, 2015. http://www.ito33.com/sites/default/files/articles/0707_ayache.pdf.

———. 2008. "I am a Creator!" ITO33. Accessed August 12, 2015. http://www.ito33.com/sites/default/files/articles/0807_nail.pdf.

———. 2010. *The Blank Swan: The End of Probability*. Chichester, UK: Wiley.

———. 2011. "In the Middle of The Event." In *The Medium of Contingency*, edited by Robin Mackay, 19–35. New York: Sequence Press.

Ayres, Ian. 2005. *Optional Law: The Structure of Legal Entitlements*. Chicago: University of Chicago Press.

Badiou, Alain. 2009. *Logics of Worlds: Being and Event, 2*. London; New York: Continuum.

Bailey, Roy. 2001. *The Economics of Financial Markets*. Cambridge: Cambridge University Press.

Benjamin, Walter. 1968. *Illuminations*. Edited by Hannah Arendt. New York: Harcourt, Brace & World.

———. 1999. *The Arcades Project*. Translated by Howard Eiland and Kevin McLaughlin. Edited by Rolf Tiedemann. Cambridge: Belknap Press of Harvard University Press.

———. 2002. *Walter Benjamin: Selected Writings*. Vol. 3, *1935–1938*. Translated by Edmund Jephcott, Howard Eiland, and Others. Edited by Howard Eiland and Michael W. Jennings. Cambridge: Belknap Press of Harvard University Press.

———. 2003. *Walter Benjamin: Selected Writings*. Vol. 4, *1938–1940*. Translated by Edmund Jephcott and Others. Edited by Howard Eiland and Michael W. Jennings. Cambridge: Belknap Press of Harvard University Press.

Benveniste, Emile. 1973. *Problems in General Linguistics*. Coral Gables: University of Miami Press.

Bhattacharya, Sudipto, and Douglas Gale. 2011. "Preference Shocks, Liquidity, and Central Bank Policy." In *Liquidity and Crisis*, edited by Franklin Allen, Elena Carletti, Jan Pieter Krahnen, and Marcel Tyrell, 35–50. Oxford: Oxford University Press.

Black, Fischer. 1970. "Fundamentals of Liquidity." Unpublished manuscript. University of Chicago Business School. https://speculativematerialism.files.wordpress.com/2013/07/fischer-black-fundamentals-of-liquidity-1970.pdf.

———. 2012. "Noise." *Journal of Finance* 41:529–43. doi:10.1111/j.1540-6261.1986.tb04513.x. First published in 1986.

Black, Fischer, and Myron Scholes. 1973. "The Pricing of Options and Corporate Liabilities." *Journal of Political Economy* 81:637–54.

Blinder, Alan. 1998. *Central Banking in Theory and Practice.* Cambridge: MIT Press.

Blyth, Mark. 2013. *Austerity: The History of a Dangerous Idea.* New York: Oxford University Press.

Bourdieu, Pierre. 1972. "The Disenchantment of the World." In *Algeria 1960.* Paris: Editions de la Maison des Sciences de L'Homme.

———. 1976. *Outline of a Theory of Practice.* Translated by Richard Nice. Cambridge: Cambridge University Press.

———. 2000. *Pascalian Meditations.* Stanford: Stanford University Press.

Brealey, Richard A., and Stewart C. Myers. 2003. *Principles of Corporate Finance.* New York: McGraw-Hill.

Brown, Michael E. 1986. *The Production of Society: A Marxian Foundation for Social Theory.* Totowa, NJ: Roman and Littlefield Publishers.

Bryan, Dick. 2006. "Real Finance: Finding a Material Foundation to Global Finance." Paper presented at the Second Annual Conference of the International Forum on the Comparative Political Economy of Globalization, Renmin University of China, Beijing, China, September.

Bryan, Dick. 2012. "Fundamental Value and Materiality: a Category in Transformation." Unpublished manuscript. Cultures of Finance Working Group, New York.

Bryan, Dick, Randy Martin, and Mike Rafferty. 2009. "Financialization and Marx: Giving Labor and Capital a Financial Makeover." *Review of Radical Political Economics* 20 (10): 1–15.

Bryan, Dick, and Mike Rafferty. 2006. *Capitalism with Derivatives: A Political Economy of Financial Derivatives, Capital, and Class.* New York, NY: Palgrave-MacMillan.

Butler, Judith. 2010. "Performative Agency." *Journal of Cultural Economy* 3 (2): 147–61. Published online September 4. doi:10.1080/17530350.2010.494117

Callon, Michel. 1998. *The Laws of the Market.* London: Blackwell Publishers.

———. 2010. "Performativity, Misfires, and Politics." *Journal of Cultural Economy* 3 (2): 163–69. Published online September 4. doi:10.1080/17530350.2010.494119

Callon, Michel, and Fabian Muniesa. 2005. "Economic Markets as Calculative Collective Devices." *Organization Studies* 26 (8): 1229–50.

Cavell, Stanley. 2006. *Philosophy the Day after Tomorrow.* Cambridge: Belknap Press of Harvard University Press.

Chandler, David. 2013. *Freedom vs. Necessity in International Relations: Human-Centred Approaches to Security and Development.* London: Zed Books.

Cohen, G. A. 1995. *Self-Ownership, Freedom and Equality.* Cambridge: Cambridge University Press.

Comaroff, John L., and Jean Comaroff. 2009. *Ethnicity, Inc.* Chicago: University of Chicago Press.

Cook, Chris. 2011. "A Very Secret Agent." *Asia Times*, July 17.

Coole, Diana, and Samantha Frost, eds. 2010. *New Materialisms: Ontology, Agency, and Politics.* Durham, NC: Duke University Press.

Coppola, Frances. 2013a. "The Financialisation of Labour." *Pieria.* May 7. http://www.pieria.co.uk/articles/the_financialization_of_labour.

———. 2013b. "When governments become banks." *Coppola Comment.* January 2. www.coppolacomment.blogspot.com/2013/01/when-governments-become-banks.html.

Crozier, Michel, Samuel P. Huntington, and Joji Watanuki. 1975. *The Crisis of Democracy: Report on the Governability of Democracies to the Trilateral Commission.* New York: New York University Press.

Cullenberg, Stephen. 1994. *The Falling Rate of Profit: Recasting the Marxian Debate.* London: Pluto Press.

Dalyan, Can. 2009. "Making Markets in the South: Experts, Science, Power." *New Perspectives on Turkey* 41:241–56.

Debord, Guy. 2007. "Theory of the Dérive." *Les Lèvres Nues* 9. Translated by Ken Knabb. Berkeley, CA: Bureau of Public Secrets. Originally published in 1956.

de Goede, Marieke. 2005. *Virtue, Fortune, and Faith: A Genealogy of Finance.* Minneapolis: University of Minnesota Press.

Deleuze, Gilles. 1992. "Postscript on the Societies of Control." *October* 59:3–7. doi:10.2307/778828.

Deleuze, Gilles, and Félix Guattari. 1987. *A Thousand Plateaus: Capitalism and Schizophrenia.* Translated by Brian Massumi. Minneapolis: University of Minnesota Press.

Derman, Emanuel. 2004. *My Life as a Quant.* Hoboken, NJ: John Wiley & Sons, Inc.

Derman, Emanuel. 2011. *Models.Behaving.Badly.: Why Confusing Illusion with Reality Can Lead to Disaster, on Wall Street and in Life.* New York: Free Press.

Derman, Emanuel, and Iraj Kani. 1994. *The Volatility Smile and Its Implied Tree.* Quantitative Strategies and Research Notes. New York: Goldman, Sachs & Co.

Derman, Emanuel, and Nassim Taleb. 2005. "The Illusions of Dynamic Replication." *Quantitative Finance* 5 (4): 323–26.

Derman, Emanuel, and Paul Wilmott. 2009. "The Financial Modelers' Manifesto." *Social Science Research Network.* http://dx.doi.org/10.2139/ssrn.1324878.

Derrida, Jacques. 1982. *Margins of Philosophy.* Translated by Alan Bass. Chicago: University of Chicago Press.

Derrida, Jacques. 1992. *Given Time: I. Counterfeit Money*. Translated by Peggy Kamuf. Chicago: University of Chicago Press.

Descartes, René. 1984. *The Philosophical Writings of Descartes*. Vol. 1. Translated by John Cottingham, Robert Stoothoff, and Dugald Murdoch. Cambridge: University of Cambridge Press.

Descola, Philippe. 2013. *Beyond Nature and Culture*. Translated by Janet Lloyd. Chicago: University of Chicago Press.

Dosse, François. 1997. *History of Structuralism*. Minneapolis: University of Minnesota Press.

Duhigg, Charles, and Keith Bradsher. 2012. "How the U.S. Lost Out on iPhone Work." *New York Times*, January 22. http://www.nytimes.com/2012/01/22/business/apple-america-and-a-squeezed-middle-class.html.

Dumont, Louis. 1970. *Homo Hierarchicus: The Caste System and Its Implications*. Chicago: University of Chicago Press.

Duncan, Richard. 2012. *The New Depression: The Breakdown of the Paper Money Economy*. Hoboken, NJ: John Wiley and Sons.

Durkheim, Emile. 1995. *The Elementary Forms of Religious Life*. Translated by Karen E. Fields. New York: Free Press. Originally published in 1912.

Elyachar, Julia. 2002. "Empowerment Money: The World Bank, Non-Governmental Organizations, and the Value of Culture in Egypt." *Public Culture* 14 (3): 493–513.

———. 2005. *Markets of Dispossession: NGOs, Economic Development, and the State in Cairo*. Durham, NC: Duke University Press.

———. 2012. "Timothy Mitchell Interviewed by Julia Elyachar." *Public Culture* 24 (3): 623–42.

Etzioni, Amitai. 1993. *The Spirit of Community: The Reinvention of American Society*. New York: Simon and Schuster.

Florida, Richard. 2012. *The Rise of the Creative Class Revisited*. 10th anniversary ed. New York: Basic Books.

Foley, Duncan. 1986. *Understanding Capital: Marx's Economic Theory*. Cambridge: Harvard University Press.

Fortes, Meyer. 1973. "On the Concept of the Person among the Tallensi." In *La notion de personne en Afrique noire*, edited by R. Bastide and G. Dieterle, 238–319. Acte du Colloque international du CNRS 544. Paris: Colloques Internationaux du Centre National de la Recherche Scientifique.

Foster, John Bellamy. 2000. *Marx's Ecology: Materialism and Nature*. New York: Monthly Review Press.

Fox, Justin. 2009. *The Myth of the Rational Market: A History of Risk, Reward, and Delusion on Wall Street*. New York: Harper Business.

Frege, Gottlob. 1980. "On Sense and Reference." In *Translations from the Philosophical Writings of Gottlob Frege*, edited and translated by P. Geach and M. Black, 3rd ed. Oxford: Blackwell.

Garcia, Cardiff. 2011. "The decline of safe assets." *FT Alphaville.* December 5. http://ftalphaville.ft.com//2011/12/05/778301/the-decline-of-safe-assets/.

Geertz, Clifford. 1977. "Deep Play: Notes on the Balinese Cockfight." In *The Interpretation of Cultures*, 412–54. New York: Basic Books.

———. 1978. "The Bazaar Economy: Information and Search in Peasant Marketing." *American Economic Review* 68 (2): 28–32. doi:10.2307/1816656.

Gillman, Joseph. 1958. *The Falling Rate of Profit: Marx's Law and Its Significance to Twentieth Century Capitalism.* New York: Cameron Associates.

Gisiger, Nicolas. 2010. "Risk-Neutral Probabilities Explained." *Social Science Research Network.* http://dx.doi.org/10.2139/ssrn.1395390.

Goldman, Michael. 2005. *Imperial Nature: The World Bank and Struggles for Justice in the Age of Globalization* London: Yale University Press.

Gorton, Garry, and Andrew Metrick. 2010a. "Haircuts." Yale International Center for Finance Working Paper No. 09–15. May 12. http://papers.ssrn.com/sol3/papers.cfm?abstract_id=1447438.

———. 2010b. "Securitized Banking and the Run on Repo." Yale International Center for Finance Working Paper No. 09–14. November 9. http://papers.ssrn.com/sol3/papers.cfm?abstract_id=1440752.

Gourinchas, Pierre-Olivier, and Olivier Jeanne. 2012. "Global Safe Assets." BIS Working Paper No. 3000. December.

Graeber, David. 2011. *Debt: The First Five Thousand Years.* Brooklyn, NY: Melville House.

Greenspan, Alan. 1996. "The Challenge of Central Banking in a Democratic Society." Francis Boyer Lecture of the American Enterprise Institute, Washington, DC, December 5.

Grice, H. P. 1957. "Meaning." *Philosophical Review* 66 (3): 377–88.

Hacker, Jacob S., and Paul Pierson. 2010. *Winner-Take-All Politics: How Washington Made the Rich Richer—and Turned Its Back on the Middle Class.* New York: Simon & Schuster.

Hegel, G. W. 1969. *Hegel's Science of Logic.* Translated by A. V. Miller. Amherst, NY: Humanity Books.

Hegel, G. W. 1975. *Hegel's Logic.* Translated by William Wallace. Oxford: Oxford University Press.

Huizinga, Johan. 1971. *Homo Ludens: A Study of the Play-Element in Culture.* New York: Beacon Press.

Hull, John, and Alan White. 1987. "The Pricing of Options on Assets with Stochastic Volatilities." *Journal of Finance* 42:281–300. doi:10.1111/j.1540–6261.1987.tb02568.x.

Hyman, Louis. 2011. *Debtor Nation: The History of America in Red Ink.* Princeton: Princeton University Press.

James, Harold. 2009. *The Creation and Destruction of Value: The Globalization Cycle.* Cambridge: Harvard University Press.

Kalecki, Michal. 1943. "Political Aspects of Full Employment." *Political Quarterly* 14 (4): 322–31.

Kaminska, Izabella. 2011a. "Manufacturing quality collateral." *FT Alphaville.* November 25. http://ftalphaville.ft.com/2011/11/25/765031/.

———. 2011b. "One man's haircut is another man's unsecured risk." *FT Alphaville.* November 25. http://ftalphaville.ft.com/2011/11/25/760761/.

———. 2012a. "The Base Money Confusion." *FT Alphaville.* July 3. http://ftalphaville.ft.com/2012/07/03/1067591/the-base-money-confusion/.

———. 2012b. "The Negative Carry Universe." *FT Alphaville.* July 4. http://ftalphaville.ft.com/2012/07/04/1071311/the-negative-universe/.

———. 2012c. "On the transfer of risk and the mystery of low yields." *FT Alphaville.* June 29. http://ftalphaville.ft.com//2012/06/29/1065251/on-the-transfer-of-risk-and-the-mystery-of-low-yields/.

———. 2012d. "Pariah profits in an age of negative carry." *FT Alphaville*, July 5. http://ftalphaville.ft.com/2012Jrl7/05/1071671/pariah-profits-in-an-age-of-negative-carry.

———. 2013. "The Perpetualisation of Debt." *FT Alphaville.* January 31. http://ftalphaville.ft.com/2013/01/31/1361462/the-perpetualisation-of-debt/.

Keister, Lisa. 2011. *Faith and Money: How Religious Belief Contributes to Wealth and Poverty.* Cambridge: Cambridge University Press.

Keynes, John Maynard. 1936. *A General Theory of Employment, Interest, and Money.* London: Macmillan.

Knight, Frank. 1999a. *Selected Essays by Frank Knight, Volume 1: "What is Truth" in Economics?* Edited by Ross B. Emmett. Chicago: University of Chicago Press.

———. 1999b. *Selected Essays by Frank H. Knight, Volume 2: Laissez Faire: Pro and Con.* Edited by Ross B. Emmett. Chicago: University of Chicago Press.

———. 2002. *Risk, Uncertainty, and Profit.* Washington, DC: Beard Books.

Konings, Martijn. 2014. "State of Speculation." Paper presented at Gifts, Derivatives & Sociality Conference, New York University, New York, March.

Kripke, Saul. 1972. "Naming and Necessity." In *Semantics of Natural Language,* edited by D. Davidson and G. Harman, 253–355. Boston: Reidel.

Krippner, Greta R. 2011. *Capitalizing on Crisis: The Political Origins of the Rise of Finance.* Cambridge: Harvard University Press

Leach, Edmund. 1976. *Culture and Communication: The Logic by which Symbols Are Connected: An Introduction to the Use of Structuralist Analysis in Social Anthropology.* Cambridge: Cambridge University Press.

Lee, Benjamin. 1989. "Semiotic Origins of the Mind-Body Dualism." In *Semiotics, Self, and Society,* ed. Benjamin Lee and Greg Urban. Berlin, New York: Mouton de Gruyter.

Lee, Benjamin, and Edward LiPuma. 2014. "From Primitives to Derivatives." Unpublished manuscript.

Leonhardt, David. 2013. "The Idled Young Americans." *New York Times*, May 5. http://www.nytimes.com/2013/05/05/sunday-review/the-idled-young -americans.html.

Lepinay, Vincent-Antonin. 2014. *Codes of Finance: Engineering Derivatives in a Global Bank*. Princeton: Princeton University Press.

Lévi-Strauss, Claude. 1966. *The Savage Mind*. Chicago: University of Chicago Press.

———. 1969. *The Elementary Structures of Kinship*. Translated by James Harle Bell, John Richard von Surmer, and Rodney Needham. Boston: Beacon Press.

———. 1976. *Structural Anthropology*. Vol. 2. Translated by Monique Layton. Chicago: University of Chicago Press.

Levy, Jonathan. 2012. *Freaks of Fortune: The Emerging World of Capitalism and Risk in America*. Cambridge: Harvard University Press.

Lewis, Michael. 2004. *Moneyball: The Art of Winning an Unfair Game*. New York: W. W. Norton & Co.

———. 2010. *The Big Short: Inside the Doomsday Machine*. New York: Norton.

LiPuma, Edward. 1998. "Modernity and Forms of Personhood in Melanesia." In *Bodies and Persons: Comparative Perspectives from Africa and Melanesia*, edited by Michael Lambek and Andrew Strathern, 53–79. Cambridge: Cambridge University Press.

———. 2000. *Encompassing Others: The Magic of Modernity in Melanesia*. Ann Arbor: University of Michigan Press.

———. 2014. "The Social Dimensions of Black Scholes." Unpublished manuscript.

LiPuma, Edward, and Thomas Koelble. 2009. "Currency Devaluations and Consolidating Democracy: The Example of the South African Rand." *Economy and Society* 38:203–29.

LiPuma, Edward, and Moishe Postone. nd. "Commodities and Gifts." Unpublished manuscript.

Luce, R. Duncan and Raiffa, Howard. 1989. *Games and Decisions: Introduction and Critical Survey*. New York: Dover Publications.

MacKenzie, Donald. 2006. *An Engine, Not a Camera: How Financial Models Shape Markets*. Cambridge: MIT Press.

———. 2007. "Is Economics Performative? Option Theory and the Construction of Derivatives Markets." In *Do Economists Make Markets?*, edited by Donald MacKenzie, Fabian Muniesa, and Lucia Siu, 54–86. Princeton: Princeton University Press.

Marazzi, Christian. 2008. *Capital and Language: From the New Economy to the War Economy*. Los Angeles: Semiotext(e).

———. 2011. *The Violence of Financial Capitalism*. Los Angeles: Semiotext(e).

Marriott, McKim. 1976. "Hindu Transactions: Diversity without Dualism." In *Transaction and Meaning: Directions in the Anthropology of Exchange and*

Symbolic Behavior, edited by Bruce Kapferer, 109–42. Philadelphia, PA: Institute for the Study of Human Issues.

Marriott, McKim, and Ronald Inden. 1974. "Caste Systems." In *Encyclopaedia Britannica*, 15th ed., 3:982–91.

Martin, Randy. 2001. *On Your Marx: Relinking Socialism and the Left*. Minneapolis: University of Minnesota Press.

———. 2007. *An Empire of Indifference: American War and the Financial Logic of Risk Management*. Durham, NC: Duke University Press.

———. 2012. "A Precarious Dance, a Derivative Sociality." *TDR: The Drama Review* 56:4, Winter. New York: New York University and the Massachusetts Institute of Technology.

Marwick, Alice E. 2014. "How Your Data Are Being Deeply Mined." *New York Review of Books*, January 9. http://www.nybooks.com/articles/archives/2014/jan/09/how-your-data-are-being-deeply-mined/.

Marx, Karl. 1967a. *Capital, Volume I: The Process of Capitalist Production*. New York: International Publishers.

———. 1967b. *Capital, Volume II: The Process of Circulation of Capital*. New York: International Publishers.

———. 1967c. *Capital, Volume III*. New York: International Publishers.

———. 1969. "The Critique of the Gotha Programme." In *Marx and Engels, Selected Works, Volume 3*, 9–30. Moscow: Progress Publishers.

———. 1976. *Capital, Volume I: A Critique of Political Economy*. Translated by Ben Fowkes. London: Penguin. Originally published in 1867.

Maurer, Bill. 2013. "David Graeber's *Wunderkammer*, Debt: The First 5000 Years." *Anthropological Forum* 23, (2): 79–93.

Mauss, Marcel. 1967. *The Gift: Forms and Functions of Exchange in Archaic Societies*. Translated by Ian Cunnison. New York: Norton.

———. 1985. "A Category of the Human Mind: The Notion of Person; the Notion of Self." Translated by W. D. Halls. In *The Category of the Person: Anthropology, Philosophy, History*, edited by Michael Carrithers, Steven Collins, and Steven Lukes, 1–25. Cambridge: Cambridge University Press. Originally published in 1938.

Meadows, Donella H. 1972. *The Limits to Growth: A Report for the Club of Rome's Project on the Predicament of Mankind*. New York: Universe Books.

Mehrling, Perry. 2005. *Fischer Black and the Revolutionary Idea of Finance*. Hoboken, NJ: John Wiley & Sons, Inc.

———. 2010. *The New Lombard Street: How the Fed Became the Dealer of Last Resort*. Princeton: Princeton University Press.

Meister, Robert. 2011. "Debt and Taxes: Can the Financial Industry Save Public Universities?" *Representations* 116:128–55.

———. 2012. *After Evil: A Politics of Human Rights*. New York: Columbia University Press.

———. 2013. "An Open Letter to a Founder of Coursera." *The Conversation* (blog), May 21. Accessed September 3, 2015. http://chronicle.com/blogs/conversation/2013/05/21/can-venture-capital-deliver-on-the-promise-of-the-public-university/.

Merton, Robert C. 1973. "Theory of Rational Option Pricing." *Bell Journal of Economics and Management Science* 4 (1): 141–83.

———. 1974. "On the Pricing of Corporate Debt: The Risk Structure of Interest Rates." *Journal of Finance* 29 (2): 449–70.

Mettler, Suzanne. 2011. *The Submerged State: How Invisible Government Policies Undermine American Democracy.* Chicago: University of Chicago Press.

Mezzadra, Sandro. 2011. "The Topicality of Prehistory: A New Reading of Marx's Analysis of 'So-called Primitive Accumulation.'" *Rethinking Marxism: A Journal of Economics, Culture & Society* 23 (3): 302–21.

Mezzadra, Sandro, and Brett Neilson. 2013. "Extraction, Logistics Finance: Global Crisis and the Politics of Operations." *Radical Philosophy* 178 (March/April): 8–19.

Minsky, Hyman. 1986. *Stabilizing an Unstable Economy.* New Haven: Yale University Press.

Mirowski, Philip. 2013. *Never Let a Good Crisis Go to Waste.* London: Verso.

Mitchell, Timothy. 2002. *Rule of Experts: Egypt, Techno-Politics, Modernity.* Berkeley: University of California Press.

———. 2011. *Carbon Democracy.* London: Verso.

Miyazaki, Hirokazu. 2013. *Arbitraging Japan: Dreams of Capitalism at the End of Finance.* Berkeley: University of California Press.

Morgenson, Gretchen, and Joshua Rosner. 2011. *Reckless Endangerment: How Outsized Ambition, Greed, and Corruption led to Economic Armageddon.* New York: Times Books.

Moseley, Fred. 1991. *The Falling Rate of Profit in the Postwar United States Economy.* New York: St. Martin's Press.

Mundell, Robert. 1960. "The Monetary Dynamics of International Adjustment under Fixed and Flexible Exchange Rates." *Quarterly Journal of Economics* 84 (2): 227–57.

———. 2000. "A Reconsideration of the Twentieth Century." *American Economic Review* 90 (3): 327–40.

Neftci, Salih. 2004. *Principles of Financial Engineering.* London: Elsevier Academic Press.

Negri, Antonio. 2010. "Postface." In *Crisis in the Global Economy: Financial Markets, Social Struggles, and New Political Scenarios,* edited by Andrea Fumagalli and Sandro Mezzadra, 263–72. Los Angeles: Semiotext(e).

Pasquinelli, Matteo. 2009. "Creative Sabotage in the Factory of Art, Gentrification and the Metropolis." In *Animal Spirits: A Bestiary of the Commons,* 126–54. Rotterdam: NAi Publishers.

Paulson, Henry. 2009. *On the Brink: Inside the Race to Stop the Collapse of the Global Financial System*. New York: Business Plus.

Peirce, Charles Sanders. 1982. *The Writings of Charles S. Peirce: A Chronological Edition*. Vols. 1–6, 8. Edited by the Peirce Edition Project. Bloomington: Indiana University Press.

Poon, Martha. 2009. "From New Deal Institutions to Capital Markets: Commercial Consumer Risk Scores and the Making of Subprime Mortgage Finance." *Accounting, Organizations and Society* 34:654–74.

Postone, Moishe. 1996. *Labor, Time, and Domination: A Reinterpretation of Marx's Critical Theory*. Cambridge: Cambridge University Press.

Protess, Ben. 2012. "Jamie Dimon Shows Some Love for Volcker Rule." *New York Times* DealBook, May 21. Accessed September 3, 2015. http://dealbook .nytimes.com/2012/05/21/jamie-dimon-shows-some-love-for-volcker-rule.

Rappaport, Roy. 1979. "The Obvious Aspects of Ritual." In *Ecology, Meaning, and Religion*, 65–112. Richmond: North Atlantic Books.

———. 1999. *Ritual and Religion in the Making of Humanity*. Cambridge: Cambridge University Press.

Reinhart, Carmen M., and Kenneth S. Rogoff. 2009. *This Time Is Different: Eight Centuries of Financial Folly*. Princeton: Princeton University Press.

Riles, Annelise. 2011. *Collateral Knowledge: Legal Reasoning in the Global Financial Markets*. Chicago: University of Chicago Press.

Roberts, Alasdair. 2010. *The Logic of Discipline: Global Capitalism and the Architecture of Government*. New York: Oxford University Press.

Ross, Andrew. 2000. "The Mental Labor Problem." *Social Text* 63 (Summer): 1–32.

Roubini, Nouriel, and Stephen Mihm. 2010. *Crisis Economics: A Crash Course in the Future of Finance*. New York: Penguin.

Sahlins, Marshall. 1972. *Stone Age Economics*. Chicago: Aldine.

———. 1985. *Culture and Practical Reason*. Chicago: University of Chicago Press.

———. 1997. "The Spirit of the Gift." In *The Logic of the Gift*, edited by Alan Schrift, 70–99. New York: Routledge.

———. 2013. *What Kinship Is—And Is Not*. Chicago: University of Chicago Press.

Scarry, Elaine. 1985. *The Body in Pain: The Making and Unmaking of the World*. New York: Oxford University Press.

Schrift, Alan D. 1997. *The Logic of the Gift: Toward an Ethic of Generosity*. New York: Routledge.

Schweitzer, Arthur. 1975. "Frank Knight's Social Economics." *History of Political Economy* 7 (3): 279–92.

Searle, John R. 1969. *Speech Acts: An Essay in the Philosophy of Language*. Cambridge, New York: Cambridge University Press.

Seaver, Paul. 1985. *Wallington's World: A Puritan Artisan in Seventeenth-Century London*. Stanford: Stanford University Press.

Shiller, Robert J. 2000. *Irrational Exuberance*. Princeton: Princeton University Press.

Simmel, Georg. 1971. *Georg Simmel on Individuality and Social Forms*. Edited by Donald N. Levine. Chicago: University of Chicago Press.

Singh, Manmohan, and Peter Stella. 2012. "iMoney and Collateral." Yale International Center for Finance Working Paper No. 12/95 (April).

Smith, Adam. 1776. *An Inquiry into the Nature and Causes of the Wealth of Nations*. 2 vols. London: W. Strahan and T. Cadell.

Strange, Susan. 1986. *Casino Capitalism*. Oxford: B. Blackwell.

Strathern, Marilyn. 1988. *The Gender of the Gift: Problems with Women and Problems with Society in Melanesia*. Berkeley: University of California Press.

Taleb, Nassim. 2007. *The Black Swan: The Impact of the Highly Improbable*. New York: Random House.

Tambiah, Stanley J. 1968. "The Magical Power of Words." *Man* 3 (2): 175–208. doi:10.2307/2798500.

———. 1985. "A Performative Approach to Ritual." *Proceedings of the British Academy* 65:113–69.

Taylor, Charles. 1989. *Sources of the Self*. Cambridge: Cambridge University Press.

———. 2002. "Modern Social Imaginaries." *Public Culture* 14:91–124.

Triffin, Robert. 1960. *Gold and the Dollar Crisis: The Future of Convertibility*. New Haven: Yale University Press.

Turner, Victor. 1969. *Forest of Symbols: Aspects of Ndembu Ritual*. Ithaca: Cornell University Press.

van Gennep, Arnold. 1960. *The Rites of Passage*. Translated by Monika B. Vizedom and Gabrielle L. Caffee. Chicago: University of Chicago Press. Originally published in 1909.

Vendler, Zeno. 1972. *Res Cogitans: An Essay in Rational Psychology*. Ithaca: Cornell University Press.

Vercellone, Carlo. 2011. "The Crisis in the Law of Value and the Becoming Rent of Profit." In *Crisis in the Global Economy: Financial Markets, Social Struggles, and New Political Scenarios*, edited by Sandro Mezzadra Andrea Fumagalli, 85–118. Los Angeles: Semiotext(e).

Viveiros de Castro, Eduardo. 2012. "Cosmological Perspectivism in Amazonia and Elsewhere." In *Hau Masterclass Series*, vol. 1. http://www.haujournal .org/index.php/masterclass /issue /view /Masterclass Volume 1.

von Neumann, John, and Oskar Morgenstern. 1944. *Theory of Games and Economic Behavior*. Princeton: Princeton University Press. Originally published in 1980.

Wagner, Roy. 1974. "Are There Social Groups in the New Guinea Highlands?" In *Frontiers of Anthropology*, edited by Murray Leaf, 95–122. New York: Van Nostrand Company.

Wark, McKenzie. 2004. *A Hacker Manifesto*. Cambridge: Harvard University Press.

Weber, Max. 1992. *The Protestant Ethic and the Spirit of Capitalism*. Translated by Talcott Parsons. London: Routledge.

———. 2009. *The Protestant Ethic and the Spirit of Capitalism*. 4th ed. Translated by Stephen Kalberg. New York: Oxford University Press. Originally published in 1920.

White, Hayden. 1975. *Metahistory: The Historical Imagination in Nineteenth-Century Europe*. Baltimore: Johns Hopkins University Press.

Wosnitzer, Robert. 2014. "'Desk, Firm, God, Country': Proprietary Trading and the Speculative Ethos of Financialism." PhD diss., New York University. Pro-Quest (AAT 3624594).

Zaloom, Caitlin. 2006. *Out of the Pits: Traders and Technology from Chicago to London*. Chicago: University of Chicago Press.

Index

.